MATHEMATICS AND MIND

LOGIC AND COMPUTATION IN PHILOSOPHY

Series Editors: Wilfried Sieg (Editor-in-Chief), Clark Glymour, and Teddy Seidenfeld

This series will offer research monographs, collections of essays, and rigorous textbooks on the foundations of cognitive science emphasizing broadly conceptual studies, rather than empirical investigations. The series will contain works of the highest standards that apply theoretical analyses in logic, computation theory, probability, and philosophy to issues in the study of cognition. The books in the series will address questions that cross disciplinary lines and will interest students and researchers in logic, mathematics, computer science, philosophy, statistics, and psychology.

MATHEMATICS
AND MIND

Edited by
ALEXANDER GEORGE

New York   Oxford
OXFORD UNIVERSITY PRESS
1994

Oxford University Press

Oxford   New York   Toronto
Delhi   Bombay   Calcutta   Madras   Karachi
Kuala Lumpur   Singapore   Hong Kong   Tokyo
Nairobi   Dar es Salaam   Cape Town
Melbourne   Auckland   Madrid

and associated companies in
Berlin   Ibadan

Published by Oxford University Press, Inc.,
200 Madison Avenue, New York, New York 10016

Oxford is a registered trademark of Oxford University Press

Library of Congress Cataloging-in-Publication Data
Mathematics and mind/edited by Alexander George
p.   cm.—(Logic and computation in philosophy)
"Descendants of presentations at the Conference on the Philosophy
of Mathematics ... held at Amherst College from April 5–7, 1991"—CIP galley.
Includes bibliographical references and index.
ISBN 0-19-507929-9
1. Mathematics—Philosophy.   I. George, Alexander.   II. Series.
QA8.6.M378   1993
510'.1—dc20   92-39900

2 4 6 8 9 7 5 3 1

Printed in the United States of America
on acid-free paper

Acknowledgments

The contributions to this volume are descendants of presentations at the Conference on the Philosophy of Mathematics on the theme "Mathematics and Mind," which was held at Amherst College, April 5–7, 1991. Comments on these presentations, which do not appear in this volume, were delivered by Mary Tiles (University of Hawaii), Linda Wetzel (Georgetown University), Dan Velleman (Amherst College), Phillip Bricker (University of Massachusetts), Alexander George (Amherst College), Thomas Tymoczko (Smith College), and Samuel Mitchell (Mount Holyoke College). The conference, a gathering of some 150 participants of varied backgrounds, was made possible through generous financial assistance from the Forry Fund in Philosophy and Science and from Amherst College. It was made actual through help from members of the Department of Philosophy and especially the tireless efforts of Deirdre Smith. For her help in making the collection ready for publication, I am grateful to Nancy Board. Finally, for a different kind of support, I extend special thanks to my friends.

Amherst, Massachusetts   *A.G.*
August 1992

Contents

Contributors

George Boolos is Professor of Philosophy at the Massachusetts Institute of Technology.

Michael Dummett was formerly Wykeham Professor of Logic at Oxford University, and is a Fellow of New College.

Michael Hallett is Associate Professor of Philosophy at McGill University.

Daniel Isaacson is University Lecturer in the Philosophy of Mathematics at Oxford University, and a Fellow of Wolfson College.

Charles Parsons is Edgar Pierce Professor of Philosophy at Harvard University.

Wilfried Sieg is Professor of Philosophy at Carnegie Mellon University.

W. W. Tait is Professor of Philosophy at the University of Chicago.

MATHEMATICS AND MIND

Introduction

Alexander George

In the natural numbers, the problem of cognition presents itself to
us in its simplest form.

—Hermann Weyl

Might the study of mathematics be important for an inquiry into mind, or vice
versa? Philosophers have always been very interested in both, although
sometimes this is only half granted. Occasionally one finds the philosophy of
mathematics deemed an arcane area of specialization, rather off the main road,
of little relevance to central and enduring areas of philosophical interest.
Mathematics, on this view, is just another one of those tangential X's for which
we have a "Philosophy of X." This conception is sometimes encouraged by the
assumption that in philosophy a discussion's degree of technicality is inversely
proportional to its importance. But, of course, the view is thoroughly mistaken
(and hence the assumption, if it leads to that view, must be too): it is a challenge
to think of major philosophers who have not grappled with problems arising
from mathematics and whose reflections on the subject are not central to
their views.

It is true that on their face many of these problems do not relate to the
mysteries of human mental life, for example, problems concerning the source
of mathematical knowledge, the nature of mathematical entities, of mathematical
truth, of the applicability of mathematics to the physical world. I believe that
this is mere appearance, however, for investigation of these problems often
reveals important connections to enquiries into the nature of mental phenomena.
Mathematical knowledge, for example, is similar, in its being a priori, to an
individual's knowledge of his or her conscious mental state. There are differences,
of course, but it is interesting that these appear to be among the few domains
of knowledge whose acquisition does not rely on sensory experience.

Related to this last observation is another one: mathematical entities, like
numbers, are not found in the physical world; we cannot locate or date them.
This seems also to be the case for at least some things grasped by the mind—
thoughts, for example—which are likewise not plausibly said to exist in space
or time. One will object to this observation if one identifies a thought with the

3

grasping of that thought and the latter with some neurochemical event or state. But this would involve a kind of psychologism against which Gottlob Frege plausibly argued over a century ago. If entertaining a thought takes place at a particular moment or even location, that should not incline us to hold that the thought does as well. For surely you and I can have the same thought even though the two acts of having that thought are spatio-temporally distinct.

The route to mathematical knowledge is through ratiocination alone, nothing else being required or relevant. Mathematical truths are arrived at merely by mentally attending and reflecting. This fact alone establishes an intimate link between the study of mathematics and that of mind. Through the study of the conceptual basis of mathematics we learn about the powers of the mind, for it is just by the grace of these powers that mathematics is accessible to us. Conversely, a deeper understanding of the mind should clarify the foundations and development of mathematics.

W. V. Quine once wrote that

> we can investigate the world, and man as a part of it, and thus find out what cues he could have of what goes on around him. Subtracting his cues from his world view, we get man's net contribution as the difference. This difference marks the extent of man's conceptual sovereignty.[1]

If, in the case of mathematics, the world's "cues" are minimal or even non-existent, then "man's net contribution" is essentially the whole "world view." He would then be sovereign over this entire domain and his mathematical "world view" would tell us much about his conceptual predilections.[2]

The thought that "like is naturally apprehended by like," as Sextus Empiricus put it,[3] is one that has long motivated philosophers puzzled about the human mind to turn to mathematics—except that in this case the turn is even more natural, for mathematics is not just "naturally apprehended" by the mind, but apprehended *merely* through its exercise. Since the early Greek thinkers, philosophers have linked their views about the mind to their reflections on mathematics. This is still true today, and the three major philosophies of mathematics of the twentieth century all provide interesting examples.

According to logicism, a project first elaborated by Frege, the truths of mathematics (with the exception of geometry) were all to be rendered in a language capable of expressing only purely logical notions and, furthermore, were to be proved using only purely logical means of inference. And logic, at least according to Frege, was just the study of the laws of thought. Mathematics, then, becomes the study of objects of thought by means of rules of thought. When doing mathematics, we are essentially employing human reason to examine itself. As Frege said,

> the reason's proper study is itself. In arithmetic we are not concerned with objects which we come to know as something alien from without through the medium of the senses, but with objects given directly to our reason and, as its nearest kin, utterly transparent to it.[4]

Elsewhere, while warning that neither logic nor mathematics is concerned with any particular individual's reasoning or mind, Frege suggested that "Their task could perhaps be represented rather as the investigation of *the* mind; of *the* mind, not of minds."[5] For logicism, the concepts and the means of inference of mathematics are creatures of thought taken most generally, and so in studying the foundations of mathematics we are effectively enquiring into the structure of thought itself.

Intuitionism, as elaborated by L. E. J. Brouwer in the early decades of this century, accepts an intimate connection between mind and mathematics but in a sense reverses the direction of inquiry. Brouwer began by advancing general Kantian theses as to the "forms of conception inherent in human reason."[6] Focusing on our perception of time, Brouwer articulated what he took to be "the fundamental phenomenon of the human intellect" and drew consequences as regards "the fundamental phenomenon of mathematical thinking."[7] This led to a critique of classical mathematics as not fully intelligible and to an elaboration of an alternative conception and practice of the subject. He called this viewpoint "intuitionism" and he took it to be what follows from an accurate understanding of the nature of human thought. Michael Dummett, in more recent work, has also advanced intuitionism and criticized classical mathematics, but from an approach quite different from, and indeed at odds with, Brouwer's. Influenced instead by Ludwig Wittgenstein's later work on the mind, Dummett has based his reflections on mathematics upon general views about the nature of linguistic understanding and the ultimate unintelligibility of its privacy. What he shares with Brouwer, however, is the belief that a correct account of the mental has important consequences for mathematics and that a failure to appreciate this leads ultimately to mathematical work that is quite literally without clear meaning.

The third great foundational project is Hilbert's program, which David Hilbert formulated, also in the early decades of this century, partly in response to the increasing controversy caused by the critique of classical mathematics by intuitionists. For he wished to retain the infinitary stretches of classical mathematics in the face of both sympathy for the intuitionist's reflections on the nature of human cognition and antipathy towards the logicist project. Hilbert advanced his own "basic philosophical position" about the mind, one which he considered "requisite for mathematics and, in general, for all scientific thinking, understanding, and communication."[8] This involved the claim that reasoning requires that "something must already be given to our faculty of representation, certain extralogical concrete objects that are intuitively present as immediate experience prior to all thought."[9] Our ability to engage in logical inference depends on this "faculty of representation" and hence, Hilbert concluded, no attempt to understand mathematics solely in terms of logic could be complete. Through reflection on the nature of this "immediate experience," Hilbert sought to characterize what he called "finitary" mathematics—a very small part of mathematics, to be sure, but one that had the epistemological credentials required for a foundation—and to show how infinitary mathematics could be justified on its basis. While logicists worked from mathematics as practiced by the classical mathematician to a conception of reason, and intuitionists worked from a view of the mind to unorthodox forms of mathematical inquiry, we may see Hilbert as working from both ends: He accepted both infinitary mathematics, the Cantorian paradise "No one shall be able to drive us from,"[10] and a finitistic conception of mind. It was the task of his program to show that these two fixed points were, in fact, co-tenable.

Whatever one's judgment as to how these three different mathematico-philosophical projects have fared, one cannot miss the close relationship those who have sought to carry them out have found between the study of mathematics and that of the mind.

This tradition of research, furthermore, is not the only one to bear out such links. In more psychologically based inquiry into the nature of mind and language, we also find intriguing connections to mathematics. The linguist Noam Chomsky, for example, has occasionally speculated on what he calls the "curious property of the human mind . . . to develop certain forms of mathematical understanding"[11] and has suggested "it is possible that the number faculty developed as a by-product of the language faculty."[12] Elaborating, he suggests that

> Human language has the extremely unusual, possibly unique, property of discrete infinity, and the same is true of the human number faculty. In fact we might think of the human number faculty as essentially an "abstraction" from human language, preserving the mechanism of discrete infinity and eliminating the other special features of language.[13]

For Chomsky, it seems, a better understanding of human linguistic understanding and its acquisition might also shed light on the developmental basis of mathematics and, hence, perhaps on the conceptual structure of this domain of knowledge.

Those inquiring into mathematical foundations have also singled out something like the property of "discrete infinity" and linked our capacity to handle it to the development of symbolization and thought. Richard Dedekind, for example, opened *Was sind und was sollen die Zahlen?*, his 1888 analysis of the natural numbers, with the claim that the "unique and therefore absolutely indispensable foundation . . . [for] the whole science of numbers" was just "the ability of the mind to relate things to things, to let a thing correspond to a thing, or to represent a thing by a thing, an ability without which no thinking is possible."[14] For Dedekind, reflection on the conceptual basis of the natural number system reveals nothing less than an "ability of the mind" required for thought.

It is suggestive that precisely these "activities of the understanding," as Dedekind called them elsewhere,[15] have been brought into focus by research into the development of symbolization and mental life conducted within quite different traditions. This can also be illustrated by indicating briefly some of psychoanalyst Melanie Klein's views as presented in her 1930 paper "The Importance of Symbol-Formation in the Development of the Ego."[16] Klein claimed that all children, from birth, experience episodes of extreme anxiety, and that the manner in which they deal with these experiences will profoundly influence their mental development. This anxiety normally leads the child to expel fantasized persecuting inner objects, together with the aggressive impulses to which they give rise. These are "projected outwards," as Klein later says, into external objects (the mother's breast being the first one, according to Klein), which in turn become sources of anxiety, leading the child to ever further projections:

> Since the child desires to destroy the organs (penis, vagina, breasts) which stand for the objects, he conceives a dread of the latter. This anxiety contributes to make him equate the organs in question with other things; owing to this equation these in turn become objects of anxiety, and so he is impelled constantly to make other and new equations, which form the basis of his interest in the new objects and of symbolism.[17]

Klein's work displays not only agreement with Dedekind about the importance of "the ability of the mind to relate things to things" for the development of a normal mental life, but also an account of what prompts such activity.[18]

The preceding remarks are intended merely to introduce and render plausible the *and* in *Mathematics and Mind*. Each of the contributors to this volume has focused on a different facet of the conjunction. Michael Dummett argues that in a sense Frege was deeply right in advancing logicism, but that he was led astray by his desire to provide a foundation for all of classical mathematics. That project requires specifying truth conditions for statements involving quantification over what Dummett calls "the domains of fundamental mathematical theories." This, in turn, requires that we determine these domains, something that Dummett believes is not humanly possible, though attempts will lead ultimately to the notion of an indefinitely extensible concept. Once it is appreciated, Dummet claims, that the concepts determining "the domains of fundamental mathematical theories" are all indefinitely extensible, there will be a greater reluctance to employ classical logic in reasoning that involves quantification over them. Frege's logicism will then finally be able to shed its uncritical stance toward classical mathematics and to provide a satisfactory answer to the question "What is mathematics about?"

In his essay George Boolos takes up the topic of logicism through a historical and mathematical investigation of the logicism of Bertrand Russell, and of Russell and Whitehead. The logicization of mathematics carried out in the latter's *Principia Mathematica* has often appeared to commentators as checkered at best, depending as it does on three axioms (infinity, choice and reducibility) that have never appeared particularly logical in character on any plausible construal of logic. Boolos focuses on the axiom of infinity, which guarantees the existence of infinitely many individuals needed for the truth of the third Peano Postulate asserting the distinctness of successors of distinct numbers. He compares the manner in which Russell and Whitehead generate the Peano Postulates to Frege's derivation of arithmetic (in his *Grundlagen der Arithmetik*) from what Boolos calls Hume's Principle. Boolos concludes by examining Russell's own views about the logical character of the axiom of infinity and hence about the upshot of his work for the logicist project.

In W. W. Tait's essay, two other central mathematical principles are examined that have been advanced as logical and have been the focus of controversy in this century. These are the Law of Excluded Middle and the Axiom of Choice—the first formulated by the ancient Greeks, the second by Ernst Zermelo in 1904. Tait examines these two principles historically, the uses to which they have been put, and the reactions with which they have been met. He then develops what he calls a "construction theoretic" conception of mathematical reasoning and on its basis examines these two principles. He argues that while the Axiom of Choice is derivable within this framework, the Law of Excluded Middle is "awkward," a conclusion at odds on both counts with the attitudes towards these principles commonly taken by the mathematical community.

One of the issues that divides constructivists like intuitionists from Tait is the latter's rejection of the requirement that mathematical constructions be *effective.* Wilfried Sieg's essay takes as its topic just this notion—more specifically, the deep conceptual analysis that effectiveness received in the 1930s at the hands of Alan Turing. Sieg tracks the problem's roots to work in the foundations of mathematics and examines in detail Alonzo Church's analysis of effective calculability, which Sieg then compares with Turing's own. He notes that Turing's analysis was considered convincing by both Kurt Gödel and Church in a way that the latter's was not, and seeks to account for this response. Sieg concludes with a general discussion of two aspects of mathematical experience that his investigations bring into focus and that have been largely neglected, according to him. He argues that they suggest an approach to the study of mathematical experience—at the very least, they provide central data for it—that is not easily located within any of the usual camps in the philosophy of mathematics.

Daniel Isaacson, in his essay, agrees with Sieg in his focus on mathematical experience and his rejection of the usual terms of debate between constructivists and classical mathematicians. He seeks to articulate a conception of mathematical thought under which both Platonism and intuitionism can be subsumed. This view, which Isaacson calls "Concept Platonism," rejects the doctrine that mathematics is about *objects* (e.g., numbers, functions, sets) and that the objectivity of mathematics is to be explained in terms of such objects and the determinate properties they possess. Rather, mathematics is concerned with concepts, particular ways of abstracting from situations. He develops this view and argues that it does greater justice to what he considers primary phenomena for any adequate philosophy of mathematics.

In contrast, Charles Parsons accepts the view that arithmetic is about particular objects, namely natural numbers. In reasoning about them, they are somehow made available to us. His question here is how this comes to be, how the natural numbers can be given to us. He explores the suggestion that they are given to us in intuition. He argues that while we might take certain kinds of objects to be given to us in a Kantian-like intuition—for example, expressions of a formal language and geometric figures—natural numbers differ from these in significant ways that bar them from being objects of such intuition.

Parsons then examines the application of natural numbers with a view to isolating the point, should there be one, at which we must treat numbers as objects of intuition.

Michael Hallett takes up the topic of Parsons's essay and clarifies Hilbert's conception of intuition and its role in mathematics and theoretical inquiry more generally. He does this in the context of an examination of Hilbert's foundational work in mathematics and its bearing on his conception of abstract thought. In comparing Hilbert's approach to Frege's, Hallett shows how their views about axiomatization, although similar in many respects, diverge in significant ways. He traces how this divergence influences their understanding of mathematics and the conclusions they drew about logic and its place in an analysis of the functioning of thought.

I began with some general reasons for thinking the link between mathematics and mind an important and fruitful one to study. They were designed more to whet the appetite than to satisfy and nourish. I am confident, however, that the reader will find in the details of what follows substantive and suggestive connections between the study of mind and of mathematics. May like inspire like.

Notes

Thanks to Jyl Gentzler, Wilfried Sieg, and Dan Velleman for helpful comments on an early draft.

1. W. V. Quine, *Word and Object* (Cambridge, Mass.: MIT Press, 1960), 5.

2. Two caveats: First, Quine would not concur with our isolating (in any philosophically interesting sense) a mathematical component within man's world view. Second, not everyone would grant that the physical world's "cues" are minimal, John Stuart Mill and David Hilbert being perhaps two (different) kinds of dissenters.

3. Sextus Empiricus, *Against the Mathematicians*, VII 92, trans. Jonathan Barnes, in *Early Greek Philosophy*, ed. Jonathan Barnes (New York: Penguin, 1987), 218.

4. Gottlob Frege, *The Foundations of Arithmetic*, trans. J. L. Austin (Evanston, Ill.: Northwestern University Press, 1978), 115e.

5. Gottlob Frege, "Thoughts" (originally "Der Gedanke"), in *Collected Papers on Mathematics, Logic, and Philosophy*, ed. Brian McGuiness (1918, reprint, Oxford: Blackwell, 1984), 369.

6. L. E. J. Brouwer, "Intuitionism and Formalism," in *Philosophy of Mathematics: Selected Readings*, 2nd edn, eds. Paul Benacerraf and Hilary Putnam (1912, reprint, Cambridge: Cambridge University Press, 1983), 78.

7. Ibid., 80.

8. David Hilbert, "On the Infinite," in *From Frege to Gödel: A Source Book in Mathematical Logic, 1879–1931*, ed. Jean van Heijenoort (Harvard University Press, 1977), 376.

9. Ibid.

10. Ibid.

11. Noam Chomsky, *Rules and Representations* (New York: Columbia University Press, 1980), 249.

12. Noam Chomsky, *Language and Problems of Knowledge: The Managua Lectures* (Cambridge, Mass.: MIT Press, 1988), 169.

13. Ibid.

14. Richard Dedekind, *Essays on the Theory of Numbers*, trans. Wooster Woodruff Beman (New York: Dover, 1963), 32.

15. From Dedekind's "Letter to Keferstein," where he writes that his goal was to "divest these properties [of the natural numbers] of their specifically arithmetic character so that they are subsumed under more general notions and under activities of the understanding *without* which no thinking is possible at all but *with* which a foundation is provided for the reliability and completeness of proofs and for the construction of consistent notions and definitions" (reprinted in van Heijenoort, *From Frege to Gödel*, 100).

16. Ancestors of these views in psychoanalytic theory can be traced back to Sigmund Freud. For a discussion of Freud's writings on identification, its genesis in frustration, and its role in structuring our inner worlds, see chapter 6 of Jonathan Lear's *Love and Its Place in Nature* (Farrar, Straus and Giroux, 1990). I discuss Klein's formulations because her account is the most coherent and compelling development that I know of in this line of research. Her paper is reprinted in *Love, Guilt and Reparation and Other Works 1921–1945* (London: Virago Press, 1988).

17. P. 220. For a later development of her views, see her 1946 paper "Notes on Some Schizoid Mechanisms," in *Envy and Gratitude and Other Works 1946–1963* (New York: Free Press, 1984).

18. (Flip summary: although mathematics may induce anxiety, more deeply, *anxiety makes mathematics possible*.) According to Hanna Segal, noted for her development and application of Klein's thought, "Symbol formation is an activity of the ego attempting to deal with the anxieties stirred by its relation to the object and is generated primarily by the fear of bad objects and the fear of the loss or inaccessibility of good objects." As a result of this anxiety, "the subject in phantasy projects large parts of himself into the object, and the object becomes identified with the parts of the self that it is felt to contain. Similarly, internal objects are projected outside and identified with parts of the external world which come to represent them. These first projections and identifications are the beginning of the process of symbol formation." ("Notes on Symbol Formation," in *Delusion and Artistic Creativity and Other Psychoanalytic Essays, The Work of Hanna Segal* (London: Free Association Books and Maresfield Library, 1986), 52, 53.)

Daniel Isaacson, in unpublished research, has charted extensively and interestingly the relevance of psychoanalytic material and theory (especially Klein's) to a wide range of philosophical issues. I am grateful to him for having introduced me to these avenues of exploration.

1

What Is Mathematics About?

Michael Dummett

The two most abstract of the intellectual disciplines, philosophy and mathematics, give rise to the same perplexity: what are they *about*? The perplexity does not arise solely out of ignorance: even the practitioners of these subjects may find it difficult to answer the question. Mathematics presents itself as a science in the general sense in which history is a science, namely as a sector in the quest for truth. Even those least instructed in other sciences, however, have some general idea what it is that those sciences strive to establish the truth about. Historians aim at establishing the truth about what was done by and what happened to human beings in the past; more exactly, to human beings after they had invented writing. Physicists try to discover the general properties of matter under the widest variety of conditions; more generally, of matter and of what it propagates, such as light and heat. But what is it that mathematicians investigate?

An uninformative answer could be given by listing various types of mathematical object and mathematical structure: mathematicians study the properties of natural numbers, real numbers, ordinal numbers, groups, topological spaces, differential manifolds, lattices, *and the like*. Apart from the difficulty of explaining "and the like," such an answer is uninformative because it is given from within: one has to know some mathematics—even if, in some of the cases, only a little—if one is to understand the answer, whereas the sample answers to the questions concerning history and physics could be understood without knowing any history or physics.

Some maintain, nevertheless, that mathematics is a science like any other. The claim is unconvincing prima facie: what is immediately striking about mathematics is how *unlike* any other science it is. It is true that, in the more mathematicized sciences such as physics, there may be elaborate deductions from initial premises, just as there are in mathematics; but they play a different role. In mathematics, their purpose is to establish theorems, that is, mathematical truths; in physics, they serve to elicit consequences of a theory, which can then be used to make predictions but also to test the theory. The word "theory" is used quite differently in mathematics and in the other sciences. In physics, biology, and so forth, it carried the connotation of a hypothesis; however well established a physical or biological theory, it always remains open to refutation or revision. In mathematics, there is no such connotation. We are all familiar with the idea of observations designed to test—to confirm or refute—the general theory of relativity; but we should be unable to conceive of observations designed to test number theory or group theory.

The most determined effort to represent mathematics as empirical in character was made by John Stuart Mill; but he achieved little more than to point out, what is in any case evident, that mathematics can be *applied* to empirical reality. That, indeed, is a salient feature of mathematics that any philosophical account of it must explain; but it is not to be explained by characterizing mathematics as itself an empirical science. Our very vocabulary indicates the difference. We do not speak of "applying" a physical theory when we draw physical consequences from it, but only when we base some technological innovation upon it. Even someone who accepted all Mill's arguments would have no ground for regarding mathematics as a science like any other; it would still differ markedly from all others. For Mill, the axioms and definitions of mathematics are derived from very general facts apparent to untutored observation; but the theorems are still consequences drawn by deductive reasoning from those axioms and definitions, without further appeal to observation, let alone to refined observations made in artificially created conditions or with the help of sophisticated instruments. Moreover, as Frege pointed out, the mathematical notions whose application Mill was anxious to locate solely in physical reality have in fact far wider application. It is misleading to say that we encounter the natural numbers, for example, in the physical world; for, while physical situations may indeed need to be described by citing a natural number as the number of physical objects of some given kind, non-physical situations may equally need to be described by citing a natural number as the number of non-physical objects of some given kind, for instance as the number of different proofs of the fundamental theorem of algebra, or, indeed, of roots of an equation. The same holds good of sets. These notions are too general for us to locate them in any particular realm of reality; as Frege maintained, they apply within every sector of reality, and the laws governing them hold good, not only of what we find to exist, but of all of which we can frame intelligible thoughts.

If mathematics is not about some particular realm of empirical reality, what, then, *is* it about? Some have wished to maintain that it is indeed a science like any other, or, rather, differing from others only in that its subject-matter is a super-empirical realm of abstract entities, to which we have access by means of an intellectual faculty of intuition analogous to those sensory faculties by means of which we are aware of the physical realm. Whereas the empiricist view tied mathematics too closely to certain of its applications, this view, generally labeled "platonist," separates it too widely from them: it leaves it unintelligible how the denizens of this atemporal, supra-sensible realm could have any connection with, or bearing upon, conditions in the temporal, sensible realm that we inhabit.

Like the empiricist view, the platonist one fails to do justice to the role of proof in mathematics. For, presumably, the supra-sensible realm is as much God's creation as is the sensible one; if so, conditions in it must be as contingent as in the latter. The continuum hypothesis, for example, might *happen* to hold, even though we can apprehend neither its truth nor anything in which its truth is implicit. That there may be mathematical facts that we shall be forever incapable of establishing is a possibility admitted by some mathematicians and philosophers of mathematics, though denied by others. When admitted, however, it is normally admitted on the ground that our inferential powers are limited: there may be consequences of our initial assumptions that we are unable to draw. If these are first-order consequences, we could "in principle" draw them, since they could be elicited by reasoning each step of which was simple; but the proofs might be too long and complex for us ever to be able to hit on them, or even follow them, in practice. If they are second-order consequences, we may be unable even in principle to see that they follow. But, if we take seriously the analogy between our supposed faculty of intuition and our perceptual faculties, there is no reason why there may not be mathematical facts that are in no sense consequences of anything of which we are aware. We may observe a physical object without either perceiving all its features or being able to deduce all of them from what we do perceive; if mathematical structures are merely the inhabitants of another realm of reality, apprehended by us in a manner analogous to our perception of physical objects, there is no reason why the same should not be true of them. There are indeed hypotheses and conjectures in mathematics, as there are in astronomy; but, while both kinds may be refuted by deducing consequences and proving them to be false, the mathematical ones cannot be established simply by showing their consequences to be true. In particular, we cannot argue that the truth of a hypothesis is the only thing that would explain that of one of its verified consequences; there is nothing in mathematics that could be described as inference to the best explanation. Above all, we do not seek, in order to refute or to confirm a hypothesis, a means of refining our intuitive faculties, as astronomers seek to improve their instruments. Rather, if we suppose the hypothesis true, we seek for a *proof* of it, and it remains a mere hypothesis, whose assertion would therefore be unwarranted, until we find one. True, we seek to make our methods of proof ever more explicit and precise. This is not analogous to the improvement of the instruments, however. Methods of proof serve to elicit consequences, not to yield a more extensive evidential base; if the hypothesis is to be established, this must be done, not by testing its consequences, but by exhibiting *it* as a consequence of what we already know. Platonism can no more explain these differences between mathematics and the natural sciences than empiricism can, for both go astray by claiming to discern too close an analogy between them.

A brilliant answer to our question, but one now generally discredited, was given by Gottlob Frege and sustained by Russell and Whitehead. It was, essentially, that mathematics is not about *anything in particular*: it consists, rather, of the systematic construction of complex deductive arguments. Deductive reasoning is capable of eliciting, from comparatively meager premises and by routes far from immediately obvious, a wealth of often surprising consequences;

in mathematics, such routes are explored and the means of deriving those consequences are stored for future use in the form of propositions. Mathematical theorems, on this account, embody deductive subroutines which, once discovered, can be repeatedly used in a variety of contexts.

This answer, generally called the "logicist" thesis, was brilliant because it simultaneously explains various puzzling features of mathematics. It explains its methodology, which involves no observation, but relies on deductive proof. It explains the exalted qualification it demands for an assertion: in other sciences, a high degree of probability ranks as sufficient ground for putting forward a statement as true, but, in mathematics, it must be incontrovertibly *proved*. It explains its generality; it explains our impression of the necessity of its truths; it explains why we are so perplexed to say what it is about. Above all, it explains why mathematics has such manifold applications, and what it is for it to be applied. It allows that mathematical statements are genuinely propositions, true or false, and hence accounts for what is manifestly so, that mathematicians may be interested in determining their truth-values regardless of the uses to which they may be put; at the same time, it explains the content of those propositions as depending on the possibility of applying them, and thus justifies Frege's dictum that it is applicability alone that raises arithmetic from the rank of a game to that of a science. By contrast, Wittgenstein's account of mathematics, which lays even greater stress on application, makes the existence of pure mathematicians a phenomenon for pathology. It will be my purpose in this essay to maintain that the logicist answer, if not the exact truth of the matter, is closer to the truth than any other than has been put forward.

The classic versions of logicism both ran aground on the problem of the existence of mathematical objects, those abstract entities of which mathematical theories, taken at face-value, treat, and, above all, of the elements of the fundamental mathematical domains; the domain of the natural numbers and that of the real numbers. The aim of representing a mathematical theory as a branch of logic is in tension with recognizing it as a theory concerning objects of any kind, as its normal formulation presents it as being: for we ordinarily think of logic as comprising a set of principles independent of what objects the universe may happen to contain. Frege nevertheless believed that the truth of number theory and of analysis demanded the existence of those objects with which, on the face of it, they are concerned; and so he had to justify the belief in their existence, while reconciling it with the purely logical character of arithmetical statements. In trying to achieve this, he ran into actual contradiction. Russell and Whitehead, greatly concerned with the need to avoid contradiction, tried to construct foundations for mathematics in accordance with the more natural conception of logic as independent of the existence of any particular objects: their classes are not genuine objects at all, but mere surrogates, statements about them being explained as a disguised means of talking about properties of objects, properties of such properties, properties of properties of *those* properties, and so on upwards. Frege had never given any good reason for insisting on the genuine existence of mathematical objects; perhaps the only plausible reason lies in the difficulties encountered by Russell and Whitehead in trying to dispense with them. The price they paid for doing so was that, in order to ensure the existence of sufficiently many of their object-surrogates, they had to make assumptions that could not be rated as logical, or even likely to be true. The Axiom of Infinity, saying that there are infinitely many concrete objects, was needed to make sure that the natural numbers did not terminate; the Axiom of Reducibility, saying that there are sufficiently many properties of things of a given type definable without speaking of all properties of those things, was needed to guarantee the completeness of the real-number system.

More recently, Hartry Field has advanced what may be seen as a modification of the logicist thesis. Frege argued that the application of a mathematical theory, outside mathematics or within it, requires, to warrant it, a stronger claim than the consistency of the theory being applied. Suppose that a theorem in one mathematical theory T is proved by appeal to another, auxiliary, theory S. It is then not enough, Frege reasoned, to know that if the theory T is free from contradiction, then so is the combination of T and S: for that would warrant us in claiming no more than that we shall not involve ourselves in contradiction if we accept the theorem, whereas we wanted to be in a position to *assert* that theorem; and for that, Frege held, we must know the auxiliary theory S to be *true*. Field argues that we need claim nothing so strong as truth on behalf of a theory in order to warrant its applications. It we want to show that a mathematical theory S can be legitimately invoked as an auxiliary to some other theory T (which may be a scientific theory or another mathematical one), we need only claim something intermediate between the logical truth of S and its consistency relative to T, namely that the conjunction of T and S is a conservative extension of T. This means that anything expressible in the language of T that could be proved from T together with S could already be proved—perhaps at greater length and with greater difficulty—in the theory T on its own.

Field, too, is concerned with the existence of mathematical objects. He agrees with Frege, as against Russell and Whitehead, that the truth of a mathematical theory demands the existence of the mathematical objects of which it purports to treat: that is his reason for denying the truth of the theory, since he disbelieves in the existence of any such objects.

To give substance to the claim that, when the theory S is added to the theory T, it yields a conservative extension of T, we must be able to formulate T without reference to whatever objects of the theory S are regarded as objectionable; achieving such reformulations is the major part of Field's program. His motivation for seeking to explain the applications of mathematics without recognizing the existence of mathematical objects lies in his general disbelief in abstract objects of any kind. It is on this that criticism has centered: can he really formulate scientific theories without appeal to abstract objects?

For Frege, on the other hand, the error that blocked any reasonable philosophy of mathematics was the failure to recognize that abstract objects may be quite as objective as concrete ones (in his terminology, non-actual objects as actual ones). He characterized abstract objects much in the way that philosophers are disposed to do today, namely as objects lacking causal powers; by "objective" he meant something that is neither a content of consciousness nor created by any mental process. It is a common complaint about abstract objects that, since they have no causal powers, they cannot explain anything, and that the world would appear just the same to us if they did not exist: we can therefore have no ground to believe in their existence. For Frege, such a complaint would reveal a crude misunderstanding. He gave as an example of an object that is abstract but perfectly objective the equator. If you tried to explain to someone who had never heard of it what the equator was, you would certainly have to convey to him that it cannot be seen, that you cannot trip over it, and that you feel nothing when you cross it. If he then objected that everything would be exactly the same if there were no such thing as the equator, and that therefore we can have no reason for supposing it to exist, it would be clear that he had still not understood what sort of object we take the equator to be. What has to be done is to explain to him how the term "the equator" is used in whole sentences: how it is to be determined whether or not someone has crossed the equator, whether some natural feature lies on it or to the north or south of it, and so on. That is all that can be done, and all that needs to be done: if he still persists in objecting, there is nothing we can do but pity him for being in the grip of a misleading picture.

Thus reference to an abstract object is to be understood only by grasping the content of sentences involving such reference, and it is only by specifying the truth-conditions of such sentences that it can be explained what such an object is: it is only in the course of saying something intelligible about an object that we make genuine reference to it. This, indeed, holds good for all objects, concrete or abstract; but, because of their failure to appreciate the dependence of reference upon the context of a proposition, philosophers are tempted to dismiss the object referred to as mythological only when it is abstract, since sentences involving reference to concrete objects include those in which they are indicated by means of demonstrative terms, which is to say that concrete objects can be encountered. For Frege, however, to treat mathematical objects such as numbers as fictitious because abstract is to commit as crude a blunder as to do the same for the equator, one which springs from the same misunderstanding about what referring to an object involves.

In this, Frege was surely right. He did not, however, take his *general* defense of the existence of abstract objects as dispensing us from any work in particular cases, but only as pointing to the kind of work that needed to be done. In each case, we have to specify the truth-conditions of sentences containing terms for objects of the kind in question; in those with which he was concerned, for natural numbers, or cardinal numbers in general, and for real numbers. And this was, for him, a highly problematic task, but one that he believed he could solve. The first lesson of the contradiction was that he was woefully mistaken in that belief.

If we reject Field's all-encompassing nominalism, his program takes on a different aspect. Much of the criticism directed at it falls away, once the task is no longer that of avoiding reference to all abstract objects; it continues to be of interest because it focuses on the problem that defeated both Frege and Russell, of either justifying or explaining away reference to specifically mathematical objects, and that remains a problem even after the general objective of eliminating all reference to abstract objects has been discarded. Field's program then becomes a new strategy for resolving the problem of mathematical objects. Nevertheless, Field envisages the justification of his conservative extension thesis as being accomplished only piecemeal. For each mathematical theory, and each theory to which it is applied, the demonstration is to be carried out specifically for those two theories; no presumption is created by the successful execution of the program in one case that it will work in others. If, for example, it is shown that real analysis yields a conservative extension when adjoined to Newtonian mechanics, real analysis will not have received a general justification as a mathematical theory, but only in application to Newtonian mechanics. Now suppose that some millionaire is converted to Field's philosophy of mathematics and endows an institute to carry out Field's program for all scientific theories and all mathematical theories which find application to them; and suppose that the institute is uniformly successful: it has so far examined every existing scientific theory, and every application of mathematics made within it, and has in each case succeeded in establishing Field's claim. Then it has still not established that claim for future applications of other parts of mathematics to existing theories, nor for applications of mathematics to scientific theories yet to be devised. Long before this stage, however, we should have become dissatisfied with the institute's work. For each mathematical theory, we should surely demand a guarantee that it would always yield a conservative extension when adjoined to any scientific theory, so that it would be justified once and for all; and we should also require an explanation why it demonstrably did yield a conservative extension when adjoined to every known scientific theory. Such an explanation would have to turn on the character of the mathematical theory itself, independently of the particular scientific theories to which it was applied; and it would presumably provide the sought-for guarantee. Without such an explanation, we could hardly suppose that we had reached the fundamental truth of the matter; for it could not very well be a mere fortunate coincidence that the theories devised by the mathematicians just happened to yield conservative extensions when adjoined to the theories developed by physicists and other scientists. It is difficult to think what such a general explanation could be, unless it was that mathematical theories, if not logically true in the strict sense, have some closely related property. Field's thesis is not a single one, but a bundle of numerous particular theses; and, as such, it lacks the generality that is required of an adequate account of the applicability of mathematical theories.

Once we have achieved the required reformulation of the theory T to which some mathematical theory S is to be applied, Field's strategy is to prove a representation theorem for T. To avoid unnecessary detail, I will illustrate this by Field's own preliminary example. Here T is (an adaptation of) Hilbert's axiomatization of Euclidean geometry, while S is the theory of real numbers. T is formulated without reference to numbers of any kind, but with variables ranging only over geometrical objects; it is based on axioms governing primitive predicates expressing properties of and relations between them. In Hilbert's original formulation, there were three sorts of variable, for points, lines (determined by any two distinct points), and planes (determined by any three non-collinear points); Field prefers to conceive it as using variables only over points. In this case, there will be a four-place predicate holding between points x, y, z, and w just in case the line segment xy is congruent to the line segment zw, and a three-place predicate saying that y lies between x and z on some line. Then a partial rendering of Hilbert's representation theorem states that there will be a binary function d from the points in any model of T into the non-negative real numbers such that

$$d(x, y) = d(z, w)$$

just in case xy is congruent to zw and

$$d(x, z) = d(x, y) + d(y, z)$$

just in case y is between x and z. By laying down suitable conditions on the distance function d, we could prove a converse, namely that any structure on which was defined a function d satisfying those conditions could be converted into a model of T by explaining segment-congruence and betweenness in the manner just stated.

This helps to explain how real numbers can be used as an auxiliary device for proving results within this particular theory, namely the theory T of Euclidean geometry; it does not, of course, illuminate the uses of real numbers in other applications. Field remarks that the function d is unique only up to multiplication by a positive constant. This reflects the obvious fact that a quantity—here, a distance—does not by itself determine a real number alone, but only in conjunction with a unit. What uniquely determines a real number is a ratio between distances: if we replaced d by a function e of four arguments, giving the ratio of the distance between x and y to that between z and w (where z and w are distinct), we could reformulate the representation theorem so that e would be unique. (We should then require that xy be congruent to zw just in case $x = y$ and $z = w$ or $e(x, y, z, w) = 1$, and that y be between x and z just in case $y = z$ or $e(x, z, y, z) = e(x, y, y, z) + 1$.) We need not do this, of course; it is enough to observe that if real numbers are uniquely determined by ratios between distances, it at once follows that there will be distance functions d obtained from one another by multiplication by positive real numbers. (Any such d will be obtainable from e by setting $d(x, y) = e(x, y, a, b)$ for suitable fixed distinct a and b.) Furthermore, real numbers correspond uniquely to ratios, not merely between distances, but between quantities of any one type. Hence, given an adequate analysis, such as that aimed at in measurement theory, of what, in general, constitutes a range of quantities, we have a hope of a general explanation of why there will be a unique mapping of pairs of objects that have these quantities on to the real numbers or on to some subset of them. From these sketchy remarks, it is possible to glimpse how such a general explanation might be made to yield a theorem of which a whole range of corollaries ensuring a representation by means of real numbers would be special cases. We should then have secured the desired generality for explaining the applications of real numbers on Fieldian lines. Such a theorem would encapsulate the general principle for applying the theory of real numbers.

This, however, would do nothing to convince Field of the existence of real numbers. Frege held that real numbers *are* ratios between quantities. Once we have abandoned the superstitious nominalist horror of abstract objects in general, there would be nothing problematic about the existence of real numbers in the context of some empirical theory involving quantities of one or another kind, if they were identified with ratios between those quantities. What real numbers there were would depend upon what quantities there were: there would be no danger of our not having sufficiently many real numbers for our purposes.

The difficulty about mathematical objects thus arises because we want our mathematical theories to be pure in the sense of not depending for the existence of their objects on empirical reality, but yet to satisfy axioms guaranteeing sufficiently many objects for any applications that we may have occasion to make. The significant distinction is not between abstract objects and concrete objects, but between mathematical objects and all others, concrete or abstract. Plenty of abstract objects exist only contingently, the equator, for example: their existence is contingent upon the existence of concrete objects, and upon their behavior or the relations obtaining between them. Ratios between empirically given quantities would be dependent abstract objects of this kind. By contrast, the existence of mathematical objects is assumed to be independent of what concrete objects the world contains.

In order to confer upon a general term applying to concrete objects—the term "star," for example—a sense adequate for its use in existential statements and universal generalizations, we consider it enough that we have a sharp criterion for whether it applies to a given object, and a sharp criterion for what is to count as one such object—one star, say—and what as two distinct ones: a criterion of application and a criterion of identity. The same indeed holds true for a term, like "prime number," applying to mathematical objects, but regarded as defined over an already given domain. It is otherwise, however, for such a mathematical term as "natural number" or "real number" which determines a domain of quantification. For a term of this sort, we make a further demand: namely, that we should "grasp" the domain, that is, the totality of objects to which the term applies, in the sense of being able to circumscribe it by saying what objects, in general, it comprises—what natural numbers, or what real numbers, there are.

The reason for this difference is evident. For any kind of concrete object, or of abstract object whose existence depends upon concrete objects, external reality will determine what objects of that kind there are; but what mathematical objects there are within a fundamental domain of quantification is supposed to be independent of how things happen to be in the world, and so, if it is to be determinate, *we* must determine it. On the face of it, indeed, a criterion of application and a criterion of identity do not suffice to confer determinate truth-conditions on generalizations involving some general term, even when it is a term covering concrete objects: they can only give them a content to be construed as embodying a *claim*. So understood, an existential statement amounts to a claim to be able to give an instance; a universal statement is of the form "Any object to which the term is recognized as being applicable will be found to satisfy such-and-such a further condition." An utterance that embodies a claim is accepted as justified if the one who makes it can vindicate his claim, and rejected as unjustified if he fails to do so; a universally quantified statement is shown to be unjustified if a counterexample comes to light, but is justified only if the speaker can give adequate grounds for the conditional expectation he arouses. The difference between such an utterance and one that carries some definite truth-condition is that the claim relates to what the speaker can do or what reasons he can give, whereas the truth-condition must be capable of being stated independently of his abilities or his knowledge.

This is not, however, how we usually think of quantified statements about empirical objects. We normally suppose that, given that we are clear what has to be true of a celestial object for it to be a star, and when a star observed on one occasion is the same as one observed on another, we need do nothing more to assure definite truth-conditions to statements of the form "There is a star with such-and-such a property" or "All stars have such-and-such a property." This assumption reflects our natural realism concerning the physical universe. Whether this realism about the physical universe is sound, or (as I myself strongly suspect) ought itself to be challenged, is a question not here at issue: what matters in the present context is the contrast between what we standardly take to be needed to secure determinate truth-conditions for statements involving generality in the empirical case and in the mathematical one.

We are, indeed, usually disposed to be quite as firmly resolved that our mathematical statements should have truth-conditions that they determinately either satisfy or fail to satisfy as we are that this should hold good of our empirical statements. This is something that it never occurred to Frege to doubt. He acknowledged the necessity for specifying the truth-conditions of the statements of a mathematical theory; unfortunately, he persuaded himself that the domain of the individual variables could be determined simply by laying down the formation rules of the fundamental terms and fixing the criterion of identity for them, which he did by means of an impredicative specification, and produced an ingenious but fallacious argument to this effect.

Despite his realism about mathematics, even Frege did not think that mathematical reality determined the truth or falsity of statements quantifying over a domain of mathematical objects, without our needing to specify their truth-conditions; and his successors, mindful of the disaster that overtook him, have accepted the need to specify the domain outright, or to form some conception of it, before interpreting the primitive predicates of a theory as applying to elements of that domain. Notoriously, however, we have found little better means of accomplishing this task than Frege did. The characterizations of the domains of fundamental mathematical theories such as the theory of real numbers that we are accustomed to employ usually convince no one that any sharp conception underlies them save those who are already convinced; this leads to an impasse in the philosophy of mathematics where faith opposes incredulity without either possessing the resources to overcome the other. Moreover, this outcome seems intrinsic to the situation. A fundamental mathematical theory, for present purposes, is one from which we originally derive our conception of a totality of the relevant cardinality: it appears evident that we cannot characterize the domain of such a theory without circularity.

What is the way out of this impasse? We may approach this by asking after the error that underlay the assumptions which led Frege into contradiction—not that involved in his fallacious justification of those assumptions, but in the assumptions themselves. We have grown so accustomed to the paradoxes of set theory that we no longer marvel at them; yet their discovery was one of the most profound conceptual discoveries of all time, fully worthy to rank with the discovery of irrational numbers. Cantor saw far more deeply into the matter than Frege did: he was aware, long before, that one cannot simply assume every concept to have an extension with a determinate cardinality. Yet even he did not see all the way: for he made the distinction between concepts that do, and those that do not, have such an extension an absolute one, whereas the depth of the discovery lies in the fact that it is not. Taken as an absolute distinction, it generates irresoluble perplexity. We are thoroughly at home with the conception of transfinite cardinal numbers; but consider what happens when someone is first introduced to that conception. A certain resistance has first to be overcome: to someone who has long been used to finite cardinals, and only to them, it seems obvious that there can only be finite cardinals. A cardinal number, for him, is arrived at by counting; and the very definition of an infinite totality is that it is impossible to count it. This is not a stupid prejudice. The scholastics favored an argument to show that the human race could not always have existed, on the ground that, if it had, there would be no number that would be the number of all the human beings there had ever been, whereas for every concept there must be a number which is that of the objects falling under it. All the same, the prejudice is one that can be overcome: the beginner can be persuaded that it makes sense, after all, to speak of the number of natural numbers. Once his initial prejudice has been overcome, the next stage is to convince the beginner that there are distinct transfinite cardinal numbers: not all infinite totalities have as many members as each other. When he has become accustomed to this idea, he is extremely likely to ask, "How many transfinite cardinals are there?" How should he be answered? He is very likely to be answered by being told, "You must not ask that question." But why should he not? If it was, after all, all right to ask, "How many numbers are there?", in the sense in which "number" meant "finite cardinal," how can it be wrong to ask the same question when "number" means "finite or transfinite cardinal"? A mere prohibition leaves the matter a mystery. If gives no help to say that there are some totalities so large that no number can be assigned to them. We can gain some grasp of the idea of a totality too big to be counted, even at the stage when we think that, if it cannot be counted, it does not have a number; but, once we have accepted that totalities too big to be counted may yet have numbers, the idea of one too big even to have a number conveys nothing at all. And merely to say, "If you persist in talking about the number of all cardinal numbers, you will run into contradiction," is to wield the big stick, not to offer an explanation.

The fact revealed by the set-theoretic paradoxes was the existence of indefinitely extensible concepts—a fact of which Frege did not dream and even Cantor had only an obscure perception. An indefinitely extensible concept is one such that, if we can form a definite conception of a totality all of whose members fall under that concept, we can, by reference to that totality, characterize a larger totality of all whose members fall under it. Russell's concept *class not a member of itself* provides a beautiful example of an indefinitely extensible concept. Suppose that we have conceived of a class *C* all of whose members fall under the concept. Then it would certainly involve a contradiction to suppose *C* to be a member of itself. Hence, by considering the totality consisting of the members of *C* together with *C* itself, we have specified a more inclusive totality than *C* all of whose members fall under the concept *class not a member of itself*. Are we to say, then, that the concept *class not a member of itself* does not have an extension? We must indeed say that, by the nature of the case, we can form no conception of the totality of all objects falling under that concept, even of the totality of all objects of which we can conceive and which we should recognize as falling under that concept. On the other hand, to the question whether it is wrong to suppose that every concept defined over a determinate domain of distinguishable objects has an extension we must answer, "Surely not." Suppose that we have succeeded in specifying, or in clearly conceiving, some determinate domain of distinguishable objects, some or all of which are classes, and over which the membership relation is well defined. Then we must regard it as determinate, for an element of that domain, whether or not it is a class and, if so, whether or not it is a member of itself. A concept whose application to a determinate totality is itself determinate must pick out a determinate subtotality of elements that fall under it; and so the concept *class not a member of itself* must have a definite extension within that domain. All that we are forbidden to suppose is that any class belonging to the domain coincides with the extension of that concept. Frege's mistake thus did not lie in taking the notion of a class, or, more exactly, his notion of a value-range (the extension of a function), to be a logical rather than a mathematical one, as is sometimes said, not even in any straightforward sense, in supposing every function to have an extension; it lay in failing to perceive the notion to be an indefinitely extensible one, or, more generally, in failing to allow for indefinitely extensible concepts at all.

There can be no objection to quantifying over all objects falling under some indefinitely extensible concept, say over everything we should, given an intelligible description of it, recognize as an ordinal number, provided that we do not think of the statements formed by means of such quantification as having determinate truth-conditions; we can understand them only as making claims of the kind already sketched. They will not then satisfy the laws of classical logic, but only the weaker laws of intuitionistic logic. Abandoning classical logic will not, by itself, preserve us from contradiction if we maintain the same assumptions as before; but, since we no longer conceive ourselves to be quantifying over a fully determinate totality, we shall have no motive to do so.

Cantor's celebrated diagonal argument to show that the totality of real numbers is not denumerable has precisely the form of a principle of extension for an indefinitely extensible concept: given any denumerable totality of real numbers, we can define, *in terms of that totality*, a real number that does not belong to it. The argument does not show that the real numbers form a non-denumerable totality unless we assume at the outset that they form a determinate totality comprising all that we shall ever recognize as a real number: the alternative is to regard the concept *real number* as an indefinitely extensible one. It might be objected that no contradiction results from taking the real numbers to form a determinate totality. There is, however, no ground to suppose that treating an indefinitely extensible concept as a definite one will always lead to inconsistency; it may merely lead to our supposing ourselves to have a definite idea when we do not. This hypothesis explains the lameness of our attempts at a characterization of the supposed determinate totality of all real numbers, and relieves us of the embarrassment resulting from the apparent need for such a characterization; for the characterization of an indefinitely extensible concept demands much less than the once-for-all characterization of a determinate totality.

The adoption of this solution has a steep price, which most mathematicians would be unwilling to pay: the rejection of classical methods of argument in mathematics in favor of constructive ones. The prejudices of mathematicians do not constitute an argument, however: the important question for us is whether constructive mathematics is adequate for applications. We have so far assumed a realist view of the physical universe: would this be compatible with a less than fully realist view of mathematics? Not on the face of it; but, having taken the concept *real number*, but not yet that of *natural number*, to be indefinitely extensible, we have not yet attained a fully constructive conception of the real numbers, since they are essentially infinite objects, involving some notion such as that of an infinite sequence. By contrast, each natural number is a finite, that is, finitely describable, object: the totality of natural numbers is therefore of a radically different kind from the totality of real numbers. It does not follow that we may call it a determinate totality. Consider Frege's "proof" that every natural number has a successor: given any initial segment of the natural numbers, from 0 to n, the number of terms of that segment is again a natural number, but one larger than any term of the segment. As Frege presents it, the proof begs the question, since it rests on the assumption that we already have a domain containing the cardinal number of any subset of that domain; but the striking resemblance between this argument and that which showed the indefinite extensibility of the concept *set not a member of itself* suggests a reinterpretation of it as showing the indefinite extensibility of the concept *natural number*. The natural objection is that, when we attain the totality of all natural numbers, the supposed principle of extension ceases to apply, since the number of natural numbers is not itself a natural number. This, however, is again to assume that we have a grasp of the totality of natural numbers: but do we? Certainly we have a clear grasp of the step from any natural number to its successor; but this is merely the essential principle of extension. The totality of natural numbers contains what, from our standpoint, are enormous numbers, and yet others relatively to which those are minute, and so on indefinitely; do we really have a grasp of such a totality?

A natural response is to claim that the question has been begged. In classing *real number* as an indefinitely extensible concept, we have *assumed* that any totality of which we can have a definite conception is at most denumerable; in classing *natural number* as one, we have assumed that such a totality will be finite. Burden-of-proof controversies are always difficult to resolve; but, in this instance, it is surely clear that it is the other side that has begged the question. It is claiming to be able to convey a conception of the totality of real numbers, without circularity, to one who does not yet have it. We are assuming that the latter does not have, either, a conception of any other totality of the power of the continuum. He therefore does not *assume* as a principle that any totality of which it is possible to form a definite conception is at most denumerable: he merely has as yet no conception of any totality of higher cardinality. Likewise, a conception of the totality of the natural numbers is supposed to be conveyed to one as yet unaware of any but finite totalities; but all that he is given is a principle of extension for passing from any finite totality to a larger one. The fact is that a concept determining an intrinsically infinite totality—one whose infinity follows from the concept itself—simply *is* an indefinitely extensible one; in the long history of mankind's grappling with the notion of infinity, this fact could not be clearly perceived until the set-theoretic paradoxes forced us to recognize the existence of indefinitely extensible concepts. Not all indefinitely extensible concepts are equally exorbitant, indeed; we have been long familiar, from the work initiated by Cantor, with the fact that there is not just one uniform notion of infinity, but a variety of them: but this should not hinder us from acknowledging that every concept with an intrinsically infinite extension belongs to one or another type of indefinitely extensible one.

The recognition of this fact compels us to adopt a thoroughly constructive version of analysis: we cannot fully grasp any one real number, but only to an approximation, although there are important differences in the extent to which we can grasp them, for example between those for which we have an effective method of finding their decimal expansions and those for which we do not. This strongly suggests that the constructive theory of real numbers is *better* adapted to their applications than its classical counterpart; for, although the realist assumption is that every quantity has some determinate magnitude, represented, relatively to some unit, by a real number, it is a commonplace that we can never arrive at that magnitude save to within an approximation.

This partly answers our question how far a realist view of the physical universe could survive the replacement of classical by constructive analysis. On a constructive view of the matter, the magnitude of any quantity, relatively to a unit, may be taken to be given by a particular real number, which we may at any stage determine to a closer approximation by refinement of the measurement process; but no precise determination of it will ever be warranted, nor presumed to obtain independently of our incapacity to determine it. The assumption that it has a precise value, standing in determinate order relations to all rational numbers and known to God if not to us, stems from the realist metaphysics that informs much of our physical theory. This observation does not, however, settle whether the assumption is integral to those theories or a piece of metaphysics detachable from them; and this question cannot be answered without detailed investigation. If it should prove that the applications of any mathematical theory to physics can be adequately effected by a constructive version of that theory, it would follow that realist assumptions play no role in physical theory as such, but merely govern the interpretation we put upon our physical theories; in this case, physics itself might for practical purposes remain aloof from metaphysics. If, on the other hand, it were to prove that constructive mathematics is inadequate to yield the applications of mathematics that we actually make, and that classical mathematics is strictly required for them, it would follow that those realist assumptions do play a significant role in physics as presently understood. That would not settle the matter, of course. There would then be a metaphysical question whether the realist assumptions could be justified; if not, our physics, as well as our mathematics, would call for revision along constructive lines.

But would it not be better to adopt Field's approach, rather than one calling for a revision of practice on the part of the majority of mathematicians? What the answer ought to be if there were any real promise of success for Field's enterprise is hard to say; but there is a simple reason why he has provided none. He proposes to infer the conservativeness of a given mathematical theory with respect to a given physical theory from the relevant representation theorem by means of a uniform argument resting upon the consistency of a version of ZF with Urelemente. Why, then, does he believe ZF to be consistent? Most people do, indeed: but then most people are not nominalists. They believe ZF to be consistent because they suppose themselves in possession of a perhaps hazily conceived intuitive model of the theory; Field can have no such reason. Any such intuitive model must involve a conception of the totality of ordinals less than the first strongly inaccessible one; and no explanation of the term "model" has been offered according to which the elements of a model need not be supposed to exist. The reason offered by Field himself for believing in the consistency of ZF is that "if it weren't consistent someone would have probably discovered an inconsistency in it by now"; he refers to this as inductive knowledge. To have an inductive basis for the conviction, it is not enough to observe that some theories have been discovered to be inconsistent in a relatively short time; it would be necessary also to know, of some theories not discovered to be inconsistent within around three-quarters of a century, that they *are* consistent. Without non-inductive knowledge of the consistency of some comparable mathematical theories there can be no inductive knowledge of the consistency of any mathematical theory. Field's proof of conservativeness therefore rests upon a conviction for which he can claim no ground whatever; one far more extravagant than any belief in the totality of real numbers.

I have argued that it is useless to cast around for new answers to the question what mathematics is about: the logicists already had essentially the correct answer. They were defeated by the problem of mathematical objects because they had incompatible aims: to represent mathematics as a genuine science, that is, as a body of *truths*, and not a mere auxiliary of other sciences; to keep it uncontaminated from empirical notions; and to justify classical mathematics in its entirety, and, in particular, the untrammeled use of classical logic in mathematical proofs. Field wishes to abandon the first, and others argue for abandoning the second: I have argued the abandonment of the third. On some conceptions of logic, it may be protested that this is not a purely logicist account, on the ground that mathematical objects still do not qualify to be called logical objects; but this is little more than a boundary dispute. If the domains of the fundamental mathematical theories are taken to be given by indefinitely extensible concepts, then we have what Frege sought and failed to find: a way of characterizing them that renders our right to refer to them unproblematic while yet leaving the existence of their elements independent of any contingent states of affairs. If the price of this solution to the problem of the basis of those theories is that argumentation within mathematics is compelled to become more cautious than that which classical mathematicians have been accustomed to use, and more sensitive to distinctions to which they have been accustomed to be indifferent, it is a price worth paying, especially if the resulting versions of the theories indeed prove more apt for their applications.

2

The Advantages of Honest Toil over Theft

George Boolos

> He [Russell] had a secret craving to have proved *some* straight
> mathematical theorem. As a matter of fact there *is* one: "$2^{2^a} > \aleph_0$ if
> *a* is infinite." Perfectly good mathematics.
>
> —J. R. Littlewood[1]

In the section of his and Martha Kneale's *Development of Logic* called "Russell's
Theory of Logical Types," William Kneale writes:

> It is essential for mathematics that there should be no end of the sequence of
> natural numbers, and so Russell finds himself driven to introduce a special
> Axiom of Infinity, according to which there is some type with an infinity of
> instances, and that presumably the type of individuals, which comes lowest in
> the hierarchy. Without this axiom, he tells us, we should have no guarantee
> against the disastrous possibility that the supply of numbers would give out at
> some highest number, i.e., the number of members in the largest admissible set.
> There is something profoundly unsatisfactory about the axiom of infinity.
> It cannot be described as a truth of logic in any reasonable use of that phrase,
> and so the introduction of it as a primitive proposition of logic amounts in
> effect to abandonment of Frege's project of exhibiting arithmetic as a develop-
> ment of logic.... But even if we abandon all hope of carrying out Frege's
> programme in full and say boldly that Russell's axiom is required as an extra-
> logical premiss for mathematics, how can we justify our acceptance of it?
> What are the individuals of which Russell speaks, and how can we tell whether
> there are infinitely many of them?... [H]e even suggests that there may be [no
> individuals] because everything which appears to be an individual is in fact a
> class or complex of some kind. With regard to [this] possibility, which seems
> very mysterious, he adds cheerfully that if it is realized, the axiom of infinity
> must obviously be true for the types which there are in the world. But he does
> not profess to know for certain what the situation is, and he ends by saying
> that there is no known method of discovering whether the axiom of infinity is
> true or false. [Footnote in Kneale and Kneale: *Introduction to Mathematical
> Philosophy*, p. 143.][2]

The irritated tone of Kneale's commentary is noticeable, but one might
well think that something more like utter exasperation with Russell's procedure

is called for: In *Principia Mathematica*,[3] a work supposedly intended to show arithmetic to be a part of logic, more than *950* pages of text[4] precede the official introduction of the axiom of infinity. Just once in volume I is the axiom mentioned, in the introduction to the second edition, on page xxiv. On page 335, Russell states:

> We might, of course, have included among our primitive propositions the assumption that more than one individual exists, or some assumption from which this would follow, such as
>
> $$(\exists\phi, x, y).\phi!x. \sim \phi!y.$$
>
> But very few of the propositions which we might wish to prove depend upon this assumption, and we have therefore excluded it. It should be observed that many philosophers, being monists, deny this assumption.

The wisecrack may distract the reader from the outrageous claim that few of the propositions we might wish to prove depend on the assumption that there are at least two individuals.

Perhaps there are only a few propositions that depend *just* on that assumption and on nothing stronger; but the existence of the cardinal number 2, equivalent in *Principia* to the existence of at least two individuals, is one of those, and without its truth the development of arithmetic is impossible. The importance of the propositions depending on this axiom that we might wish to prove may offset the smallness of their number.

And of course a much stronger statement is needed than that of the existence of at least two individuals. The first two Peano postulates, in the order given them by Russell in *Introduction to Mathematical Philosophy*, assert that zero is a (natural) number and that the successor of a number is a number; the fourth states that zero is not the successor of a number; the fifth is the principle of mathematical induction. These are very easily proved in *Principia* without the assumption of any special axiom. The third, however, states that different numbers have different successors; together with the first three and Russell's definitions of *zero, successor,* and *natural number,* it implies the truth of the axiom of infinity, which asserts there are infinitely many individuals. The first four Peano postulates are theorems of every formal system for arithmetic that I know of; it is hard to see how any development of *arithmetic* could fail to deliver them.

Three axioms of *Principia* have struck commentators as having diminished claims to *logical* truth: those of reducibility, choice, and infinity. (Russell calls the axiom of choice the "multiplicative axiom.") Of these only the axiom of infinity is required for a *Principia*-style development of the arithmetic of the natural numbers, basic to all mathematics, but it is the only one of the three of which no mention is made in the first edition of volume I, where indeed not a word is spoken of the need to assume a special axiom guaranteeing the truth of the third Peano postulate.

In order to determine whether Russell has unjustifiably minimized the role of the axiom of infinity by thus tucking it away, to raise certain further worries, to point out certain perhaps underappreciated virtues of his procedure, and to compare his with the sublime (and therefore consistent) account of number found in Frege's *Grundlagen der Arithmetik*, we shall have to race over some all too familiar material: the development of arithmetic in the modernized theory of types *TT*, which, for the sake of simplicity and ignoring Russell's own strenuous efforts to dispense with classes, we shall pretend was the theory Russell was expounding. The version we shall explain is essentially the one given in Gödel's "On formally undecidable propositions of *Principia Mathematica*, etc." but without symbols for zero and successor, and without the assumption that the natural numbers are individuals.

In *TT*, the objects of type 0 are the *individuals*, whatever they are; those of type $n + 1$ are the classes of objects of type n, n a natural number. Objects of types 1, 2, and 3 we shall call *sets*, *classes*, and *class-classes*, respectively. Variables $x_n, y_n, z_n, \ldots$ range over objects of type n; for every natural number n, there is an axiom

$$\forall x_{n+1} \forall y_{n+1} (\forall z_n (z \in x \leftrightarrow z \in y) \rightarrow x = y)$$

of extensionality and infinitely many comprehension axioms

$$\exists y_{n+1} \forall x_n (x \in y \leftrightarrow \phi)$$

ϕ a formula not containing y_{n+1} free.[5]

We shall frequently use $a, b, c, \ldots$ as variables ranging over individuals (in addition to $x_0, y_0, z_0, \ldots$); $x, y, z, \ldots$, over sets; $m, n, A, B, C, \ldots$, over classes; and $X, Y, Z, \ldots$, over class-classes.

Λ is the null set; V is the universal set, that is, the set of all individuals. $\varnothing$ is the null class; 0, alias zero, is $\{\Lambda\}$. Like those that follow, these sets and classes all exist by comprehension and are unique by extensionality. $x - a$ is $\{b: b \in x \wedge b \neq a\}$, $y + a$ is $\{b: b \in y \vee b = a\}$, and sA, alias the successor of A, is $\{x: \exists a (a \in x \wedge x - a \in A)\}$.

À la Frege and Russell, n is a number if and only if

$$\forall X (0 \in X \wedge \forall A (A \in X \rightarrow sA \in X) \rightarrow n \in X)$$

that is, iff n belongs to every class-class to which zero and the successor of every member belong. $m, n, \ldots$ range over (natural) numbers.

The first, second, and fifth Peano postulates are trivial to prove. (*Applications* of induction of course require comprehension.) And it is very easy to prove the fourth, that 0 is not the successor of a number: every member x of sn is non-empty but 0 has an empty member. The difficulty is to see that different numbers have different successors. This will turn out to be the case iff $\varnothing$ is not a number.

Infin ax, introduced in section 120 of *Principia Mathematica*, reads

$$\alpha \in \text{NC induct} . \supset_\alpha . \exists! \alpha$$

In our terminology, for all n, n has at least one member; equivalently, $\emptyset$ is not a number.

Not only is it more than dubious whether any version of the axiom of infinity can be regarded as a logical truth, this formulation disguises what is being asserted more than need be. As usual, define a set x to be finite if and only if

$$\forall A(\Lambda \in A \wedge \forall y \forall a(y \in A \rightarrow y + a \in A) \rightarrow x \in A)$$

A less ad hoc formulation of the axiom of infinity is V, the set of individuals, is not finite. Of course, the two versions are fairly easily interderivable. Thus it might be thought a matter of "taste" which one assumes. Perhaps so, but it would be absurd to claim that "$\emptyset$ is not a number" expresses the statement that there are infinitely many individuals as directly as does "V is not finite."

However that may be, I shall want to argue that this lapse from perspicuity is the only charge against Russell mentioned in this essay that can be made to stick and that in *Principia Mathematica* Russell has in no way given us grounds for complaint that he has disguised, obscured, or minimized the role of the axiom of infinity.

If, following Russell, we say that x sm y if and only if there is a one-to-one function with domain x and range y, then with the aid of a lemma provable by induction on n, and asserting that if $x \in n$, then x sm y iff $y \in n$, it is easy enough to show that $\emptyset$ is not a number if and only if the third Peano postulate holds, that is, iff different numbers have different successors.

The proofs, found in Appendix I, are short and routine. They show how short the logical distance is between the axiom of infinity and the third Peano postulate. One could well think it not much less of a cheat for Russell to have assumed the axiom of infinity and then derived the third Peano postulate from it than it would have been for him to proclaim the postulate a truth of logic outright.

Russell once wrote, sarcastically, I believe, that "The method of 'postulating' what we want has many advantages; they are the same as the advantages of theft over honest toil. Let us leave them to others and proceed with our honest toil."[6]

Russell's procedure may seem to suffer further when compared with the account of number found in Frege's *Grundlagen der Arithmetik*. It will be recalled that in sections 74–83 of that work, Frege outlines a derivation of (second-order) arithmetic in the logical system given in his *Begriffsschrift* from the principle that the number belonging to the concept F is the same as that belonging to the concept G if and only if the objects falling under F are in one-one correspondence with those falling under G. Frege derives this principle, sometimes called the number principle, or Hume's principle, from an inconsistent theory of objects, extensions (a species of object), and concepts of various levels. A number is defined as the extension of some second-level concept under which falls some first level concept along with all and only those first-level concepts that are equinumerous with it. Being extensions, numbers are objects. Frege's criterion for the identity of extensions, that extensions of concepts (of the same level) are identical if and only if the same entities fall under them, is inconsistent, not only with respect to extensions of first-level concepts, as Russell showed, but also with respect to extensions of concepts of any higher level. Thus it is clear that the theory Frege implicitly employed in *Grundlagen* to define *number* is inconsistent.

Suitably formalized, however, Hume's principle can be shown to be equiconsistent with the arithmetic that Frege wished to derive from it: a proof of a contradiction in the system that results when Hume's principle is adjoined to the logic of the *Begriffsschrift* can (easily) be turned into a contradiction in second-order arithmetic, and, as Frege in effect showed, vice versa.[7] The derivation of arithmetic from Hume's principle that Frege sketched can be elaborated into formal deductions of the (infinitely many) axioms of second-order arithmetic. The most remarkable part of Frege's argument is his proof that every natural number has a successor. It utilizes a much more interesting mathematical idea than any found in Russell's derivation of the Peano postulates: *zero*, *successor of*, and *natural number* having been defined, and *less than* being defined as the ancestral of the relation an object bears to any of its successors, the number of objects less than or equal to any given natural number *a* can be shown to be a successor of *a*.

Recall also that Frege wished to show how numbers could be "conceived as logical objects." It is clear enough that before Russell's communication to him of the Contradiction, Frege supposed that the identification of numbers with certain sorts of *extensions* expressed a recognition of numbers as logical objects, and that the mere recognition of the truth of Hume's principle did not. As many commentators have noted, what is perhaps not clear is why Frege should have supposed this. Questions of consistency aside (!), what is there about extensions that makes *them*, and not numbers, logical objects in the absence of an account such as Frege tried to give? Extensions of concepts are supposed to be the same if and only if the objects falling under one of the concepts are identical with those falling under the other. To say when numbers are the same, simply change "extensions of" to "numbers belonging to" and change "identical" to "in one-one correspondence" in the foregoing sentence. Although it certainly requires a somewhat more complex formula to express that some objects are in one-one correspondence with others than to express that some objects are identical with others, one may reasonably doubt whether that difference entitles us to conclude that extensions are logical objects, but numbers are not.

Frege, it is also well known, failed to find a way out: his proposed solution to the difficulty turned out to be inconsistent with the assertion that there are at least two numbers. There is a modification of the notion of an extension that works, however. Say that a concept *F* is *small* iff the objects falling under *F* cannot be put in one-one correspondence with all the things there are. Say that *F* equiv *G* if and only if, if either *F* or *G* is small then the same objects fall under both. Equiv is an equivalence relation. Introduce subtensions by assuming that the subtension *F* of the concept *F* is identical with *G* if and only if F equiv G. This assumption can be shown to be consistent relative to second-order arithmetic, and can be used to define numbers: let $0 = *[x: x \neq x]$, that is, let $0 = *F$, where $\forall x(Fx \leftrightarrow x \neq x)$; let $sy = *[x: x = y]$; and let x be a number iff, as usual, $\forall F(F0 \wedge \forall y(Fy \rightarrow Fsy) \rightarrow Fx)$. The development of arithmetic then proceeds smoothly enough. (Peano three is no problem since $\exists x\, x = x$; thus $0 \neq *[x: x = x]$; thus there are at least two objects; thus for every y, $[x: x = y]$ is small.)

If subtensions are logical objects, then we have a way of recognizing numbers as logical objects; if not, despite their resemblance to extensions and the consistency of the axiom governing them, then we have even less reason than before to agree with the view that extensions, "had Rule V been consistent," would be logical objects.

Whether extensions, subtensions, or numbers are logical objects or not, it may seem, from a Fregean point of view, that Russell's definition of the numbers as certain sorts of class fails in two respects: invoking the axiom of infinity invalidates a claim to have shown numbers to be *logical* objects; defining them as certain classes (of sets of individuals) forbids him from thinking he has shown them to be logical *objects*. To show numbers to be objects, Russell would have had to show which individuals they are.

My aim so far has been to depict Russell's account of number in the worst possible light, as a series of tedious definitions and deductions in an inadequate theory to which an inelegantly formulated axiom has been surreptitiously adjoined with no justification other than to derive an indispensable but otherwise unobtainable theorem, and in which the definitions, moreover, obviously fail to satisfy one basic requirement of the enterprise of setting up a theory of number at all.

What, then, did Russell achieve? The answer may be found by reflecting on the "perfectly good" piece of mathematics mentioned in Littlewood's remark. This proposition and its proof, found in volume II at *124.57, constitute, I want to claim, the mathematical core of the theory of natural numbers given in *Principia Mathematica*.[8]

Never forget that the natural numbers form not merely an infinite totality, but one that is *Dedekind* infinite. Assuming now some theory of sets such as ZF, we say that a set is *finite* if and only if (as in the definition given previously) it belongs to all classes (here = sets) that contain the null set and contain all results of adjoining to any member any one object. Equivalently, a set x is finite if and only if there is a natural number i such that x can be put into one-one correspondence with the set of natural numbers less than i. A set is *Dedekind infinite* if and only if it can be put in one-one correspondence with a proper subset of itself. Equivalently, a set x is Dedekind infinite if there is a one-one correspondence between the set of all natural numbers and a subset of x (not necessarily a proper subset). The set of natural numbers is, trivially, Dedekind infinite according to either of these equivalent definitions. A set is infinite if and only if it is not finite, Dedekind finite if and only if not Dedekind infinite. It is easy to show that no finite set is Dedekind infinite; it requires some assumption that is not a theorem of ZF such as the axiom of choice to show that no infinite set is Dedekind finite. Russell, who was admirably clear on the distinction, called the finite sets "inductive" and the Dedekind infinite sets "reflexive"; it is a pity that this excellent terminology has not become standard.

According to the theorem Littlewood ascribed to Russell, if a is an infinite number, then $2^{2^a} > \aleph_0$. What does the theorem mean? Theorems about cardinal numbers are often best understood as encrypted theorems about one-one correspondences. After decoding, the theorem states that if x is an infinite set (with cardinal number a), then the set of natural numbers (which has cardinal number $\aleph_0$) can be mapped one-one into the power set $\mathcal{PP}x$ of the power set $\mathcal{P}x$ of x (which thus has cardinal number 2^{2^a}; thus $\aleph_0 \leq 2^{2^a}$), that is, that $\mathcal{PP}x$ is Dedekind infinite; but that there is no one-one correspondence between the set of natural numbers and the power set of the power set of x (thus $\aleph_0 \neq 2^{2^a}$, and so $2^{2^a} > \aleph_0$). The more interesting half of the theorem is thus that if x is an infinite set, then $\mathcal{PP}x$ is Dedekind infinite.

How, then, may this half of the theorem be proved? Let x be an infinite set. The null set is a subset of x of cardinality 0. If y is a subset of x of cardinality n, then since y is a finite subset of the infinite set x, y is not identical with x; thus there is some element a of x not in y and $y \cup \{a\}$ is a subset of x of cardinality $n + 1$. By mathematical induction, for every natural number n, there is a subset of x of cardinality n. Thus for each finite n the set S_n of subsets of x of cardinality n is nonempty, and if $m \neq n$, S_m and S_n are disjoint and hence distinct. Each S_n is a subset of the power set $\mathcal{P}x$ of x. Thus $n \mapsto S_n$ is a one-one function from the set of natural numbers into $\mathcal{PP}x$.

(The other half of the theorem, according to which $2^{2^a} \neq \aleph_0$, is immediate: if $2^{2^a} = \aleph_0$, then since $a < 2^a < 2^{2^a}$ by Cantor's theorem, $a < \aleph_0$, a is finite, and then so are 2^a, 2^{2^a}, and $\aleph_0$, impossible. I am not sure whether Littlewood had this, the "*strictly*-less-than," half of the theorem in mind when he made his remark.)

Thus, although one can point to a specific place in *Principia* where Russell proved the theorem ascribed to him by Littlewood, it would not be unreasonable to give: "*PM*, passim" as a citation for the theorem. To belabor the obvious: call the members of the infinite set x *individuals*. Then $\mathcal{PP}x$ comes to type 2 and S_n to the Russellian version of n; the Dedekind infinity of $\mathcal{PP}x$ is witnessed by S_0 and the function, which assigns S_{n+1} to each S_n and A itself to each member A of $\mathcal{PP}x$ not of the form S_n.

Put in Russellian terminology, the point is that Russell did not assume the type of individuals to be reflexive. He supposed it non-inductive and showed that it follows from that weaker supposition that type 2 is reflexive, and thus includes a subcollection similar to the set of natural numbers.

Not only can it not be proved in set theory without choice that there are no infinite Dedekind finite sets, it cannot even be proved that there do not exist infinite sets *whose power set* is Dedekind finite. And by adapting to the theory of types the Fraenkel–Mostowski method for showing the independence of various forms of the axiom of choice from set theory with individuals it can be shown that it is consistent with the theory of types supplemented with the axiom of infinity that the type of all individuals is infinite whereas the type of sets, that is, all classes of individuals, and hence the type of all individuals as well, is Dedekind finite.[9]

The idea of the proof is simple. Working in the theory of types, we shall build a model $\{T_0, T_1, T_2, \ldots\}$ of the theory of types in which T_0 is infinite, but in which there is no one-one mapping of the Russell numbers into T_1.

Begin with an infinite (Dedekind infinite if you like) set T_0, of individuals. Define a permutation π to be a one-one function whose domain and range are T_0. Say that π fixes a set x of individuals if for every $a \in x$, $\pi a = a$. Now suppose T_n defined, and $\pi\alpha$ defined for all α in T_n. If β is a subset of T_n, let $\pi\beta = \{\pi\alpha: \alpha \in \beta\}$, and let T_{n+1} be the set of those subsets β of T_n such that for some *finite* set x of individuals, $\pi\beta = \beta$ for all π that fix x. Thus each T_n is a subset, in general a proper subset, of type n.

It is easy to see that T_1 consists of the sets of individuals that are either finite or have a finite complement (relative to T_0). If n is a Russell number, then $\pi n = n$, for *every* π, and thus n is in T_2 (take $x = \Lambda$); similarly for the set N of Russell numbers: $\pi N = N$ for every π, and therefore N is in T_3.

The sets T_n, together with the sets belonging to them, turn out to form a model $\mathcal{M}$ of the theory of types and the statements that there are infinitely many individuals but Dedekind finitely many classes of individuals. The details of the proof are given in Appendix II.

Russell showed that there are Dedekind infinitely many classes of classes of individuals from the assumption that there are infinitely many individuals. But, as we have just observed, Dedekind infinity could not have been found any lower: without the aid of some such assumption as the axiom of choice it cannot be proved from the axiom of infinity that the individuals or the classes of them form a Dedekind infinite totality.

Of course there is a simpler reason why the numbers must first appear two types up if only the axiom of infinity is assumed. In the theory of types there is no way to define the numbers as sets of individuals and hence no way to define them as individuals. More precisely, for every formula $\phi(x)$ containing exactly the (set) variable x free, the sentence $\exists! 3x\phi(x)$[10] expressing the existence of exactly three sets satisfying $\phi(x)$ is not a theorem of the theory of types. Thus there are no formulae $0(x)$, $1(x)$, and $2(x)$ such that $\iota x0(x)$, $\iota x1(x)$, and $\iota x2(x)$ can be proved to exist and differ from one another; otherwise $\exists! 3x(0(x) \vee 1(x) \vee 2(x))$ would be provable.

In fact, it can be shown more generally that for any formula $\phi(x)$ of TT and any integer $i > 2$, the sentence

$$[\exists! ix\phi(x) \to \bigvee \{\exists! na\ a = a: n \leq i \text{ and for some } \sigma \subseteq \{0, \ldots, n\},$$
$$i = \sum \{nCr: r \in \sigma\}\}]$$

is provable in TT (nCr is the binomial coefficient). As the only rows of Pascal's triangle from which 3 can be obtained by summing entries are 121 and 1331, for any formula $\phi(x)$, $\exists! 3x\phi(x) \to \exists! 2a\ a = a \vee \exists! 3a\ a = a$ is provable in TT. Since $\exists! 2a\ a = a \vee \exists! 3a\ a = a$ is not a theorem, neither is $\exists! 3x\phi(x)$. Thus, if our resources are confined to those of the theory of types with the axiom of infinity, the natural numbers cannot be classes of individuals. (The mod 2 numbers could be, however.)

In his first proof that every set can be well ordered, Zermelo in effect showed how to extend the theory of types plus the axiom of infinity to make it possible to define the numbers as individuals. It will be instructive to examine the extension and definition, which it is perhaps not too farfetched to take to formalize the theory of arithmetic of Frege's interlocutor at the beginning of *Die Grundlagen der Arithmetik*, who, according to Frege, will likely invite us to "*select* something for ourselves—anything we please—to call one."

Let us add to the language of the theory a symbol θ for a function f whose values for arguments of type 1 are of type 0. And now let us take as a new axiom a strengthened version of the axiom of choice for type 1:[11]

$$\exists a\ a \in x \rightarrow \theta x \in x\ (*)$$

We can now define 0 as fT_0, 1 as $f(T_0 - 0)$, 2 as $f(T_0 - 0 - 1)$, etc. (Had we asked Frege's man on the street to tell us what two was, he would surely have invited us to select something *else*—anything *else* we please—and call it two.)

By the argument of Zermelo's proof, there is a unique well-ordering R of T_0 in which $f(T_0 - A)$ is the R-least element of $T_0 - A$, for any proper initial segment A of R. We may then define b to be the successor of a if aRb and for no c, $aRcRb$, and a to be a natural number if every b such that bRa or $b = a$ is zero or a successor. The axiom of infinity here guarantees that every natural number has a successor.

Thus, simply by adding a new function symbol to the language of the theory of types and a suitable axiom governing the function denoted by it, we have found a way to "recognize" the numbers as individuals. Of course, there was no need to bring in a *function* symbol; we could have adhered more closely to the syntactic style of the theory of types by introducing a constant $\mathscr{C}$ of type 4, along with the axiom

$$\exists a\ a \in x \rightarrow \exists!\ a(a \in x \land \{\{x\}, \{x, \{a\}\}\} \in \mathscr{C})$$

"But," it may be objected, "isn't that cheating? We are trying to find individuals with which to identify the natural numbers. However, not any old means of finding them is allowed. We have to use means that are recognizably logical. I don't see that the importation of a brand-new function sign, designating who knows what function (or the use of a higher-type constant: there's no difference), counts as a logical means of finding individuals that can serve as the natural numbers. We don't know which function θ denotes; you've just pulled something out of thin air to do the work you wanted to have done."

Let us note this objection for now and examine another means of recognizing the numbers as individuals.

Suppose that we add to the theory of types a function sign $^{\#}$ whose values for arguments of type 1 are of type 0 and take as a new axiom

$$^\#x = {}^\#y \leftrightarrow x \text{ sm } y$$

("sm" abbreviates "is similar to," defined as usual).

Then, as Frege showed in *Grundlagen*, if, *working without axioms of extensionality, the axiom of infinity or any version of the axiom of choice*, we define 0 as

$$\iota a \, \exists y (\forall c \, c \notin y \wedge a = {}^\#y)$$

define c to succeed b iff

$$\exists a \, \exists y \, \exists z (z = y + a \wedge a \notin y \wedge b = {}^\#y \wedge c = {}^\#z)$$

and define a to be a natural number iff

$$\forall x (0 \in x \wedge \forall b \forall c (b \in x \wedge c \text{ succeeds } b \to c \in x) \to a \in x)$$

then we can prove the Peano postulates, together with all necessary existence and uniqueness assumptions. It is an immediate consequence that the individuals form a Dedekind infinite totality, and that the axiom of infinity therefore holds after all. Moreover, the numbers have indeed been defined as individuals.

For all its excellences, this method of obtaining the natural numbers at the lowest level of the type hierarchy is as much subject to the objection that we have no idea which function the new symbol refers to as was the postulation previously described of a *particular* choice function f for type 1 (e.g., if π is a permutation of T_0, then where a is the value of $^\#x$ and b that of $^\#y$, $\pi a = \pi b$ iff x sm y holds[12]). It can be said with equal justice in both cases that nothing establishes, determines, fixes the function to which the newly introduced function symbol refers. No one struggled harder than Frege to overcome the apparent lack of fixity of the function referred to by "the number of (belonging to)." But it has often been remarked that whatever other problems may have beset Rule V of *Grundgesetze*, for Frege to use that axiom to introduce extensions and then to define a number as a certain sort of extension, is to advance little if at all in settling the question to which items number words refer: if we are uncertain whether numbers are conquerors, we are not going to be helped out of the slough by being told that numbers are extensions. (I think Michael Dummett pointed this out to me more than thirty years ago.)

It may be thought that we know what it is for one item to bear the relation indicated by "$\in$" to another better than we know which particular function is designated by "the number of," and certainly better than we know which function is designated by θ. To the extent that this is so, or supposed so, Russell's treatment of the numbers will be, or seem, *ideologically* superior to Frege's in the sense of Quine, superior in respect to the clarity or determinacy of the notions of which it avails itself. Russell may assume as an axiom a statement that Frege can prove, but Frege utilizes a notion that can neither be expressed in Russell's language, a sublanguage of Frege's, nor, apparently, freed from a very familiar sort of indeterminacy.

Of course, there is indeterminacy aplenty in the theory of types. As in the theory of complex numbers, i and $-i$ are indiscernible—any truth remains true in which "i" and "$-i$" are everywhere interchanged—so in the theory of types "$\in$" and "$\notin$" may be uniformly interchanged at any one type (thanks to the existence of a unique complement in its type for every item not of the type of individuals). More exactly, for any n, if ϕ is a theorem of the theory of types, then so is the result of replacing every atomic formula of the form $x_n \in y_{n+1}$ in ϕ with its negation. (In set theory we cannot perform this sort of switch: $\exists y \forall x \neg x \in y$ is, but $\exists y \forall x x \in y$ is not, a theorem of set theory.) Moreover, such interchange can be performed at any other type independently of whether it is performed at any others. Thus the theory of types is indeterminate in at least $2^{\aleph_0}$ ways.

But this sort of indeterminacy also infects the theory of objects and first- and higher-level concepts that was employed by Frege: we are free to interpret the predication Fx as asserting that the value of x fails to fall under the concept denoted by F. Thus, in any event a *new* sort of indeterminacy arises with the introduction of either $^\#$ or θ.

Of course the axiom $^\#x = {}^\#y \leftrightarrow x$ sm y (Hume's principle) is not to be regarded as a *definition* of number; it is merely a consistent principle whose addition to a suitable higher-order (indeed, second-order) logic yields a system in which the basic notions of the arithmetic of natural numbers can be defined and their most familiar properties proved. Thus, with the aid of a familiar-seeming principle. Frege has given a remarkably simple axiomatization of arithmetic whose consistency is not at present subject to doubt. (The tragedy of Russell's paradox was to obscure from Frege and from us the great interest of his actual positive accomplishment.) It has been my aim these last few pages to point out a number of respects in which Russell's account of arithmetic stands comparison with the one Frege is now known to have provided.

The construction of the numbers with the aid of a choice function, which was sketched earlier, shows, I think, that Hume's principle cannot be thought to be *the* foundation of arithmetic. One of zero's properties, and a very important one too, is that it is the number of things there are that are not self-identical; but, as our discussion of Frege's man in the street showed, there is also a perfectly sensical alternative development of the idea that 0, or 1 (if you prefer to begin the number series there), is the "typical object." It is also to be noted that there is no trace in the construction of the idea that 2, for example, is the class of all couples; nor is use made in the construction of a function injecting Russell numbers into the individuals.

Moreover, by the trick of reserving 0 for the number of things that are self-identical and "pushing each natural number up one," we can define $^\#$ so as to prove Hume's principle in the theory of types plus the axiom of infinity and our strengthened version (*) of choice.

I now want to take up the question whether Russell's introduction of the axiom of infinity in volume II of *Principia Mathematica* amounts, as Kneale put it, "to abandonment of Frege's project of exhibiting arithmetic as a development of logic." Of course the axiom of infinity cannot be counted as a truth of logic, and no one was clearer on that score than Russell himself.

> From the fact that the infinite is not self-contradictory, but is also not demonstrable logically, we must conclude that nothing can be known *a priori* as to whether the number of things in the world is finite or infinite. The conclusion is, therefore, to adopt a Leibnizian phraseology, that some of the possible worlds are finite, some infinite, and we have no means of knowing to which of these two kinds our actual world belongs. The axiom of infinity will be true in some possible worlds and false in others; whether it is true or false in this world we cannot tell. . . .
>
> We may take the axiom of infinity as an example of a proposition which, though it can be enunciated in logical terms, cannot be asserted by logic to be true. . . . We are left to empirical observation to determine whether there are as many as *n* individuals in the world. . . . There does not even seem any logical necessity why there should be even one individual [Footnote in original: The primitive propositions in *Principia Mathematica* are such as to allow the inference that at least one individual exists. But I now view this as a defect in logical purity.]—why in fact there should be any world at all.[13]

In *Principia Mathematica*, Whitehead and Russell say:

> If, for example, Nc'Indiv = *v*, then this proposition is false for any higher type; but this proposition, Nc'Indiv = *v*, is one which cannot be proved logically; in fact it is only ascertainable by a census, not by logic. Thus among the propositions which can be proved by logic, there are some which can only be proved for higher types, but none which can only be proved for lower types. . . .
>
> "Infin ax," like "Mult ax," is an arithmetical hypothesis which some will consider self-evident, but which we prefer to keep as a hypothesis, and to adduce in that form whenever it is relevant. Like "Mult ax," it states an existence theorem. . . .
>
> It seems plain that there is nothing in logic to necessitate its truth or falsehood, and that it can only be legitimately believed or disbelieved on empirical grounds.[14.]

And in volume III:

> Great difficulties are caused, in this section ["Generalization of number"], by the existence-theorems and the question of types. These difficulties disappear if the axiom of infinity is assumed, but it seems improper to make the theory of (say) 2/3 depend upon the assumption that the number of objects in the universe is not finite. We have, accordingly, taken pains not to make this assumption, except where, as in the theory of real numbers, it is really essential, and not merely convenient. When the axiom of infinity is required, it is always explicitly stated in the hypothesis, so that our propositions, as enunciated, are true even if the axiom of infinity is false.[15]

But if Russell made it plain that he did not consider the axiom of infinity to be a truth of logic, "asserted by logic to be true," what becomes of the project of showing arithmetic to be a development of logic, of logicism? Russell was a logicist, wasn't he?

To determine whether or not he was, it might just be advisable to consult his writings instead of common opinion. It turns out that Russell was rather more cautious in certain works than in others in proclaiming that mathematics can be reduced to logic, or is identical with it. The question whether Russell was or was not a logicist cannot, I think, be given a direct answer, and ought to be replaced with a question of the form, "Was Russell a logicist in work X?" What can be said is that he expressed logicist views in certain works and refrained—significantly, it seems to me—from expressing them in others, notably *Principia Mathematica*, in which, as it happens, there are rather few remarks on the relation between logic and mathematics; perhaps Whitehead and Russell considered it unnecessary to supply many, for the work is, after all, an extended disquisition upon just that subject. Those there are, however, make it doubtful that the authors should be considered logicists, that is, defenders of the view that mathematics, or arithmetic, or at least the Peano postulates, can be derived by logical means alone from statements true solely in virtue of logic and appropriate definitions of mathematical notions. *Principia* is not quite 2,000 pages long, and it is hard to be perfectly certain that one has not overlooked a significant remark or failed to put together separated comments that would make it plain that its authors do after all count as logicists. However, there appears to be only one section of *Principia* that explicitly deals with the relation between logic and mathematics, at the beginning of the introduction to the first edition. There Russell and Whitehead list three aims of the logic that occupies part I of *Principia*. They are, in reverse order, the avoidance of the contradictions, the precise symbolic expression of mathematical propositions, and the one that concerns us:

> effecting the greatest possible analysis of the ideas with which it deals and of the processes by which it conducts demonstrations, and ... diminishing to the utmost the number of the undefined ideas and undemonstrated propositions (called respectively *primitive ideas* and *primitive propositions*) from which it starts.[16]

Later, the first aim is described, rather differently, as "the complete enumeration of all the ideas and steps in reasoning employed in mathematics."[17]

It is evident that one who claims to have enumerated all the ideas and steps involved in mathematical reasoning need not imply that that reasoning is logical reasoning, or even that the third Peano postulate is a truth of logic. However justly, it might well be said that Zermelo–Fraenkel set theory provides such an enumeration; to say so is, obviously, not to be committed to the view that its axioms are logical truths. Russell's second description of his first aim provides no reason to take him to be committed to the central thesis of logicism.

Nor does his first description. The most thorough analysis possible of mathematical ideas and argumentation might well have as its outcome that the third Peano postulate is equivalent to the axiom of infinity, but leave entirely open the question whether the latter is a truth of logic. Russell repeatedly states that it is not one, and he did not take it to be a primitive proposition; moreover, he claimed to have proved from primitive propositions only the conditional with consequent Peano three and antecedent Infin ax.

One may distinguish, as Carnap has usefully done,[18] two theses of logicism, the first of which states that the concepts of mathematics can be explicitly defined from logical concepts; the second, that the theorems of mathematics can be deduced from logical axioms by logical means alone. We may call these the *definability thesis* and the *provability thesis* of logicism.

Establishing the definability thesis will show that all truths of mathematics can be expressed in the vocabulary of pure logic. But it is important to distinguish truths expressed in the vocabulary of pure logic from truths that are true "by virtue of logic alone," that is, *logical truths* or *truths of logic* properly so called. Russell's way of making this distinction was between propositions that are "enunciated in logical terms" and those that are "asserted by logic to be true."[19] "$\exists x \exists y \, x \neq y$" is a truth, and expressed in logical vocabulary, which Russell, correctly in my view, did not regard as a logical truth. One who accepts the theory of types will almost surely regard Infin ax as true and in logical vocabulary, but one who so regards it need not therefore take it to be a logical truth. Establishing both theses would certainly show the truths of mathematics to be logical truths, but establishing the definability thesis alone does not suffice to do this, and hence certainly does not establish the provability thesis. No one, I take it, counts as a full-fledged logicist who does not endorse the provability thesis as well as the definability thesis.

It seems fair to take Russell's aim in *Principia* to have been the systematic exposition of a sufficiently large portion of mathematics to enable the reader to see that, and how, the whole of the subject could be treated in its system, in the sense that every concept of mathematics could be defined in terms of the primitive ideas of the system and every theorem of mathematics either proved from its primitive propositions, *or suitably related* to other propositions of mathematics. In *Principia*, then, Russell was an advocate of the definability thesis, but not of the provability thesis of logicism. It was never part of his aim there to show that (say) Peano three, as opposed to "If Infin ax then Peano three," could be derived from the primitive propositions of the system. Whitehead and Russell might have paraphrased Boole and called their work *The Logical Analysis of Mathematics*. To provide such an *analysis*, however, it is not requisite to derive from logic the whole of elementary mathematics.

Once the idea is abandoned that the aim of *Principia* is to vindicate full-fledged logicism, to exhibit arithmetic as a development of logic, there is little to object to in Russell's *modus operandi*. The axiom of infinity is introduced at the appropriate point: in subsection *120 "Inductive cardinals," of section C, "FINITE AND INFINITE," of part III, "CARDINAL ARITHMETIC" (with which volume II begins). Part I of *Principia* is entitled "MATHEMATICAL LOGIC;" part II, "PROLEGOMENA TO CARDINAL ARITHMETIC." Where else should the axiom of infinity have been introduced?

When pronouncing on the relation of logic to mathematics, Russell is significantly less circumspect in the exoteric *Introduction to Mathematical Philosophy* than he is in *Principia*:

> Pure logic, and pure mathematics (which is the same thing), aims at being true, in Leibnizian phraseology, in all possible worlds, not only in this higgledy-piggledy job-lot of a world in which chance has imprisoned us. . . .

> The consequence is that it has now become wholly impossible to draw a line between the two; in fact, the two are one. . . . The proof of their identity is, of course, a matter of detail. . . . If there are still those who do not admit the identity of logic and mathematics, we may challenge them to indicate at what point in the successive definitions and deductions of *Principia Mathematica* they consider that logic ends and mathematics begins. It will then be obvious that any answer must be arbitrary. . . .

> Assuming that the number of individuals in the universe is not finite, we have now succeeded not only in defining Peano's three primitive ideas, but in seeing how to prove his five primitive propositions, by means of primitive ideas and propositions belonging to logic.[20]

These remarks and others that might be cited might well lead one to take Russell to be advocating a position he himself has given the best of reasons for rejecting, since he has elsewhere been as explicit as possible that he does not regard the axiom of infinity as a logical truth. To the challenge Russell lays down, one may respond that every proposition deduced in *Principia* is indeed a truth of logic, but Peano three, a proposition of mathematics if any is, has not been deduced there.

The last quotation, however, suggests a more charitable reading of *Introduction to Mathematical Philosophy*, under which one may interpret Russell to be claiming the identity of the concepts of mathematics with those of logic, the derivability of all the Peano axioms but the third, and the provability of "if Infin ax then Peano three." On this reading, the frequent omissions of an important qualification of the logicist thesis must be thought careless, if not propagandistic. In *Introduction to Mathematical Philosophy*, then, Russell can perhaps be considered to espouse the definability thesis of logicism, but to hedge significantly on the question whether the provability thesis holds. It is therefore arguable that Russell does not significantly change his mind between the writing of *Principia Mathematica* and *Introduction to Mathematical Philosophy*, and that in neither work should he be seen as fully committed to logicism.

Appendix I

LEMMA. If $x \in n$, then x sm y iff $y \in n$.

PROOF. INDUCTION. The lemma is trivial if $n = 0$, since Λ sm y iff $y = \Lambda$. Suppose $x \in sn$. Then for some $a \in x$, $x - a \in n$. Suppose x sm y via f. Then $fa \in y$, $x - a$ sm $y - fa$, $y - fa \in n$ by the i.h., and $y \in sn$. Conversely, suppose $y \in sn$. Then for some $b \in y$, $y - b \in n$. By the i.h., $x - a$ sm $y - b$ via some f, and thus x sm y via g, where domain$(g) = x$, $gc = fc$ for $c \in x - a$, and $ga = b$.

THEOREM. $\emptyset$ is not a number iff different numbers have different successors.

PROOF. Suppose that $\varnothing$ is a number. $\varnothing$ is empty. 0 is not empty. By induction we may assume that for some number n, n is not empty, but sn, which is a number, is empty. Thus $n \neq sn$. Since sn is empty and $ssn = \{x: \exists a(a \in x \wedge x - a \in sn)\}$, ssn is also empty, and by Ext, $sn = ssn$. Since ssn is also a number, n and sn are different numbers with the same successor. Conversely, assume that $\varnothing$ is not a number, m, n are numbers and $sm = sn$. Since sm is a number, $sm \neq \varnothing$, and for some x, $x \in sm = sn$. Then for some a, b, $a \in x$, $b \in x$, $x - a \in m$ and $x - b \in n$. Then $x - a$ sm $x - b$ via f, where domain$(f) = x - a$, $fb = a$ if $b \in x - a$, and $fc = c$ for $c \in x - a$, $c \neq b$. If $z \in m$, z sm $x - a$ by the lemma, whence z sm $x - b$, and $z \in n$ by the lemma again. Similarly, if $z \in n$, $z \in m$. By Ext, $m = n$.

Appendix II

In $\mathcal{M}$, T_0 satisfies the formula "x is infinite": since there is in fact no one-one function from any finite set of natural numbers onto T_0, no function in $\mathcal{M}$ witnesses the finitude of T_0.

We now show that T_1 does not satisfy "x is Dedekind infinite" in $\mathcal{M}$.

Suppose that $f, \in \mathcal{M}$, witnesses the Dedekind infinity of T_1. Abbreviate "$\iota z\{\{n\}, \{n, \{z\}\}\} \in f$" by "$fn$." Then f is a one-one function with domain N such that for every n in N, $fn \in T_1$. Since $f \in \mathcal{M}$, there is some finite $x \subseteq T_0$, such that $\pi f = f$ for every π that fixes x. There are only finitely many y such that $y \subseteq x$ or $T_0 - y \subseteq x$. Thus, for some n in N and some finite $y \subseteq T_0$, y is not a subset of x, and either $fn = y$ or $fn = T_0 - y$. Let a be an individual in $y - x$, and let b be an individual in neither y nor x (some such b exists since x and y are finite and there are infinitely many individuals). Let π permute a and b but do nothing else. π fixes x; so $\pi f = f$. Then if $fn = y$, $\pi y = \pi fn = \pi f \pi n = fn = y$, and if $fn = T_0 - y$, then $y = T_0 - fn$, and since $\pi T_0 - T_0$, $\pi y = \pi(T_0 - fn) = \pi T_0 - \pi fn = T_0 - \pi f \pi n = T_0 - fn = y$. In either case $\pi y = y$, $a \in y$, whence $b = \pi a \in \pi y = y$. But $b \notin y$, contradiction.

We now show that $\mathcal{M}$ is a model of the theory of types.

That extensionality holds in $\mathcal{M}$ is clear: if $x, y \in T_{n+1}$, $x \neq y$, then for some z, $z \in x$ xor $z \in y$. But then $z \in T_n$.

As for comprehension, let $x^1, \ldots, x^n$ be a list containing all variables free in a formula ψ; each x^i ranges over some one type or other. By induction on ψ, for any π, any objects $o^1, \ldots, o^n$ of the appropriate types, $\mathcal{M} \vDash \psi(o^1, \ldots, o^n)$ iff $\mathcal{M} \vDash \psi(\pi o^1, \ldots, \pi o^n)$.

Now let x_n be a variable ranging over type n, $x_n, x^1, \ldots, x^m$ be a list containing all variables free in a formula ϕ. We must see that for any objects $o^1, \ldots, o^m$ in $\mathcal{M}$ of the appropriate types $\{o \in T_n: \mathcal{M} \vDash \phi(o, o^1, \ldots, o^m)\} \in T_{n+1}$. Notice that for each n, T_n is a definable subset of type n, and therefore for each formula ϕ, "$\mathcal{M} \vDash \phi(o, o^1, \ldots, o^m)$" defines a definable relation. It thus suffices to show that if $q = \{o \in T_n: \mathcal{M} \vDash \phi(o, o^1, \ldots, o^m)\}$, then for some finite $z \subseteq T_0$, $\pi q = q$ for every π that fixes z.

For each i, $1 \leq i \leq m$, let z_i be a finite subset of T_0 such that $\pi o^i = o^i$ for every π that fixes z_i. Let $z = z_1 \cup \cdots \cup z_m$. Suppose π fixes z. We show that $\pi q = q$. π fixes $z_1, \ldots, z_m$, and so $\pi o^i = o^i$, $1 \leq i \leq m$, $\pi T_n = T_n$. Suppose $o \in \pi q$. Then $\pi^{-1} o \in q$; $\pi^{-1} o \in T_n$ and $\mathcal{M} \vDash \phi(\pi^{-1} o, o^1, \ldots, o^m)$; $o \in \pi T_n$ and $\mathcal{M} \vDash \phi(o, \pi o^1, \ldots, \pi o^m)$; $o \in T_n$ and $\mathcal{M} \vDash \phi(o, o^1, \ldots, o^m)$; and so $o \in q$. Thus $\pi q \subseteq q$. And if $o \in q$, then $\pi^{-1} o \in \pi^{-1} q$, whence, similarly, $\pi^{-1} o \in q$, and $o \in \pi q$. So $q \subseteq \pi q \subseteq q$, done.

Notes

I am grateful to Tony Anderson, David Auerbach, Richard Cartwright, Philippe de Rouilhan, Michael Hallett, Elliott Mendelson, Michael Resnik and Linda Wetzel for helpful comments. Research for this paper was carried out under grant no. SES-8808755 from the National Science Foundation.

1. Littlewood (1986), 128.
2. Kneale and Kneale (1984), 657–672, esp. 669.
3. Whitehead and Russell (1927).
4. More than 800 in the first edition.
5. We will often drop type subscripts when the type of a variable is clear from context.
6. Russell (1919), 71.
7. Cf. Boolos (1990) and (1987).
8. The theorem is erroneously ascribed to Tarski in one well-known excellent text: Levy (1979), 80.
9. Cf. Jech (1973), chap. 4, and Felgner (1971), chap. 3.
10. That is, $\exists x \exists y \exists z (\phi(x) \wedge \phi(y) \wedge \phi(z) \wedge x \neq y \wedge x \neq z \wedge y \neq z \wedge$
$$\forall w(\phi(w) \rightarrow w = x \vee w = y \vee w = z)).$$
11. By replacing items with their singletons, we can see that "choice drops down"; thus, if we had introduced a function sign ρ and a strengthened version of choice for type $n + 1$:

$$\exists x_n x_n \in x_{n+1} \rightarrow \rho x_{n+1} \in x_{n+1}$$

we could then have defined a suitable θ and proved (*).
12. The "Irving Caesar" problem.
13. Russell (1919), 141, 202–203.
14. Quotations from Whitehead and Russell (1927), vol. II, x, 203, 183, respectively.
15. Whitehead and Russell (1927), vol. III, 234.
16. Whitehead and Russell (1927), vol. I, 1.
17. Whitehead and Russell (1927), vol. I, 2–3.
18. Carnap (1983).
19. Russell (1919), 202–203.
20. Quotations from Russell (1919), 192, 194–195, 24–25, respectively.

References

Boolos, G. 1987. The consistency of Frege's *Foundations of Arithmetic*. In J. J. Thomson, ed., *On Being and Saying*. Cambridge, Mass., MIT Press, 3–20.

Boolos, G. 1990. The standard of equality of numbers. In *Meaning and Method: Essays in Honor of Hilary Putnam*. Edited by G. Boolos. Cambridge University Press, 261–277.

Carnap, R. 1983. The logicist foundations of mathematics. In P. Benacerraf and H. Putnam, eds., *Philosophy of Mathematics: Selected Readings*, 2nd ed. Cambridge University Press, 41–52.

Felgner, U. 1971. *Models of ZF-Set Theory: Lecture Notes in Mathematics*, vol. 233. Berlin, Springer-Verlag.

Frege, G. 1879. *Begriffsschrift*. Halle, Verlag von Louis Nebert.

———. 1884. *Die Grundlagen der Arithmetik*. Breslau, W. Koebner.

———. 1893, 1903. *Grundgesetze der Arithmetik*, Vols. I, II. Jena, Hermann Pohle.

Jech, T. 1973. *The Axiom of Choice*. Amsterdam, North-Holland.

Kneale, W., and M. Kneale. 1984. *The Development of Logic*. Oxford University Press.

Lévy, A. 1979. *Basic Set Theory*. Berlin, Springer-Verlag.

Littlewood, J. E. 1986. *Littlewood's Miscellany*. Edited by B. Bollobás. Cambridge University Press.

Russell, B. 1919. *Introduction to Mathematical Philosophy*. London, Allen and Unwin.

Whitehead, A. N., and B. Russell. 1927. *Principia Mathematica*, 2nd ed. Cambridge University Press.

3

The Law of Excluded Middle and the Axiom of Choice

W. W. Tait

I

With the gradual introduction into mathematics of the notions of an arbitrary function and an arbitrary set in the nineteenth and early twentieth centuries, two principles of logic became subject to controversy; and the controversies concerning them are curiously related.

One of the principles is the Law of Excluded Middle:

(LEM) $\neg A \vee A$

which is an ancient principle, explicitly formulated by the Stoics. An equivalent principle is the Law of Double Negation Elimination:

$(\neg\neg E)$ $\neg\neg A \rightarrow A$

When I say without further qualification that two principles are equivalent or that one principle follows from another, I mean that the relationship can be established using principles that are themselves noncontroversial.[1]

The other logical principle in question is the axiom of choice, which was first explicitly formulated in Zermelo (1904). I will express this principle by

(AC) $\forall x: A \exists y: B . \Phi(x, y) \rightarrow \exists f: B^A \forall x: A . \Phi(x, fx)$

A and B are types of objects and B^A is the type of functions with domain of definition A and whose values are of type B:

$\forall x: A$ means *For all objects x of type A*

$\exists x: A$ means *For some object x of type A*

where fx and, sometimes, $f(x)$ denote the value of f for the argument x of type A.

Note that I speak of *types* here and not of sets. A type A of object is determined when it is determined how we are to construct and reason about objects of type A. A mathematical object x is introduced or constructed *as* an object of some type A. It is not appropriate to ask for a proof that x is of type A (see section IX). As Gödel (1947, 1964)[2] pointed out, the original notion of a set is that of a set of objects of some type. Thus, we can pass from the type A to the type $P(A)$ of all sets of objects of type A. From the principles of construction and reasoning about A and the general logical principles concerning the operation P (see sections VIII–X), the principles of construction and reasoning about $P(A)$ are derived. (The conception of set underlying Zermelo–Fraenkel set theory, on the other hand, is obtained by iterating the operation P "transfinitely," starting with some particular type (of *urelements*) such as the null type 0; see section XIII.) If y is of type $P(A)$ and the object x of type A is an element of y, then we noted that it is not appropriate to ask for a proof that x is of type A, but it is certainly appropriate to ask for a proof that x is an element of y. In this we can see an important difference between the notion of a type and that of a set.

Zermelo's formulation of AC was

(AC′) For every set u of non-empty sets, there is a *choice function f* for u, that is, f is defined on u and, for all $x \in u, fx \in x$

AC and AC′ are equivalent under the assumption of LEM.[3] Zermelo first introduced AC′ in order to prove the Well-ordering Principle:

(WOP) Every set can be well ordered

AC′ easily follows from WOP; but the derivation of WOP from AC′ requires the use of LEM.[4]

II

Today, there is a small minority of mathematicians who adopt an intuitionistic or, more generally, a constructive point of view and who consequently reject LEM. For them, $A \lor B$ can be asserted only if we have proved one of A or B and so $\neg A \lor A$ can be asserted only if we have either proved or refuted A. For them also, as we shall see, AC is a law of logic. There is likewise a small minority for whom LEM is a law of logic, but who entertain the possibility that the Axiom of Determinacy is true and so must reject AC as a principle of logic. But the majority of mathematicians accept both principles in practice. Nevertheless, there is a clear difference in attitude toward them. LEM is not so much accepted as it is never questioned. The acceptance of AC has been more uneasy.

For Zermelo, who was by no means a constructivist, AC was also a law of logic. His argument (1908) is that it was implicitly used in mathematics and that many important results in mathematics depend upon it—and that this is the only justification that one can give for *any* logical principle. He is certainly right that AC was used implicitly in mathematics before he explicitly formulated it. Of course, Cantor used it implicitly over and over again in his work on set theory and transfinite numbers. An instance in analysis attributed to Cantor is in the proof that a real-valued function defined on $[a, b]$, which is sequentially continuous at $x \in [a, b]$ is continuous at x.[5] Another example is Dedekind's proof (1911) that any *Dedekind finite* set (i.e., one that is not equipollent to any of its proper subsets) is finite (i.e., equipollent to $\{1, \ldots, n\}$ for some n). An ironic example, in view of Lebesgue's later rejection of AC after it had been explicitly formulated, is his implicit use of it (1902) to prove that Lebesgue measure on the real line is countably additive.[6] It would be interesting to know whether, *before* Zermelo's explicit statement of AC, there was any single instance in which an argument was rejected because of a step in the argument that amounted to an implicit use of AC.

Even into the middle of the twentieth century there have been examples of implicit applications of AC in expositions of analysis and algebra, in which the authors make the inference from antecedent to conclusion as though it were simply a principle of logic.[7] But in the twentieth century generally, among those explicitly aware of AC, a more ambivalent attitude is expressed, both in analysis[8] and in algebra.[9] To whatever extent in these instances AC has been regarded as a law of logic, it seems to have been on Zermelo's grounds: it is essential to the proof of many results that we are inclined to regard as part of mathematics. But there is no sense that it is a law of logic because it follows from the meanings of $\forall$ and $\exists$.

Indeed, if one defines $\exists x : A$ to mean $\neg \forall x : A \neg$, it is difficult to see why AC, which now has the form

$$\text{(AC'')} \quad \forall x : A \neg \forall y : B . \neg \Phi(x, y) \rightarrow \neg \forall f : B^A \neg \forall x : A . \Phi(x, fx)$$

should count as a law of logic. I would like to argue in this essay that $\exists$ is not reducible to $\forall$ and $\neg$ and that, on the correct analysis of $\exists$, AC is indeed a law of logic, derivable from the basic inferences that define the logical operations $\forall$ and $\exists$.

III

The assumption of LEM in elementary arithmetic is unproblematic. Providing that we interpret $A \vee B$ and $\exists x : \mathcal{N}. \Phi(x)$ as meaning $\neg(\neg A \wedge \neg B)$ and $\neg \forall x : \mathcal{N}. \neg \Phi(x)$, respectively, and providing that we can prove $\neg \neg \Phi(x, \ldots, y) \rightarrow \Phi(x, \ldots, y)$ for all the atomic formulas in question, then we can prove it for all fomulas built up from them by means of the propositional connectives and the quantifiers over the type $\mathcal{N}$ of the natural numbers. In geometry, LEM was assumed by Euclid in the form that, for two like magnitudes (line segments, bounded surfaces, etc.) b and c, $b = c$ or $b \neq c$. Translated into analytic geometry, this becomes the assertion that, for any two real numbers b and c,

$b = c$ or $b \neq c$, which is not justifiable from a constructivist point of view. But, if we pay attention to the kind of constructions actually admitted in Euclid's *Elements*, it suffices to consider the least subfield of the real numbers closed under square roots of positive numbers, for which these instances are constructively justified.

So long as such notions as number and function were either insufficiently or too restrictively clarified, it is not clear when there was essential use of LEM in mathematics. The earliest instance of an (almost) rigorous proof in analysis involving an essential application of LEM may have been Bolzano's proof (1817) of the theorem:

> If $M(x)$ is a property of real numbers x that does not hold for all x but, for some r_0, $x < r_0$ implies $M(x)$, then there is a greatest r such that $x < r$ implies $M(x)$.[10]

From this theorem (and the first precise and correct definition ever given of the notion of a real-valued function defined in an open interval being continuous), Bolzano derived the Intermediate Value Theorem (if f is a continuous real-valued function defined on the interval $[a, b]$ and $f(a) < 0 < f(b)$, then $f(x) = 0$ for some $x \in [a, b]$). Another immediate consequence of the theorem is the Bolzano–Weierstrass Theorem (every infinite bounded set of real numbers has a limit point).[11] It is unlikely that any of these three theorems is constructively valid, because the principles actually used in constructive mathematics are compatible with the assumption that all functions are computable (in the sense of Post and Turing). But there are examples of computably continuous real-valued computable functions f defined on $[0, 1]$ with $f(0) < 0 < f(1)$ but such that there is no computable real number x in $[0, 1]$ with $f(x) = 0$. (f is computably continuous when there is computable function g of type $\mathcal{N}^{\mathcal{N}}$ such that for each m and all x and y in $[0, 1]$, $|x - y| < 1/g(m)$ implies that $|f(x) - f(y)| < 1/m$.)

It is interesting to consider why the reaction to the essential application of LEM came so late in the nineteenth century. Bolzano's paper was not generally known, but only four years later Cauchy published essentially the same proof of the Intermediate Value Theorem (based on a somewhat less precise definition of continuity), which was well known. The easy answer is that the paradoxes of set theory encouraged a more conservative conception of mathematics. But this cannot explain Kronecker's opposition in the 1880s, which preceded the discovery of the paradoxes. As a matter of fact, I do not know if Kronecker ever rejected LEM explicitly. But, as Harold M. Edwards (1988, 1989) notes, Kronecker's objection was to a style of mathematics that, as it turns out, requires the use of LEM and AC. Specifically, he wanted to limit concepts in mathematics to those for which there is an algorithm for deciding whether or not they hold—and so for which LEM is derivable. Strangely, it was initially only in Brouwer (1908) that criticism focused on LEM. In particular, the so-called French constructivists—Borel, Baire, and Lebesgue—did not challenge LEM at all in this period, but rather AC.

IV

Let me turn now to Lebesgue's rejection of AC. In a letter to Borel in 1905,[12] he begins by agreeing that Zermelo "has very cleverly shown that" WOP follows from AC. His doubts concern AC. He takes up Hadamard's distinction between demonstrating the existence of an object and defining it. His point is that AC asserts the existence of the function f without defining how fx is to be determined for each value of x. His own view is that "we can only build solidly *by granting that it is impossible to demonstrate the existence of an object without defining it*" (p. 265). But he then goes on to make a puzzling remark:

> when Cantor's well-known argument is interpreted as saying that *there exists a non-denumerable infinity of numbers*, no means is given to name such an infinity.... This sort of existence can be used in an argument in the following fashion: A property is true if negating it leads to the assertion that all numbers can be arranged in a denumerable sequence. I believe that this kind of existence can enter an argument only in such a fashion (p. 266).

Concerning his notion of definition Lebesgue writes, "Here the word *define* always means *to name a property characterizing what is to be defined*" (p. 266). Of course, to say that a proposition leads to the assertion that the set of real numbers is denumerable is equivalent to saying that it is inconsistent. So here Lebesgue is affirming the principle $\neg\neg E$ or, equivalently, LEM. But, as we have noted, this is already implied in a special case by his acceptance of Zermelo's proof of WOP from Zermelo's axiom of choice AC′.

Now Lebesgue's actual example is by itself confusing. Why can't I define the set of all real numbers—or rather, why haven't I defined it already with the definite description: "the set of all real numbers"? The property characterizing what is to be defined in this case is the property of being a set containing all and only real numbers. It is the fact that this set is non-denumerable that is the content of Cantor's theorem, not the fact of its existence. But leave that aside.

It is still hard to square all of the things Lebesgue is saying here. First, if a proof of $\exists y : B . \Psi(y)$ must involve defining a witness b (i.e., such that $\Psi(b)$) and a proof of $\Psi(b)$, then a proof of the antecedent of AC:

(1) $\forall x : A \exists y : B . \Phi(x, y)$

must yield a definition, for each x of type A, of the corresponding witness y and a proof of $\Phi(x, y)$. For certainly a proof of (1) should yield, for each such x, a proof of $\exists y : B . \Phi(x, y)$. But then let fx be the witness y so defined by this proof. So then we have a proof of $\Phi(x, fx)$ as a function of x. Thus, we have a means of transforming any proof of (1) into the definition of a function f of type B^A and, for each x, a proof of $\Phi(x, fx)$. In other words, we have a means of transforming any proof of (1) into a definition of f and a proof of $\forall x : A . \Phi(x, fx)$. We have defined a means of transforming an arbitrary proof of the antecedent of AC into a proof of its conclusion:

$$\exists f : B^A \forall x : A . \Phi(x, fx)$$

But what more should be required of a proof of AC?

So Lebesgue's conception of mathematical proof of existence should have led him to accept AC. Therefore, since he accepted Zermelo's proof of WOP from AC', which involves an instance of $\neg\neg E$, he ought to have accepted the inference of AC' from AC and so to have regarded WOP as proved. His point of view is simply not coherent.

V

Is Lebesgue's acceptance of LEM compatible with his view that a proof of $\exists y : B . \Phi(y)$ should include a definition of a witness? Suppose that we obtained this proof from a proof of $\neg\neg \exists y : B . \Phi(y)$ by $\neg\neg E$. Why should we believe in this case that a proof of $\neg\neg \exists y : B . (y)$ yields a definition of a witness? But now we should begin to consider what is to be meant by a "definition" of a witness b. Brouwer and the later intuitionists or, more generally, constructivists likewise require a proof of $\exists y : B . \Phi(y)$ to define a witness, but in a sense not available to Lebesgue. For example, if B is $\mathcal{N}(0) = \mathcal{N}$, then the proof should effectively yield a numeral t in the sequence $0, 0', 0'', \ldots, 0^{(n)}, \ldots$ and a proof of $\Phi(t)$. If B is $\mathcal{N}(k + 1) = \mathcal{N}^{\mathcal{N}(k)}$, then the proof should yield an (extensional) function $f \in \mathcal{N}(k + 1)$ and a proof of $\Phi(f)$. But to give such a function from the constructivist point of view is to give a rule for computing f. That is, if $k = 0$, from each numeral $0^{(n)}$, the rule should enable us to effectively determine the value $f(n)$ of the function. If $k > 0$, the rule should enable us to determine the value $f(u)$ of the function from any rule determining the object u of type $\mathcal{N}(k - 1)$. To say that f is extensional means that, if x and y are of type $\mathcal{N}(k)$ and $x = y$, then $fx = fy$. (Equality of functions f and g in B^A means that $fx = gy$ for all x and y of type A such that $x = y$.) Thus, functions are given intensionally, by rules of computation, but they respect extensionality.

There are well-known examples, simpler than the Intermediate Value Theorem, to show that LEM is not compatible with this constructive point of view.[13]

VI

There is a circularity in the constructivist notion of a function (i.e., of a "constructive" function).[14] A function f of type $\mathcal{N}^{\mathcal{N}}$, for example, is to be given by a rule r for computing, for all n, $0^{(f(n))}$ from $0^{(n)}$. Now there are simple rules, such as "add 10," which clearly define objects of type $\mathcal{N}^{\mathcal{N}}$ in this sense: From $0^{(n)}$ we construct $0^{(n + 10)}$. But how do we know in general whether a given rule is well defined, in the sense that it yields a unique numeral for each input $0^{(m)}$? Certainly, if we consider the rules that express the behavior of arbitrary Turing machines, then it is not decidable whether or not an arbitrary such rule defines an object of type $\mathcal{N}^{\mathcal{N}}$. So there is no escape from it: To be given a function of type $\mathcal{N}^{\mathcal{N}}$ is not only to be given a rule, but a rule r for which it is true that r determines such a function. But, for the constructivist, this can only mean that we have proved that it determines a function. In other words, to give a function of this type, we must give a rule r and a proof of

$$\forall n : \mathcal{N} \exists k : \mathcal{N} \text{ (from input } 0^{(n)}, r \text{ yields output } 0^{(k)})$$

But, by AC, to be given a proof of this is to be given a function g of type $\mathcal{N}^{\mathcal{N}}$ such that

$$\forall n : \mathcal{N} \text{ (from input } 0^{(n)}, r \text{ yields output } 0^{(g(n))})$$

So we have succeeded in explaining the notion of a function of type $\mathcal{N}^{\mathcal{N}}$ in terms of the notion of a function of type $\mathcal{N}^{\mathcal{N}}$.

VII

There are really two parts to the constructivist conception of mathematical reasoning. One part concerns the basic role of the notions of constructing an object of a given type—for example, of type $\mathcal{N}(k)$ for some k—and of constructing a proof of a proposition. The second part concerns the "effective" or "computable" character of these objects or proofs.

I truly wish that the term "constructive" had been reserved for just the first part, since it seems most appropriately applied to the view that the basic notion of mathematics is that of construction, without further specification of what kinds of construction are to be permitted. Then I could have called the view that I wish to present a "constructivist" view. But the term has been preempted for the narrower conception. So I will call the conception that I want to present the "construction theoretic" conception. As you will see immediately, I could also have called it a "proof theoretic" conception.

There are, at first blush, two kinds of construction involved: constructions of proofs of some proposition and constructions of objects of some type. But I will argue that, from the point of view of foundations of mathematics, there is no difference between the two notions. A proposition may be regarded as a type of object, namely the type of its proofs. Conversely, a type A may be regarded as a proposition, namely the proposition whose proofs are the objects of type A. So a proposition A is true just in case there is an object of type A.[15]

The identification of propositions with types has two sides. The first is technical and unproblematic. If we simply translate the relation of proposition to proof as the relation of type to object, it turns out that there is a considerable economy, which we shall illustrate in sections IX and XI. The rules of proof for propositions correspond exactly to rules of construction of objects of the corresponding type. So every proposition that we recognize as such may, from the point of view of proof theory, be treated as a type (see note 23). The other side of the identification needs argument. For it implies that a proposition is determined when it is determined proof theoretically, that is, when it is determined *qua* type. On this view, truth can only mean provability.

Remark. There is a possibility of confusion here. First, both of the concepts truth and proof are usually applied to sentences. It should be clear that propositions in my sense are not sentences and so I am using the terms in a somewhat non-standard way. But, of course, we can simply stipulate that an object of type A is also to count as a proof of "A." Secondly, when I say that truth can only mean provability, I do not mean that "A is true" is defined to mean "A is provable" for each type A. "A is true" means, simply, that A. So the force of the identification of truth with provability is simply that the only warrant for asserting A is a proof of A. In particular, the so-called Principle of Bivalence (A is true or A is false, for every A) is not the speculative principle that, for every type A, A is provable or A is refutable. Rather, it is just LEM.

We shall certainly have to return to this identification of truth with provability. For there are many who would argue that truth is a prior notion which cannot be captured by the notion of proof. For one who holds this opinion, the identification of propositions as types would be unsatisfactory. For it would be inadequate to simply specify how to construct objects of the various types A. We would also have to explain the conditions under which A is true (and explain in these terms why the objects of type A should count as proofs of A). But let me leave this challenge aside for the moment and develop the proposition-as-type picture a bit.

VIII

Consider, for example, two propositions/types A and B. What should we require of a proof f of the implication $A \rightarrow B$? We implicitly gave the answer earlier in the discussion of Lebesgue's inconsistent stance toward AC: namely, the only requirement should be that, given any proof x of A, f should yield a proof of B, f should be a function from A to B. In other words, the proposition $A \rightarrow B$ is just the type of functions from type A to type B:

$$A \rightarrow B = B^A$$

Similarly, all that should be required of a proof c of the conjunction $A \& B$ is that it yield proofs x and y of A and B, respectively. So c is just the pair (x, y). Thus, from the construction theoretic point of view, $A \& B$ is nothing but the type $A \times B$ of all pairs (x, y), where x is of type A and y is of type B:

$$A \& B = A \times B$$

The absurd proposition **0** is the proposition without proofs; it corresponds to the null type $\emptyset$:

$$\mathbf{0} = \emptyset$$

Negation can, of course, be defined by

$$\neg A = A \rightarrow \mathbf{0}$$

If we introduce the two-element type $\mathbf{2} = \{\top, \bot\}$, then the type $P(A)$ of all sets of objects of type A is defined by

$$P(A) = A \rightarrow \mathbf{2}$$

If f is of type $P(A)$ and x is of type A, we define elementhood in f by

$$x \in_A f \text{ iff } fx = \top$$

Let Φ be a function that assigns to each x of type A a type $\Phi(x)$. Then, in analogy with the case $A \rightarrow B$, a proof f of the proposition $\forall x : A . \Phi(x)$ should clearly associate with each x of type A a proof of $\Phi(x)$. And, moreover, nothing more than this should be required of such a proof. So f is just a function with domain of definition A and such that, for each x of type A, fx is of type $\Phi(x)$. In other words, $\forall x : A . \Phi(x)$ is the Cartesian product of the $\Phi(x)$'s:

$$\forall x : A . \Phi(x) = \Pi x : A . \Phi(x)^{16}$$

A proof of the proposition $\exists x : A . \Phi(x)$ should—as Lebesgue and the constructivists believe—determine an object x of type A and a proof y of $\Phi(x)$. And the determination of such objects x and y should be sufficient for a proof of $\exists x : A . \Phi(x)$. So a proof of this proposition is just a pair (x, y), where x is of type A and y is of type $\Phi(x)$. So $\exists x : A . \Phi(x)$ is just the disjoint union of the $\Phi(x)$'s:

$$\exists x : A . \Phi(x) = \Sigma x : A . \Phi(x)$$

Notice that $A \rightarrow B$ and $A \,\&\, B$ are the special cases of $\forall x : A . \Phi(x)$ and $\exists x : A . \Phi(x)$, respectively, in which Φ is the constant function with value B. So, in further discussion, we need not mention the propositional constants $\rightarrow$ and $\&$.

Although the only types we have introduced are $\mathbf{0}$ and $\mathbf{2}$, we speak of type-valued functions Φ defined on the type A. If we were to try to give a complete inventory of the building blocks of mathematical reasoning, we would have to specify the operations by means of which such type-valued functions are constructed. Actually, the general treatment of this problem is more complex than just considering type-valued functions defined on types. Consider the proposition

$$\forall x : A \exists y : \Phi(x) . \Psi(x, y)$$

where Φ is a type-valued function defined on A and Ψ is a type-valued function defined for pairs (x, y), where x is of type A and y is of type $\Phi(x)$. Thus, the range of the second argument y of Ψ is not a single type, but rather depends on the first argument x. Or consider the proposition

$$\forall x : A \exists y : \Phi(x) \forall z : \Psi(x, y) . X(x, y, z)$$

where A is a type, Φ is a type-valued function defined on A, Ψ is a type-valued function defined for pairs (x, y), where x is of type A and y is of type $\Phi(x)$, and χ is a type-valued function defined for triples (x, y, z), where x is of type A, y is of type $\Phi(x)$ and z is of type $\Psi(x, y)$. In general, we would have to consider sequences

$$\Gamma = \Phi_0, \Phi_1, \Phi_2, \ldots, \Phi_n$$

where $n \geq 0$, Φ_0 is a type such that, for all x_1 of type Φ_0, $\Phi_1(x_1)$ is a type such that, for all x_2 of type $\Phi_1(x_1)$, $\Phi_2(x_1, x_2)$ is a type such that ... such that, for all x_n of type $\Phi_{n-1}(x_1, \ldots, x_{n-1})$, $\Phi_n(x_1, \ldots, x_n)$ is a type. The members of such a sequence Γ are called *open types* and the sequence Γ itself is called a *base* of open types. For $i \leq n$, $\phi_0, \ldots, \phi_{i-1}$ is the *base* of ϕ_i. The sequence $x_1, \ldots, x_n$ is called an *argument* for the base Γ.

For our present purposes, we can ignore the principles by means of which bases of open types are constructed. We shall also ignore the initial part of bases. Thus, in any context, we may suppose that a base Γ and an argument $x_1, \ldots, x_n$ for Γ are given. Then our "types" A are all of the form $\Phi_{n+1}(x_1, \ldots, x_n, x_{n+1})$, where $\Gamma, \Phi_{n+1} = \Phi_0, \ldots, \Phi_n, \Phi_{n+1}$ is a base which extends the base Γ and x_{n+1} is of type $\Phi_n(x_1, \ldots, x_n)$. Similarly, if Φ is "a type-valued function" defined on $A = \Phi_{n+1}(x_1, \ldots, x_{n+1})$, then, for x of type A, $\Phi(x)$ is $\Phi_{n+2}(x_1, \ldots, x_n, x_{n+1}, x)$. So $\Gamma, \Phi_{n+1}, \Phi_{n+2}$ is a base with argument $x_1, \ldots, x_{n+1}, x$.

There is one special type-valued function defined on **2** that we should mention, the open type **T** with $\mathbf{T}\top = \neg\mathbf{0}$ and $\mathbf{T}\bot = \mathbf{0}$. Let $\mathbf{1} = \neg\mathbf{0} (= \mathbf{0} \to \mathbf{0})$. Then clearly the null function $\mathbf{n}$ on **0** (see section X) is of type **1**. In terms of this open type we may define, for any types A and B, the open type $\langle A, B \rangle$ with base 2 by

$$\langle A, B \rangle x = [(\mathbf{T}x \to A) \& (\neg\mathbf{T}x \to B)]$$

Writing $C \equiv D$ as an abbreviation for $(C \to D) \& (D \to C)$, one easily proves that $\langle A, B \rangle\top \equiv A$ and $\langle A, B \rangle\bot \equiv B$.[17] It follows that we may introduce disjunction $A \vee B$ by

$$A \vee B = \exists x : \mathbf{2} . \langle A, B \rangle x$$

IX

We should say something now about the construction of objects/proofs. We have described **0** and **2** as the "null type" and "two-element type," respectively; and we have described $\forall x : A . \Phi(x)$ as a type of "functions" and $\exists x : A . \Phi(x)$ as a type of "pairs." But these descriptions should be regarded as informal and preliminary, hinting at how objects of these types are to be constructed and how objects of other types can be constructed from them. Ultimately, we have explained these types only when we have specified what constructions can be performed.

This remark is very important as an answer, in the context of the construction theoretic point of view, to the argument that there is a circularity in the constructivist's notion of a function of type $A \to B$. If it made sense to ask whether the principles we introduce are correct for the notions of function and pair, for example, then we would have the analogue of the circle described in section VI, namely, an infinite regress:

x is of type A

y is a proof that x is of type A

z is a proof that y is a proof that x is of type A

But there is no such infinite regress. The principles for constructing functions or pairs of a given type $\forall x : A . \Phi(x)$ or $\exists x : A . \Phi(x)$, respectively, *exhibit* what these concepts mean, to the extent that their meanings are determined; and it is not appropriate to ask for a proof that the constructions are valid.

It must be noted in connection with this discussion that the relation of equality is not identity and the notion "x is of type A" or "x is a proof of A" in intentional. For example, two functions are equal iff they have equal values for equal arguments. Let Φ be a type-valued function defined on $A \to B$, let b and c be equal objects of type $A \to B$, and let x be constructed as a proof of $\Phi(b)$. It does not follow that x is a proof of $\Phi(c)$, even though $\Phi(b) = \Phi(c)$. The fact that $b = c$ and so $\Phi(b) = \Phi(c)$ may itself require nontrivial proof. (Since we are mainly interested in proof theory in this essay, that is, in what can be proved, and the notion of two proofs being equal is not important in this respect, we can ignore the notion of equality.)

The implication of these remarks is that so-called propositions of the form "x is of type A" can be true but never have proofs. This apparently contradicts our construction theoretic point of view. The resolution of the apparent contradiction is that "x is of type A" is not a genuine mathematical proposition at all. x is something that we construct and the construction *is* of an object of a particular type. If the construction is according to the principles of construction that we have laid down, x shows its type and so "x is of type A" is either "true" or it is nonsense. It is, in any case, not susceptible to proof (see the preliminary remark about "types" in section I). For example, 0 is of type $\mathcal{N}$. It is not as though the term "0" has a prior meaning and then we must determine the type of its reference. If 0 is not a number (whatever that could possibly mean), then the symbol "0" is meaningless.

To say that the notion of a function of a given type is only determined when we have specified the principles governing our use of it is not, of course, to say that there was no notion of function until it was so analyzed. But we do not have to think of this prior notion as something that goes beyond the kinds of constructions of and inferences about functions that were habitually made. If we did, then circularity would reappear: How are we to show that the principles we introduce are really valid for the notion of function? (In just this way, the circle is ineliminable in constructive mathematics, because whatever principles of logic are given, they must ultimately answer the challenge of whether they really yield "constructive objects." The notion of being constructive is intended as a measure of correctness for any particular principle considered.) The sense in which there was a prior notion of function, which we have analyzed by means of these principles, is simply that there was a prior usage of the word "function" in mathematics and these principles are both a part of that usage and serve to derive the rest. There remains no ghost of the notion of function to which the principles are accountable.

Only empirical explanation is possible for why we have come to accept the basic principles that we do and why we apply them as we do—for why we have mathematics and for why it is as it is. But it is only within the framework of mathematics as determined by this practice that we can speak of mathematical necessity. In this sense, which I believe Wittgenstein was first to fully grasp, mathematical necessity rides on the back of empirical contingency. Notice that this view of things leaves no room for so-called epistemological foundations of mathematics or for "foundations of mathematics" in the sense of attempting to show that mathematics is "true" as opposed to showing that in mathematics a particular proposition is true.

X

Concerning the principles of logic themselves, associated with each of the "logical constants" 0, 2, $\forall$ and $\exists$ are certain rules for construction of objects (rules of proof):

(0) For each type A, there is a unique function of type $0 \rightarrow A$

Recall that we are ignoring initial segments of bases. Thus, 0 and A will be $\Phi_{n+1}(x_1, \ldots, x_n, x_{n+1})$ and $\Phi'_{n+1}(x_1, \ldots, x_n, x_{n+1})$, where Γ, Φ_{n+1} and Γ, Φ'_{n+1} are bases and $x_1, \ldots, x_n, x_{n+1}$ is an argument for both bases. In this case, the unique function of type $0 \rightarrow A$ depends, too, on the argument $x_1, \ldots, x_n, x_{n+1}$. This remark will apply to the following principles as well, though I will not spell it out.

From the point of view of types, the existence of a unique object of type

$0 \to A$ for all A expresses simply that 0 is null. From the point of view of logic, $0 \to A$ expresses that every proposition follows from absurdity.

2(a) $\top$ and $\perp$ are objects of type **2**.

2(b) If Φ is a type-valued function defined on **2**, there is a unique function f of type

$$\Phi(\top) \to (\Phi(\perp) \to \forall x : \mathbf{2}. \Phi(x))$$

such that, for x and y of types $\Phi(\top)$ and $\Phi(\perp)$, respectively,

$$fxy\top = x \qquad fxy\perp = y$$

(b) expresses what it means to say that $\top$ and $\perp$ are the only objects of type **2**.

∀(a) For all pairs of types A and B, there is an object K of type

$$A \to (B \to A)$$

∀(b) If Φ and Ψ are type-valued functions defined on the type A, then there is an object S of type

$$\forall x : A(\Phi(x) \to \Psi(x)) \to (\forall x : A . \Phi(x) \to \forall x : A . \Psi(x))$$

∀(c) If b is of type A and f is of type $\forall x : A . \Phi(x)$, then fb is of type $\Phi(b)$.

From the type theoretic point of view, (c) introduces the operation of applying a function to an argument. We are using the notation "fb" instead of "$f(b)$" for application of the function f to the argument b. If the value fb is itself a function with argument (c), then fbc denotes the value of fb for this argument, and so on.

From the logical point of view, (c) is the principle of Universal Quantifier Instantiation and when $\forall x : A . \Phi(x)$ is $A \to B$, it is the principle of Modus Ponens.

The functions K and S of (a) and (b) are defined by the equations

$$Kab = a \qquad Sfga = fa(ga)$$

In logic, the type

$$A \to (B \to A)$$

of **∀**(a) and the special case

$$(A \to (B \to C)) \to ((A \to B) \to (A \to B))$$

of the type of **∀**(b) are the axioms for implication; and

$$A \to \forall x : B . A$$

(which is just $A \rightarrow (B \rightarrow A)$) and

$$\forall x : A(\Phi(x) \rightarrow \Psi(x)) \rightarrow (\forall x : A . \Phi(x) \rightarrow \forall x : A . \Psi(x))$$

are the axioms for universal quantification. From the type theoretic point of view, K and S are Schönfinkel's combinators.[18]

Speaking informally, but in a way that can be made rigorous, there is the following result due essentially to Schönfinkel: let $t(x)$ be a term of type $\Phi(x)$ built up by means of our rules from the variable x of type A. Then there is an object f of type $\forall x : A . \Phi(x)$ such that, for all b of type A,

$$fb = t(b)$$

f is usually denoted by

$$\lambda x : A . t(x) \text{ or } \lambda x . t(x)$$

when the type of x is given in the context. From the logical point of view, $t(x)$ is a proof of $\Phi(x)$, and so the construction of f is a derivation of the principle of Universal Quantifier Introduction. In the case that $\forall x : A . \Phi(x)$ is $A \rightarrow B$, introducing the variable x of type A amounts to introducing the hypothesis that A. So $t(x)$ represents a proof of B from the assumption that A. In this case, Schönfinkel's construction of f corresponds to the usual proof of the Deduction Theorem in predicate logic.

∃. Let Φ be a type-valued function defined on A.

(a) There is a function P of type $\forall x : A(\Phi(x) \rightarrow \exists x : A . \Phi(x))$.
(b) There is a function P_0 of type $\exists x : A . \Phi(x) \rightarrow A$.
(c) There is a function P_1 of type $\forall y : (\exists x . \Phi(x)) . \Phi(P_0(y))$.

When b is of type A and c is of type $\Phi(b)$, then Pbc is the pair (b, c). If d is of type $\exists x : A . \Phi(x)$, then d is a pair (b, c). In that case, $P_0(d) = b$ and $P_1(d) = c$. So we have the equations

$$P_0(Pbc) = b$$
$$P_1(Pbc) = c$$
$$P(P_0 d)(P_1 d) = d$$

∃(a) is certainly familiar from predicate logic. But (b) and (c) are very different from the corresponding "elimination rule" for ∃ in predicate logic, namely

(1) From $\exists x : A . \Phi(x)$ and $\forall x : A(\Phi(x) \rightarrow B)$, infer B

We can derive (1), however. If b is of type $\exists x : A . \Phi(x)$ and c is of type $\forall x : A(\Phi(x) \rightarrow B)$, then $c(P_0 b)(P_1 b)$ is of type B.

We know that, in classical first-order predicate logic, $\exists$(a) and (1) are sufficient, for the simple reason that we can prove the Completeness Theorem. I believe that $\exists$(a) and (1) suffice in intuitionistic first-order predicate logic, too, in the sense that any first-order formula proved using $\exists$(b–c) and without $\neg\neg E$ can be proved using (1) and without $\neg\neg E$. (I think that I once proved this; but I cannot find notes on it and can only remember ways in which it *cannot* be proved. So it should stand as a conjecture.)

Why were the inference rules for $\exists$ given as $\exists$(a) and (1)? Frege defined $\exists x$ as $\neg\forall x\neg$ and $\exists$(a) and (1) are the natural duals of the rules for $\forall$. But Gentzen was interested in intuitionistic systems as well as classical ones, where $\exists x$ is not equivalent to $\neg\forall x\neg$, and still gave $\exists$(a) and (1) as the inference rules for $\exists$ in his system of natural deduction. The reason is clear: If the type $\exists x : A . \Phi(x)$ is a first-order formula, then A is the domain of individuals and the type $\exists x : A . \Phi(x) \to A$ of (b) is not a first-order formula and still less is the type $\forall y : (\exists x : A . \Phi(x)) . \Phi(P_0(y))$ of (c). So, to the extent that Gentzen wished to restrict his attention to first-order predicate logic, $\exists$(b–c) were not available to him.

In terms of the rules of construction associated with $\forall$ and $\exists$, we can prove AC, making rigorous the argument previously given that Lebesgue should have accepted this principle. Namely, let u be a proof of the antecedent $\forall x : A \exists y : B . \Phi(x, y)$. Let x be of type A. Then $P_0(ux)$ is of type B and $P_1(ux)$ is a proof of $\Phi(x, P_0(ux))$. So $s(u) = \lambda x . P_0(ux)$ is of type $A \to B$ and $t(u) = \lambda x . P_1(ux)$ is a proof of $\forall x : A . \Phi(x, fx)$. $\lambda u . Ps(u)t(u)$ is therefore a proof of $\forall x : A \exists y : B . \Phi(x, y) \to \exists f : (A \to B)\forall x : A . \Phi(x, fx)$.

Incidentally, this proof of AC is entirely within constructive logic. Yet it is sometimes said in the literature on constructive mathematics that the Axiom of Choice does not generally hold in our sense. That is, from $\forall x \exists y \phi(x, y)$, where x and y range over some domains, we may constructively conclude that there is a nonextensional operation O such that $\forall x \phi(x, O(x))$; but in general O may not be a function because equal x's may not yield equal $O(x)$'s. But, in the examples provided, the scope of x is not a type in our sense but rather is a set. Thus, one example is that for every real number x there is an integer y that is greater than x. In fact, we can constructively prove that, for any Cauchy sequence z, there is an integer y which is greater than (the real number represented by) x. But the proof does not yield the same y for sequences x and x' which represent the same real number. But this is not really a counter-example to our previous argument that AC is a theorem of constructive logic. For, if we code rational numbers as natural numbers and $\mathcal{N}$ is the type of natural numbers, then the Cauchy sequences form a subset of $\mathcal{N}^{\mathcal{N}}$. The premise of the proposed instance of the Axiom of Choice is therefore $\forall x : \mathcal{N}^{\mathcal{N}}$ [x is a Cauchy sequence $\to \exists y(x < y)$]. This cannot be constructively reduced to the antecedent of an instance of AC, since "x is a Cauchy sequence" is not a constructively decidable property of numerical functions. It is true that, from x of type $\mathcal{N}^{\mathcal{N}}$ and a proof p that x is a Cauchy sequence, we may obtain $y = f(x, p)$, where f is an (extensional) function. But it will depend essentially upon p and not just upon x.

Finally, what distinguishes classical from constructive logic is the principle

$\neg\neg$ For every type A, there is an object D of type $\neg\neg A \to A$

The completely circular argument for this principle is this: If there is an object x of type A, then the function on $\neg\neg A$ with constant value x is of type $\neg\neg A \to A$. If there is no object of type A, then $\neg A$ is true and so $\neg\neg A$ is false. In this case, the null function is of type $\neg\neg A \to A$. But we are assuming that either there is an object of type A or not. That is precisely the assumption that A or not, that is, it is the assumption of LEM.

We can see now that it is LEM and not AC that is awkward. Every principle other than $\neg\neg$ introduces only objects that are uniquely characterized. But, in general, there is no uniquely characterizable function from $\neg\neg A$ to A.

Of course, for particular A we may be able to define D. For example, if A is either $\mathbf{0}$ or $\mathbf{2}$, we can derive $\neg\neg E$. If Φ is a type-valued function on C and we can derive $\neg\neg E$ for Φ, that is, if

(2) $\forall x : C(\neg\neg\Phi(x) \to \Phi(x))$

is derivable, then so is $\neg\neg\forall x : C.\Phi(x) \to \forall x : C.\Phi(x).$[19] In particular, if we can derive $\neg\neg E$ for B, then we can derive it for $A \to B \ (= \forall x : A.B)$. It follows that we can derive $\neg\neg E$ for any negation $\neg A$. So the crucial case is

(3) $\neg\neg\exists x : C.\Phi(x) \to \exists x : C.\Phi(x)$

Even when (2) is derivable, we may not be able to derive (3) without $\neg\neg$. Yet by $\neg\neg$ there is a function D of this type. So, for every proof u of $\neg\neg\exists x : C.\Phi(x)$, Du is of type $\exists x : C.\Phi(x)$ and $P_0(Du)$ is of type C. Let $f = \lambda u . P_0(Du)$. For each proof u of $\neg\neg\exists x : C.\Phi(x)$, f "chooses" an object $P_0(Du)$ of type C. But we may have no information about which object of type C it is.

However awkward this is, it is a fact of life in classical mathematics.

Using $\neg\neg$, we derive LEM and hence

(4) $\forall x : A.(\Phi(x) \lor \neg\Phi(x))$[20]

Recall that for x of type A and f of type $\mathbf{P}(A)$, $x \in_A f$ means $fx = \top$. Clearly, we can express this by

$x \in_A f =_{\text{Def}} \mathbf{T}(fx)$

since the right-hand side is true just in case it is equal to $\mathbf{1}$, which is the case iff $fx = \top$. Let f be a proof of (4). Then for each x of type A, $\mathbf{P}_0(fx)$ is of type $\mathbf{2}$ and $\mathbf{P}_1(fx)$ is a proof of $\Phi(x)$ iff $\mathbf{P}_0(fx) = \top$. So $g = \lambda x : A.\mathbf{P}_0(fx)$ is of type $\mathbf{P}(A)$ and we can prove

$\forall x : A(x \in_A g \equiv \Phi(x))$[21]

So we can derive the *Comprehension Axiom*:

(CA) $\exists g : P(A) \forall x : A(x \in_A g \equiv \Phi(x))$

This, too, is a principle of logic from the present point of view!

To return to the discussion of $\exists$, using the principle $\neg\neg$, we can prove

$\exists x : A . \Phi(x) \equiv \neg \forall x : A \neg \Phi(x)^{22}$

It follows that in classical logic we can prove

(AC'') $\forall x : A \neg \forall y : B \neg \Phi(x, y) \rightarrow \neg \forall f : A \rightarrow B \neg \forall x : A . \Phi(x, fx)$

XI

In Gentzen's system of natural deduction for first-order predicate logic, he is able to formulate the rules of inference in such a way that, if there is a proof of a formula Φ from assumptions $\Psi, \ldots, \chi$, then there is such a proof in which the only logical constants occurring in the proof are those that occur in one of $\Phi, \Psi, \ldots$, or χ. It is interesting to note that this is not so in general. If the constant $\exists$ and the rules $\exists$(a–c) are dropped, the AC'' cannot be proved, even though it does not contain the constant $\exists$ (when $\Phi(x)$ does not). First-order predicate logic really is very special. It is too bad that the influence of Skølem and, later among philosophers, Quine has allowed it to dominate our notion of logic.

XII

One might wish to consider using the fact just mentioned, that AC'' cannot be proved without introducing the operation $\exists$, to reject AC'' in classical logic and to take $\exists x$ to mean $\neg \forall x \neg$, thus rejecting the Axiom of Choice, AC. But, so long as we adopt the construction theoretic point of view toward propositions, this is not a viable option. For, if Φ is a type-valued function defined on the type A, then $\Sigma x : A . \Phi(x)$ *is* a well-defined type, governed by the rules $\exists$(a–c). On what grounds could we reject it as a proposition? But then, as we have noted, we can prove the equivalence of $\Sigma x : A . \Phi(x)$ with $\neg \forall x : A . \neg \Phi(x)$ and so can prove AC'.

The only alternative would seem to be to reject the construction theoretic point of view. The grounds for this rejection would presumably be that, to define a proposition, it does not suffice merely to specify the conditions for constructing proofs of it and the proofs from it as hypothesis. After all, to prove a proposition should mean to show that it is true. So, the alternative might go, truth is a prior notion. We have specified a meaningful proposition only when we have specified the conditions under which it is true—and then *that* should tell us what is to count as a valid proof.

Two considerations might seem to support this alternative. One is that no notion of proof that is codifiable in a formal system can be adequate to the notion of mathematical truth, on account of Gödel's incompleteness theorems.

The other consideration is based upon a picture of mathematical propositions as being about some SUPER-MODEL. So the question of whether a proposition is true is a semantical question, about that model, and independent of whatever principles of proof we accept. I have discussed this picture in Tait (1986) and do not wish to say much about it here. Models are things that we construct in mathematics and what we know of these models is what we can prove. The semantical notion of truth in *these* models is consequent upon the notion of proof. The SUPER-MODEL picture is offered as the only way to account for how propositions that seem to refer to numbers and functions and the like can be meaningful and true—offered most often by those who wish to undermine the meaningfulness or truth of such propositions by noting the manifest absurdity of the SUPER-MODEL picture. The plausibility of the view that only in terms of this picture can we account for the meaningfulness or truth of mathematical propositions is supposed to come from a comparison with the case of propositions about ordinary sensible objects, where the "model" is the physical world. Here, the story goes, we can see how the language works and how we can ascertain truths. For we can perceive the objects and facts in this model and, for example, by pointing, we can give meaning to our words. Some 106 years after the publication of Frege's *Foundations of Arithmetic* and some 38 years after the publication of Wittgenstein's *Philosophical Investigations*, the lesson of the dreadful inadequacy of this view of language—whether it be the language of ordinary sense experience or the language of mathematics—has still not been absorbed.

Let me turn now to the first consideration, based upon Gödel's incompleteness theorems.

XIII

Our discussion of the theory of types, as an account of the framework of mathematics, is incomplete: namely, consider some operation F which, applied to a type A, yields a type $F(A)$. A basic construction in mathematics is that of "iterating" F "transfinitely." Zermelo–Fraenkel set theory, for example, is based on the idea of iterating the operation P of passing from a type A to its "power type" $P(A)$ transfinitely. If one wishes a distinction to be made between logic and mathematics, perhaps we should say that the transition lies at this point: What we have been discussing up to now is logic. (I think it is essentially what some category theorists call "local set theory.")

The natural way to analyze the notion of iteration is in terms of the "incomplete type" Ω of ordinals. With each ordinal α we introduce the type Ω_α, which we can essentially identify with the segment of ordinals $< \alpha$—so that $\alpha < \beta$ means that α is of type Ω_β. The fact that $<$ well-orders Ω is expressed by a principle of definition of both types and objects by recursion—a special case of which is the forementioned iteration of the operation F on types. But what about rules for the construction of ordinals? Clearly, we should specify that there is a least ordinal 0 and a function $S: \Omega \to \Omega$ of successor. On the other hand, we cannot give an exhaustive set of rules for the construction of limit ordinals and this is why I refer to Ω as "incomplete." The reason for this is that any such set of valid rules for constructing ordinals of type Ω should determine a least ordinal α such that Ω_α is already closed under these rules. This principle, to which I shall refer as the *General Reflection Principle*, is somewhat vaguely stated. Indeed, although we can explicate particular cases of it yielding higher and higher ordinals, it seems impossible that there could be a precise and entirely adequate mathematical formulation of the principle. But one example is this: 0 is of the (incomplete) type Ω and, whever α is of type Ω, then so is $S\alpha$. Hence, there is a least ordinal ω such that 0 is of type ω and, whenever α is of type ω, then so is $S\alpha$. In other words, ω is the least limit ordinal, and so we have derived the usual Axiom of Infinity. Other relatively simple applications of the General Reflection Principle yield much stronger axioms of infinity, including the Axiom of Replacement and the existence of (strongly) inaccessible cardinals.

Now, in the present context, Gödel's incompleteness theorem concerns a sufficiently strong (but necessarily partial) theory T of the types, including the incomplete type Ω and incomplete types $A(\Omega)$ built up from it by means of the logical operations $0, 2, \forall$ and $\exists$. In our terms, the theorem asserts that there is a type $A = \forall x : \mathcal{N}.\Phi(x)$ constructible in T, which has no object constructible in T, but such that A is "true." The argument that A is true is that, for each n of type $\mathcal{N}, \Phi(n)$ is provable in T and that the principles of proof formalized in T are valid. So there may seem to be a wedge between the notion of proof and the notion of truth.

But the wedge is only between the notion of truth and the notion of proof in T. $\Phi(n)$ is not an incomplete type for n of type $\mathcal{N}$. In fact, $\Phi(x)$ is expressed by a formula of elementary arithmetic. By an application of the General Reflection Principle, from the fact that T is valid, we obtain the existence of an ordinal $\alpha \geq \omega$ such that $T(\Omega_\alpha)$ is a valid theory, where $T(\Omega_\alpha)$ is obtained by replacing each incomplete type $B(\Omega)$ by the (complete) type $B(\Omega_\alpha)$. But, from the existence of such an ordinal, we can prove A.[23]

It is important to see that the argument is not the trivial one that, seeing that A is true but not provable in T, we may extend T to a system in which A is provable. For this is true just because we can always add A itself to T as an axiom. Rather, my point is that the extension is not ad hoc but involves a simple application of the General Reflection Principle. The incompleteness manifested by Gödel's theorem, as Gödel himself noted, is an incompleteness of expression resulting from the essential incompleteness of Ω—in other words, from the fact that no matter what principles for constructing limit ordinals we have accepted, reflection will yield new principles that we should accept.[24] It is not an incompleteness of logic.

Of course, in this discussion of incompleteness, I am speaking only of the incompleteness exposed to Gödel's theorem. But then it was only this incompleteness that was supposed to show the difference between proof and truth, since we always know that the undecidable proposition produced is true. But there are other cases of incompleteness, such as the Continuum Hypothesis, in which the proof of undecidability does not yield a truth value. In these cases, it is unlikely that either proof or refutation will be possible just using the General Reflection Principle.

Notes

1. To derive LEM from $\neg\neg$E, note that both $\neg A$ and A imply $\neg A \vee A$; and so $\neg(\neg A \vee A)$ implies both $\neg\neg A$ and $\neg A$—a contradiction. So $\neg\neg(\neg A \vee A)$. Hence, by $\neg\neg$E, $\neg A \vee A$. To derive $\neg\neg$E from LEM, note that from the premises $\neg A \vee A$, $\neg\neg A$, and $\neg A$ we obtain the contradiction $\neg\neg A \wedge \neg A$, and so anything follows and, in particular, A follows. A also follows from the premises $\neg A \vee A$, $\neg\neg A$, and A. So, by disjunction elimination, A follows from $\neg A \vee A$ and $\neg\neg A$. Hence $\neg\neg A \rightarrow A$ follows from $\neg A \vee A$. It is an easy exercise to show that this argument can be transformed into a derivation of each of LEM and $\neg\neg$E from each other on the basis of the rules of proof in section X.

2. See pp. 262–263 and, in particular, fn. 14 of the 1964 version.

3. If u is a set of objects of type $A = P(B)$ and $\Phi(x, y)$ is the formula $x \in u \rightarrow y \in x$, then $\forall x : A \exists y : B . \Phi(x, y)$ follows using LEM from $\forall x : A(x \in u \rightarrow \exists y(y \in x))$. The latter proposition simply asserts that u is a set of nonempty sets and $\forall x : A \Phi(x, fx)$ asserts that f is a choice function for u. So AC' follows from AC. Conversely, if $\forall x : A \exists y : B . \Phi(x, y)$, then the set u of all sets $v(x) = \{y \text{ of type } B \,|\, \Phi(x, y)\}$ of type $P(B)$ for x of type A is a set of nonempty sets. A choice function f for u satisfies $\forall x : A . \Phi(x, fv(x))$; and so AC follows from AC'.

4. To derive AC' from WOP, well-order $\bigcup u$, the set of all elements of elements of u, and define the choice function f on u by the condition that fx is the least element of x in the given well-ordering. In the other direction, AC is a valid principle in constructive mathematics. But there is certainly no constructive proof that the set of real numbers (e.g., in the sense of Bishop, 1967) is well-orderable. Zermelo's argument was this: Let u be a set and f a choice function for the set $u - \{\varnothing\}$ of all nonempty subsets of u. $\langle v, <_v \rangle$ is called an "f-set" iff v is a subset of u and $<_v$ well-orders v and, for each $x \in v$, $x = f\{y \in v \,|\, y <_v x\}$. Let w be the set of all elements of u which are in v for some f-set $\langle v, <_v \rangle$. For x and y in w, let $x <_w y$ mean that $x <_v y$ for some f-set $\langle v, <_v \rangle$. Zermelo proves that $\langle w, <_w \rangle$ is an f-set. If $w = u$, then we are done, since $<_w$ well-orders w. He argues that $w = u$ as follows. If $\neg w = u$, then $u - w$ is a nonempty subset of u. Let $x = f(u - w)$ and define $\langle p, <_p \rangle$ by $p = w \cup \{x\}$ and $y <_p z$ iff $y <_w z$ or else $y \in w$ and $z = x$. Zermelo shows that $\langle p, <_p \rangle$ must be an f-set and so $p \subseteq w$. But that implies $x \in w$, a contradiction. So $\neg\neg w = u$. But now he makes us of $\neg\neg$E to infer $w = u$. (He does not make this last step explicit, of course.)

5. See Heine (1872), p. 183. f is sequentially continuous at x iff for every sequence $\langle x_n \,|\, n < \infty \rangle$ of numbers in $[a, b]$, is $\lim_{n \to \infty} x_n = x$, then $\lim_{n \to \infty} f(x_n) = f(x)$.

6. See pp. 237–239. Let m be the Lebesgue measure on the interval $[a, b]$. To show that m is countably additive, Lebesgue assumes that $A_1, A_2, \ldots$ are disjoint measurable subsets of $[a, b]$ and that $A = \bigcup_{n < \omega} A_n$. Let $\varepsilon > 0$. For each n he chooses (essentially) an open set $G_n \supseteq A_n$ and a closed set $F_n \subseteq A_n$ such that $m(G_n - F_n) \leq \varepsilon/2^{n+1}$. If m^* and m_* denote outer and inner measure, respectively, then $m^*(A) - m_*(A) \leq \sum_n m(G_n) - \sum_n m(F_n) = \sum_n m(G_n - F_n) \leq \varepsilon$. So A is measurable and both $m(A)$ and $\sum_n m(A_n)$ are in

the interval $[\sum_n m(F_n), \sum_n m(G_n)]$ for arbitrary $\varepsilon > 0$ and so are equal. But the choice of F_n and G_n for each n requires AC.

7. For example, Walter Rudin (1953), without anywhere mentioning AC, applies it when he argues that the countable union of countable sets is countable. He also uses it when he proves that if the complex number b is a limit point of a set E of complex numbers, then $b = \text{Lim}_{n \to \infty} a_n$, where each a_n is in E. An even more impressive example is in van der Waerden (1937), in which the author explicitly rejects AC and WOP in the preface and then goes on to "prove" that a countable union of countable sets is countable. Most interesting of all, I think, is the proof of the Hausdorff Maximality Theorem, Zorn's Lemma, and WOP in Dunford and Schwartz (1958), which uses AC without ever mentioning that principle by name. Since the authors surely knew that these principles are all equivalent to AC, this would seem to be a case of conscious acceptance of AC as a principle of logic.

8. In Hille and Phillips (1957), a more ambivalent attitude is expressed. The authors note that Zorn's Lemma is equivalent to AC and write "... its use has been found to be essential to many parts of the theory of abstract spaces" (p. 3). Graves (1946) devotes a section (section 10 of chapter 13) to AC:

> Some mathematicians have made strenuous efforts to avoid using such logical tools, and some even regard as doubtful all proofs of existence which give no means of identifying an object whose existence is being asserted. An existence proof depending on the axiom of choice is necessarily of this character, and such proofs enter into many parts of mathematics. Since the axiom of choice has a way of slipping into proofs without being noticed, it is well for the student to become thoroughly familiar with its various forms. The consistency of this axiom with the other axioms of set theory has been demonstrated by Gödel. Its use in mathematics is now generally regarded as well justified, but some mathematicians make a practice of systematically pointing out the occasions of its use. (p. 322)

This passage expresses something of the same ambivalence. It also raises two points. One is Gödel's proof that the constructible sets form an inner model of Zermelo–Fraenkel set theory (ZF) that satisfies AC. So a proposition proved in ZF + AC (together possibly with additional assumptions that are also valid of the inner model of constructible sets) will at least be valid in this inner model. The other point raised concerns the nature of existence proofs. But, as we shall shortly see, there is confusion here. It is not applications of AC that lead to existence proofs which give no means of identifying an object of the kind proved to exist. Rather, it is applications of LEM. (As I remarked at the beginning of this essay, the controversies concerning these two principles are curiously related.)

9. In Jacobson's *Lectures in Abstract Algebra*, in three volumes, AC is not mentioned until volume 2 (1953), where Zorn's Lemma is used to show, for example, that every vector space has a basis. It is invoked again in volume 3 (1964) to prove that every field has an algebraic closure. But he nowhere discusses the logical status of the principle. He refers in volume 3 to Kelley (1955) for a discussion. But Kelley does not discuss the logical status either. He assumes the Hausdorff Maximal Principle "as an axiom" and then simply proves a number of equivalents to it, including AC and Zorn's Lemma. In Lang (1965), Zorn's Lemma is described among the "Prerequisites" with the simple statement that it will be used.

10. The following familiar argument is a slight simplification of Bolzano's proof: Let $N(y)$ mean that $M(x)$ holds for all $x < y$. Then the assumptions of the theorem imply that $N(r_0)$ and that, for some $s_0 > r_0$, $\neg N(s_0)$. Having defined $r_0 \le r_1 \le \cdots \le r_n < s_n \le \cdots \le s_1 \le s_0$ such that $N(r_i)$ and $\neg N(s_i)$ for all $i \le n$, let $t_n = 1/2(s_n - r_n)$ and

define r_{n+1} and s_{n+1} by

> If $N(t_n)$, set $r_{n+1} = r_n + t_n$ and $s_{n+1} = s_n$
>
> If $\neg N(t_n)$, set $r_{n+1} = r_n$ and $s_{n+1} = s_n - t_n$

He notes that the sequence $\langle r_n \mid n < \infty \rangle$ satisfies the condition of being (what we now call) a Cauchy sequence, and concludes that it converges to the required greatest r such that $N(r)$. This last step was without foundation, of course, until Weierstrass and others proved, on the basis of a definition of the real numbers, that every Cauchy sequence has a limit. It is the definition (*) that requires LEM for its justification. We need to assume

> (**) $\neg N(t_n) \vee N(t_n)$

in order to be assured that r_{n+1} and s_{n+1} are defined. But there is no reason to believe that we can prove for any n (much less for all of them) (**) without invoking LEM (or some principle such as $\neg\neg E$ which implies it).

The above proof of Bolzano's theorem is a slight simplification of Bolzano's proof (pp. 42–80). He checks at each stage n to see whether $r_n = r_{n+k}$ for all k. If so, he stops because $r = r_k$ is the solution. In either case, he notes that if $d = r_0 - s_0$, then the solution is

> (***) $r = r_0 + d(1/2^k + 1/2^m + 1/2^n + \cdots)$

where $k < m < n < \cdots$ is a (possibly null) finite or infinite increasing sequence of positive integers.

11. Gregory H. Moore's remarks (1982) on Bolzano's proof are puzzling. On p. 13 he writes that Bolzano did not use the bisection argument in his proof. "What Bolzano actually did was to give an algorithm for approximating the least upper bound of a bounded subset of $\mathscr{R}$ by summing powers of 2." But the terms of the approximation were obtained by repeated bisection. It would seem that Moore is denying the use of the bisection method on the grounds that Bolzano unnecessarily complicates it. Moore's remarks are in the context of a discussion of Cauchy's proof of the Intermediate Value Theorem, which uses the same subdivision argument (with 2 replaced by an arbitrary $m > 1$). A difference is that Cauchy applies the method directly to prove the existence of an intermediate value, whereas Bolzano obtains the least intermediate value by an application of his theorem. The situation becomes even more confusing when, on pp. 17–18, Moore indicates that all Bolzano contributed to the proof of the Bolzano–Weierstrass Theorem was the "rudiments of [Weierstrass's] method of proof." But, leaving aside the question of method of proof, the one-dimensional case of the Bolzano–Weierstrass Theorem is a simple corollary of the above theorem. Let $A \subseteq [c, d]$ be infinite and let $M = \{x \le d \mid x < c$ or $A \cap [c, x]$ is finite$\}$. M is a proper subset of $\mathscr{R}$, every $x < c$ is in M. So there is a greatest number u such that every $x < u$ is in M. Clearly, u is the least limit point of A.

Bolzano actually proves the Intermediate Value Theorem in the equivalent form that if f and g are continuous functions on $[a, b]$, $f(a) < g(a)$, and $g(b) < f(b)$, then $f(x) = g(x)$ for some x in $[a, b]$.

12. Baire et al. (1905), pp. 265–266.

13. Consider an arbitrary function $f \in \mathscr{N}^{\mathscr{N}}$. By LEM,

> $\exists y : \mathscr{N}(fy = 0) \vee \neg \exists x : \mathscr{N}(fx = 0)$

and so

> (*) $\exists y : \mathscr{N}(fy = 0 \vee \neg \exists x : \mathscr{N}(fx = 0))$

An effective determination of a witness $t = 0^{(n)}$ for (8) would reduce the question of whether f has a zero to the question of whether $f(t) = 0$; and if f is a computable function, then we can decide this (at least in the idealized sense which does not take account of our limitations as computors). But this proof does not depend on the particular choice of f at all and so we can preface (8) with $\forall f : \mathcal{N}(1)$. So, by AC, we have a proof of

(**) $\exists G : \mathcal{N}(2) \forall f : \mathcal{N}(1)[f(Gf) = 0 \lor \forall x : \mathcal{N}(fx \neq 0)]$

It is known that no computable G satisfies this condition when f is understood to range over computable functions. Constructivists generally do not accept the Post–Turing analysis of computability as an analysis of their notion of a constructive function. But, as we have noted, it does not seem that constructive methods so far employed lead to functions which are not (Post–Turing) computable. In any case, it should be clear that there is no reason to believe (**) to be constructively valid. And, certainly, the classical proof of (*) does not itself effectively determine a witness.

14. I have discussed this circularity in Tait (1983).

15. This, of course, is not to say that our interest in A *qua* proposition is the same as our interest in it *qua* type. As a proposition, we are generally interested only in whether A is true, i.e., in whether there is some object of type A. As a type, we are interested in *what kinds* of objects of type A there are. For example, we are interested in propositions of the form $\exists x : A . \Phi(x)$.

16. There are at least two prima facie objections to this identification that should be mentioned, especially one to which I subscribed at one time. The more superficial one is that a proof of $\forall x : A . \Phi(x)$ need not associate a particular proof of $\Phi(x)$ with each x of type A. It would suffice that it associate a nonempty set $u(x)$ of such proofs for each x of type A. This makes sense when formalizing the notion of proof in a universe in which AC fails (cf. Barwise, 1975). But in the presence of AC the two notions of proof are equivalent. For a choice function for the $u(x)$'s immediately yields a function in $\prod_{x : A} \Phi(x)$. The other objection, the one I once believed, applies also to our definition of $A \to B$ as a type. It is that a proof is something that we can grasp as a proof—it is something that we can construct and for which it is then inappropriate to ask for a proof that it is indeed a proof. This still seems to be correct: this is the way to talk about proofs. But the other part of the objection is that functions of type $\prod_{x : A} \Phi(x)$ need not have that character because we can conceive of functions that we could never construct, for example, "random" sequences in $P(\mathcal{N}) = \mathcal{N} \to \mathbf{2}$. It is this that I no longer believe. Its initial plausibility lies in the fact that if, when we speak of what is constructible, we are speaking of construction by specific means, such as are formalized in some formal system, then clearly there are functions of type $P(\mathcal{N})$, for example, which we cannot construct. For example, the functions constructible in a formal system are countable in number and there are an uncountable number of functions of type $P(\mathcal{N})$. But the notion of what is constructible is not restricted to some formal system, but is open-ended (see section XIII). The proof that $P(\mathcal{N})$ is uncountable does not depend on any "random" sequences of numbers. So how can it imply that there are such sequences?

17. We assume the notation of section X. Let u be a proof of $\langle A, B \rangle \top$. $P_0 u$ is a proof of $\mathbf{1} \to A$ and so $P_0 u \mathbf{n}$ is a proof of A (where $\mathbf{n}$ is of type $\mathbf{0} \to \mathbf{0}$). Hence $q = \lambda u . P_0 u \mathbf{n}$ is a proof of $\langle A, B \rangle \top \to A$. If v is a proof of A and x is a variable of type $\mathbf{1}$, then $\lambda x . v$ is a proof of $\mathbf{1} \to A$ and, by the principle $\mathbf{0}$ of section X, there is a proof e of $\mathbf{0} \to B$. So $P(\lambda x . v) e$ is a proof of $\langle A, B \rangle \top$. Hence $r = \lambda v . P(\lambda x . v) e$ is a proof of $A \to \langle A, B \rangle \top$. Finally, Pqr is a proof of $\langle A, B \rangle \top \equiv A$. Similarly for the other case.

18. This relationship between the theory of typed combinators and the logic of $\to$ was first noted in H. Curry and R. Feys (1958, pp. 312–315). The notion of "reduction"

of a term in Combinator theory is precisely D. Prawitz's notion of reduction of a formal proof in the system of natural deduction for $\to$ (see Prawitz, 1965). The extension to the logic of $\forall$ was due to W. Howard, in notes that were privately circulated in 1969 and published in 1980, who chose to consider the lambda calculus and the sequence calculus in place of combinator theory and natural deduction. An extension to the logic of $\exists$ appears in Martin-Löf (1982).

19. By the principle $\mathbf{0}$, we have $\mathbf{n}$ of type $\neg\mathbf{0}$ $(= \mathbf{0} \to \mathbf{0})$. So, if x is of type $\neg\neg\mathbf{0}$, then $\lambda x.xf$ is of type $\neg\neg\mathbf{0} \to \mathbf{0}$. If y is of type $\neg\neg\mathbf{2}$, then $\lambda y.\perp$ is a proof of $\neg\neg\mathbf{2} \to \mathbf{2}$.

Note that if p is a proof of $A \to B$, z is a variable of type A, and y is a variable of type $\neg B$, then $\lambda y\lambda z.y(pz)$ is a proof of $\neg B \to \neg A$. By $\forall$(c), there is a proof of $\forall x:C.\Phi(x) \to \Phi(u)$, where u is a variable of type C. So by two applications of the observation just made, there is a proof f of $\neg\neg\forall x:C.\Phi(x) \to \neg\neg\Phi(u)$. If g is a proof of (2) and y is a variable of type $\neg\neg\forall x:C.\Phi(x)$, then $t(u, y) = gu(fy)$ is a proof of $\Phi(u)$ and $\lambda y\lambda u.t(u, y)$ is a proof of $\neg\neg\forall x:C.\Phi(x) \to \forall x:C.\Phi(x)$.

20. Let x and y be variables of types A and $\neg A$, respectively. $\lambda x.P\perp x$ and $\lambda y.P\top y$ are of types $A \to \neg A \vee A$ and $\neg A \to \neg A \vee A$, respectively. By the observation in the previous note, there are proofs p and q of $\neg(A \vee \neg A) \to \neg\neg A$ and $\neg(A \vee \neg A) \to \neg\neg A$, respectively. If u is a variable of type $\neg(\neg A \vee \neg A)$, then $r = \lambda u.(uq)(up)$ is a proof of $\neg\neg(\neg A \vee A)$. So $t = Dr$ is a proof of $A \vee \neg A$.

Let Φ be a type-valued function defined on C and apply the above result to $\Phi(x)$, where x is a variable of type C. There is a term $t(x)$ of type $\Phi(x) \vee \neg\Phi(x)$ and so $\lambda x.t(x)$ is a proof of (4).

21. This follows from the fact that we can prove $B \equiv \mathbf{T}(P_0 p)$ given a proof p of $B \vee \neg B$. Let $r = P_0 p$. r is of type $\mathbf{2}$ and $P_1 p$ is a proof of $\langle B, \neg B\rangle r$. By note 20 we have proofs of $\langle B, \neg B\rangle\top \equiv B$ and $\langle B, \neg B\rangle\perp \equiv \neg B$, respectively. Let x be a variable of type B and y a variable of type $\neg B$. $\lambda x.\mathbf{n}$ is a proof of $B \to \mathbf{T}\top$ and $\lambda y.yx$ is a proof of $\neg B \to \mathbf{T}\perp$ (depending on x). Therefore, we have proofs u and $v(x)$ of $\langle B, \neg B\rangle\top \to \mathbf{T}\top$ and $\langle B, \neg B\rangle\perp \to \mathbf{T}\perp$, respectively. So by $\mathbf{2}$(b), there is a proof (depending upon x) of $\forall z:\mathbf{2}.(\langle B, \neg B\rangle z \to \mathbf{T}z)$ and hence a proof $t(x)$ of $\langle B, \neg B\rangle r \to \mathbf{T}r$. So $\lambda x.t(x)(P_1 p)$ is a proof of $B \to \mathbf{T}r$. A similar construction yields a proof of $\neg B \to \neg\mathbf{T}r$.

22. In one direction, namely

(*) $\exists x:A.\Phi(x) \to \neg\forall x:A.\neg\Phi(x)$

$\neg\neg$ is not needed. Let u be a proof of $\exists x:A.\Phi(x)$ and let v be a proof of $\forall x:A.\neg\Phi(x)$. Then $P_1 u$ is a proof of $\Phi(P_0 u)$ and $v(P_0 u)$ is a proof of $\neg\Phi(P_0 u) = \Phi(P_0 u) \to \mathbf{0}$. So $v(P_0 u)(P_1 u)$ is a proof of $\mathbf{0}$. It follows that $\lambda u\lambda v:[v(P_0 u)(P_1 u)]$ is a proof of (*). But now let u be of type $\neg\forall x:A.\neg\Phi(x)$, let v be of type $\neg\exists x:A.\Phi(x)$, let y be of type A, and let z be of type $\Phi(y)$. Pzy is a proof of $\exists x:A.\Phi(x)$ and so $v(Pzy)$ is a proof of $\mathbf{0}$. Hence, $\lambda y.v(Pzy)$ is a proof of $\neg\Phi(z)$ and so $b(v) = \lambda z\lambda y.v(Pzy)$ is a proof of $\forall x:A.\neg\Phi(x)$. $ub(v)$ is therefore a proof of $\mathbf{0}$ and so $c(u) = \lambda v.ub(v)$ is a proof of $\neg\neg\exists x:A.\Phi(x)$. Here is where the nonconstructive principle $\neg\neg$ comes in: $Dc(u)$ is a proof of $\exists x:A.\Phi(x)$ and so $\lambda u.Dc(u)$ is a proof of $\neg\forall x:A.\neg\Phi(x) \to \exists x:A.\Phi(x)$.

23. The truth predicate True(x) for $T(\Omega_\alpha)$ can be defined. So we can prove that, for each name "C" of a type in $T(\Omega_\alpha)$,

True("C") iff C

and for each type-valued function Ψ on $\mathcal{N}$ expressed in $T(\Omega_\alpha)$, we can prove

$\forall n:\mathcal{N}.\text{True}("\Psi(0^{(n)})") \to \text{True}("\forall n:\mathcal{N}.\Psi(0^{(n)})")$

and

$$\forall n : \mathcal{N}\left[\text{``}\Psi(0^{(n)})\text{''} \text{ is provable in } T(\Omega_\alpha) \to \text{True}(\text{``}\Psi(0^{(n)})\text{''})\right]$$

So, since we have $\forall n : \mathcal{N}.$ $[\text{``}\Phi(0^{(n)})\text{''}$ is provable in $T]$, we can indeed prove A.

24. It is interesting to note that there is another notion of "reflection" involved here. For one might say that truth of the Gödel sentence A is obtained by "reflection" in the sense that it is by reflecting on the validity of the principles formalized in T that we know that A is true. This is connected with our General Reflection Principle in the following way: It is only in a proper meta-theory T' relative to T that we may possibly speak about the validity of the principles of T and he truth of sentences of T. It is T together with the assertion of the existence of an α such that the principles of T are valid in Ω_α that provides the required meta-theory.

References

Aspray, W. and P. Kitcher, eds. 1988. *History and Philosophy of Modern Mathematics.* Minnesota Studies in the Philosophy of Science, vol. 11. Minneapolis, University of Minnesota Press.

Baire, R., E. Borel, J. Hadamard, and H. Lebesgue. 1905. Cinq lettres sur la théorie des ensembles. *Bulletin de la Société Mathématique de France* 33, 261–73.

Barwise, J. 1975. *Admissible Sets and Structures.* Berlin, Springer-Verlag.

Benacerraf, P. and H. Putnam. 1983. *Philosophy of Mathematics: Selected Readings,* 2nd ed. Cambridge, Cambridge University Press.

Bishop, E. 1967. *Foundations of Constructive Analysis.* New York, McGraw-Hill.

Bolzano, B. 1817. *Rein analytischer Beweis des Lehrsatzes, das zwischen je zwey Werthen, die ein entgegensetztes Resultat gewären, wenigstens eine reele Wurzel der Gleichung liege* (Prague); translated by S. B. Russ in *Historia Mathematica* 7 (1980), 156–165.

Brouwer, L. E. J. 1908. De Onbetrouwbaarheid der logische principes. *Tijdschrift voor Wijsbegeerte* 2, 152–158; translated as The unreliability of the logical principles in Brouwer (1975), 107–111.

———. 1975. *Collected Works,* Vol. I. A. Heyting, ed. Amsterdam, North-Holland.

Cohen, L. J., J. Los, H. Pfeiffer, and K.-P. Podewski. 1982. *Logic, Methodology and Philosophy of Science VI.* Amsterdam, North-Holland.

Curry, H. and R. Feys. 1958. *Combinatory Logic I.* Amsterdam, North-Holland.

Dedekind, R. 1911. *Was sind und was sollen die Zahlen?,* 3rd ed. Braunschweig, Vieweg.

Dunford, N. and J. T. Swartz. 1958. *Linear Operators I.* New York, Interscience.

Edwards, H. 1988. Kronecker's place in history. In Aspray and Kitcher (1988), 139–144.

———. 1989. Kronecker's views on the foundation of mathematics. In Rowe and McCleary (1989), 67–77.

Gödel, K. 1947. What is Cantor's continuum problem? *American Mathematical Monthly* 54, 515–525.

———. 1964. A revised version of Gödel (1947). In Benacerraf and Putnam (1983).

———. 1990. *Kurt Gödel: Collected Works,* Vol. II. S. Feferman et al., eds. Oxford, Oxford University Press.

Graves, L. M. 1946. *The Theory of Functions of Real Variables.* New York, McGraw-Hill.

Heine, E. 1872. Die Elemente der Functionenlehre. *Journal für die reine und angewandte Mathematik (Crelle)* 74, 17–188.

Hille, E. and R. S. Phillips. 1957. *Functional Analysis and Semi-groups*. Providence, R.I., American Mathematical Society.

Hindley, J. and J. Sheldon, eds. 1980. *To H. B. Curry: Essays on Combinatory Logic, Lambda Calculus and Formalism*. London, Academic Press.

Howard, W. 1980. The formulae-as-types notion of construction. In Hindley and Seldin (1980), 107–124.

Jacobson, N. 1953. *Lectures in Abstract Algebra II*. New York, Van Nostrand.

———. 1964. *Lectures in Abstract Algebra III*. New York, Van Nostrand.

Kelley, J. L. 1955. *General Topology*. New York, Van Nostrand.

Lang, S. 1965. *Algebra*. Reading, MA, Addison-Wesley.

Lebesgue, H. 1902. Intégrale, longueur, aire. *Annali di matematica pura ed applicata* 7(3), 231–259.

Martin-Löf, P. 1982. Constructive mathematics and computer programming. In Cohen et al. (1982), 153–178.

Moore, G. 1982. *Zermelo's Axiom of Choice: Its Origins, Development and Influence*. New York, Springer-Verlag.

Prawitz, D. 1965. *Natural Deduction: A Proof-Theoretic Study*. Stockholm, Almqvist & Wiksell.

Rowe, D. E. and J. McCleary, eds. 1989. *The History of Modern Mathematics*, Vol. I: *Ideas and Their Reception*. San Diego, Academic Press.

Rudin, W. 1953. *Principles of Mathematical Analysis*. New York, McGraw-Hill.

Tait, W. 1983. Against intuitionism: Constructive mathematics is part of classical mathematics. *Journal of Philosophical Logic* 12, 173–195.

———. 1986. Proof and truth: The Platonism of mathematics. *Synthese* 69, 341–70.

van der Waerden, B. L. 1937. *Moderne Algebra*, 2nd ed. Berlin, Julius Springer.

van Heijenoort, J. 1967. *From Frege to Gödel: A Source Book in Mathematical Logic, 1879–1931*. Cambridge, MA, Harvard University Press.

Zermelo, E. 1904. Beweise, das jede menge wohlgeordet werden kann (Aus einem an Herrn Hilbert gerichten Briefe). *Mathematische Annalen* 59, 514–516; translated in van Heijenoort (1967).

———. 1908. Neuer Beweise für die Möglichkeit einer Wohlordnung. *Mathematische Annalen* 65, 107–128.

4

Mechanical Procedures and Mathematical Experience

Wilfried Sieg

Turing's "Machines." These machines are *humans* who calculate.
—Ludwig Wittgenstein

Wittgenstein's terse remark[1] captures the feature of Alan Turing's analysis of calculability that makes it epistemologically relevant. Focusing on the epistemology of mathematics, I will contrast this feature with two striking aspects of mathematical experience implicit in repeated remarks of Kurt Gödel. The first, the *conceptional* aspect, is connected to the notion of mechanical computability through his assertion that "with this concept one has for the first time succeeded in giving an absolute definition of an interesting epistemological notion"; the second, the *quasi-constructive* one, is related to axiomatic set theory through his claim that its axioms "can be supplemented without arbitrariness by new axioms which are only the natural continuation of the series of those set up so far." Gödel speculated on how the second aspect might give rise to a humanly effective procedure that cannot be mechanically calculated and thus provide a reason for his belief that the class of mental procedures is not exhausted by mechanical ones. Leaving this latter speculation aside, Gödel's remarks point to data that underlie the two aspects and "challenge," in the words of Charles Parsons (in press, 19), "any theory of meaning and evidence in mathematics."[2]

Not that I will present a theory accounting for these data; rather, I will mainly clarify the first datum by reflecting on the question that is at the root of Turing's analysis and central for mathematical logic, as well as for cognitive psychology and artificial intelligence. In its sober mathematical form the question simply asks, "What is an effectively calculable function?" The equivalent answers given in the mid-1930s are widely taken to be of fundamental significance also for the less sober question, "Are we (reducible to) machines?" After all, Turing's answer to the mathematical question used the concept of an idealized computing machine. Turing presented his characterization in 1936 to give a negative solution to Hilbert's *Entscheidungsproblem*, and his characterization is

71

generally accepted as correct or, at least, as more convincing than others. But what are the reasons for such a judgment? It seems to me that this issue has yet to be treated adequately.[3]

When approaching the original question, it is important to note its emergence from work in the foundations of mathematics. The first part of my essay provides this background by presenting epistemological concerns that motivated the use of effectively decidable notions in mathematics as well as in logic and by summarizing (meta-) mathematical issues that required an analysis of effective calculability. The second part starts out with a discussion of general recursive functions as introduced by (Herbrand and) Gödel, but it focuses on Church's main argument for the proposal to identify recursiveness with the informal notion of effective calculability. Thus, *Church's Thesis* is at the center of the second part. I will point out unsatisfactory aspects of Church's argument, but also the centrality of the concept *calculability in a logic* for this early discussion. That prepares the ground for *Turing's Analysis* of mechanical processes carried out by a human computor. The third part refines and generalizes that analysis, isolates *Turing's Thesis* as asserting that a human computor satisfies certain finiteness conditions, and argues for the pertinency and correctness of this thesis.[4]

The generalized form of the analysis allows me to connect Turing's considerations in a most informative way with Church's argument and Gödel's proposal. These systematic connections reinforce the conceptual core of the early investigations and weaken, if not undermine, the "argument from confluence of different notions" in favor of Church's Thesis. Turing's analysis was in perfect accord with Church's views, as can be gathered from the 1937 review Church wrote of Turing's paper. In his review Church asserted it is "*immediately clear*" that the notion of Turing computability "can be identified with ... the notion of effectiveness as it appears in certain mathematical problems (various forms of the Entscheidungsproblem ... and in general any problem which concerns the discovery of an algorithm)." Gödel was also convinced by Turing's analysis of the correctness of Church's Thesis and used the adequacy of Turing's notion to establish rigorous consequences for the mind and machine problem. The fourth part of this essay presents these Gödelian consequences and two closely related, but more general, aspects of mathematical experience alluded to in Gödel's remarks that were quoted previously. But note that these features are separable from Gödel's Platonism; they are more subtly attuned, I will argue, to the practice of mathematics.

1. Background

The precise connection between the informal notion of effective calculability and the mathematical notion of computability is brought to light, as section 3 will show in detail, by Turing's analysis of effectively calculable functions. According to Turing (1939), "A function is said to be 'effectively calculable' if its values can be found by some purely mechanical process,"[5] and mechanical process—with a specifically human touch—was characterized by Turing through axiomatic conditions and was shown to be equivalent to Turing machine computation. For a critical appreciation of the analysis and its remarkable pertinency, it is crucial to be clear about the mathematical and philosophical context in which it arose; indeed, in section 3.2 I argue that the general "problematic" *required* an analysis of the kind Turing offered.

1.1. Effectiveness in Mathematics and Logic

The problematic of effective calculability emerged within two traditions in logic and mathematics where proper symbolic representations of problems and their algorithmic solution were sought.[6] These traditions met briefly in Leibniz; he viewed algorithmic solutions of mathematical and logical problems as paradigms of problem solving in general. Remember that he recommended to disputants in *any* field to sit down at a table, take pens in their hands, and say "Calculemus!" His recommendation was clearly based on high hopes for his *lingua characterica* and *calculus ratiocinator*. This is relevant pre-history; relevant history begins in the second half of the nineteenth century with detailed work in the foundations of mathematics, in particular, with the so-called arithmetization of analysis and the axiomatic characterization of the real numbers. Dirichlet had demanded that a systematic arithmetization should show that *any* theorem of algebra and higher analysis could be formulated as a theorem about natural numbers. In this way, I assume, he hoped to clarify the role of analytic methods in number theory; recall that it was he who had introduced such methods in the proof of his famous theorem on arithmetic progressions. Dedekind and Kronecker, both deeply influenced by Dirichlet, sought to give an arithmetization satisfying Dirichlet's demand, but they proceeded in radically different ways. Their pertinent essays brought out conflicting philosophical positions that have influenced, directly or indirectly, the subsequent foundational discussion. But—and I would like to emphasize this very strongly—these positions evolved from and influenced their closely related mathematical work in algebraic number theory. (The background and the evolution of their work should be the focus of a case study concerned with the revolutionary changes in mathematics during the nineteenth century.)

Kronecker admitted only natural numbers as objects of analysis outright; from them he constructed, in now familiar ways, integers and rationals. Even algebraic reals were introduced, because they could be isolated effectively as roots of algebraic equations. The general notion of irrational number, however, was rejected in consequence of two restrictive methodological conditions to which mathematical considerations have to conform: (1) concepts must be decidable in finitely many steps, and (2) existence proofs must be carried out in such a way that they present objects of the required kind. Consequently, for Kronecker, infinite mathematical objects could not exist. All of this added up to a strictly arithmetic procedure, and Kronecker thought that by following it analysis could be re-obtained. More than 100 years later, we know that such a redevelopment is not as chimerical as people in the 1920s, for example Hilbert, believed.[7]

Dedekind opposed Kronecker's methodological restrictions. With respect to the previous decidability condition he maintained that it is determined independently of our knowledge, whether an object does or does not fall under a concept. He also used infinite sets of natural numbers as respectable mathematical objects, for example, in his definition of real numbers by cuts. But how, you may ask, was the existence of such mathematical objects to be secured? Dedekind proposed to give purely logical proofs for the existence of models of axiomatically characterized notions, not of individual mathematical objects. Thus the consistency of the notions would be guaranteed. With regard to the development in his 1888 booklet, he wrote to Keferstein in a letter dated February 27, 1890:

> After the essential nature of the simply infinite system, whose abstract type is the number sequence **N**, had been recognized in my analysis ... the question arose: does such a system *exist* at all in the realm of our ideas? Without a logical proof of existence it would always remain doubtful whether the notion of such a system might not perhaps contain internal contradictions. Hence the need for such a proof.[8]

Dedekind viewed his considerations not as specific for foundational systems, but rather as paradigmatic for a general mathematical procedure intended to secure the coherence of axiomatically given notions. In sum, Dedekind tried to safeguard his axiomatic approach by consistency proofs relative to logic broadly conceived, whereas Kronecker insisted on a radical restriction of mathematical objects and methods.

Dedekind recognized that Frege's logical foundation for natural numbers agreed with his own, not only in the details of justifying induction, but also in assuming the unrestricted comprehension schema as a logical principle. Dedekind's development of his theory was uncompromisingly rigorous but mathematically informal; Frege, by contrast, insisted on giving arguments in his Begriffsschrift. With this *formula language* Frege had realized some of Leibniz's hopes and for the first time provided the means necessary to formalize mathematical proofs. His booklet *Begriffsschrift* (1879) offered not only a rich language with relations and quantifiers, but its logical calculus also required that all assumptions be explicitly listed and that each step in a proof be taken in accord with one of the antecedently specified rules. Frege correctly considered this last requirement as a sharpening of the axiomatic method he traced back to Euclid's *Elements*. With this sharpening Frege pursued the aim of recognizing the "epistemological nature" of theorems. In the introduction to *Grundgesetze der Arithmetik* (1893) he wrote:

> By insisting that the chains of inference do not have any gaps we succeed in bringing to light every axiom, assumption, hypothesis or whatever else you want to call it on which a proof rests; in this way we obtain a basis for judging the epistemological nature of the theorem.

But such a basis can be obtained, Frege realized, only if inferences do not require contentual knowledge: their applications have to be recognizable as correct on account of the form of the sentences occurring in them. Indeed, Frege claimed that in his logical system "inference is conducted like a calculation," and he continued:

> I do not mean this in a narrow sense, as if it were subject to an algorithm the same as ... ordinary addition and multiplication, but only in the sense that there is an algorithm at all, i.e., a totality of rules which governs the transition from one sentence or from two sentences to a new one in such a way that nothing happens except in conformity with these rules.[9]

Almost fifty years later, in 1933, Gödel pointed back to Frege and Peano when he formulated "the outstanding feature of the rules of inference" in a formal mathematical system. The rules, Gödel said, "refer only to the outward structure of the formulas, not to their meaning, so that they can be applied by someone who knew nothing about mathematics, or by a machine" (Gödel 1933, 1).[10] To Frege, formulas represented (abstract) propositions in a concrete way; their concrete character provided the basis for the algorithmic transitions reflecting logical inferences. For this to be really useful the representation has to be adequate, and Frege asserted, "Proper use can be made of this only if the content is not just indicated, but if it is built up from its components by means of the very same logical signs, that serve for the computation." (This continues the quote in note 9.) Frege believed that his Begriffsschrift provided the means to represent content adequately.

1.2. Finitist Mathematics

It is all too well known that Frege's precise formal (re-)presentation did not prevent Russell from deducing a contradiction from the basic laws. A contradiction could also be obtained from the principles for Dedekind's notion of system. How this problem in Dedekind's foundational work already stirred Hilbert's concerned interest in the last few years of the nineteenth century is detailed in Sieg (1990a). But it was only in his paper of 1904 that Hilbert proposed a radically new, although still vague, approach to the consistency problem for mathematical theories. He suggested using the finiteness of mathematical proofs in order to establish directly, not through models, that contradictions could not be derived within particular mathematical theories. During the early 1920s he turned the issue into an elementary arithmetical problem and strategically joined the developments arising out of Frege's formal logical work with Kronecker's requirements for "genuine" mathematics (in order to save Dedekind's conception of the subject).[11]

The possibility of mechanically drawing inferences and of algorithmically solving some problems was not considered by Frege to be among the *logically* significant achievements of his *Begriffsschrift*. But Hilbert grasped the potential of this formal aspect, radicalized it, and exploited it for programmatic purposes, namely, to justify finitistically the use of classical theories **T** for establishing finitist statements without taking into account the problematic content of **T**.[12] That amounted to giving a finitist proof of the *reflection principle*

$$\mathrm{Pr}_T(x, `\phi') \to \phi$$

where Pr_T is the finitist proof predicate for **T**, ϕ a finitist statement, and 'ϕ' its translation in the language of **T**. This is directly related to the consistency problem, because the reflection principle is equivalent to the consistency statement for **T** under well-known conditions. It is perhaps worthwhile to mention that the connection to the nineteenth-century issues in the foundations of analysis was emphasized also by the independently minded Herbrand (1929b), who described a special case of the general consequence to be drawn from a finitist consistency proof for the system of *Principia Mathematica*:

> If an arithmetical theorem has been proved by using incommensurable numbers or analytic functions, then it can also be proved by using only purely arithmetic elements (integers and functions defined by recursion). Examples of this are Dedekind's theorem of prime numbers, and class field theory. (p. 43)[13]

It seemed that proof theoretic investigations would resolve the earlier methodological problems in a most satisfactory way because of the restricted character of finitist mathematics. Hilbert took finitist mathematics to be an elementary part of arithmetic, and it was assumed to coincide with the part of mathematics accepted by Kronecker and Brouwer.[14] Thus, for his meta-mathematical investigations, Hilbert joined the constructivist tradition in mathematics, crucial requirements of which had been formulated by Kronecker. The latter's views had influenced the French discussion surrounding the validity of the axiom of choice and of set theoretic methods in general at the very beginning of the twentieth century, and they were alive and well in Germany even during the 1920s.[15] The epistemological motivation for the restrictions was quite explicit in those discussions. As far as the still-evolving program of Hilbert and its direction were concerned, it was clearly formulated by Bernays in a talk at the 1921 meeting of the Deutsche Mathematiker Vereinigung in Jena:

> The assumption of such a system with particular connection properties [i.e., the assumption of the existence of a set of objects that satisfies certain axioms, W.S.] contains something as it were transcendent for mathematics, and thus the question arises, which principled position one should take with respect to it.... It would be quite hasty to deny from the very beginning any farther-reaching kind of intuitive evidence; nevertheless, we certainly want to take into account the tendency of the exact sciences to eliminate the more subtle organs of knowledge and use only the most primitive means of [acquiring] knowledge. From this perspective we are going to try [to determine] whether or not it is possible to justify those transcendent assumptions in such a way that only *primitive intuitive knowledge is being applied*. (1922, 11)[16]

Bernays goes on to discuss how Hilbert's approach addresses this problem and how it combines what is "positively fruitful" in the attempts of the intuitionists and logicists to provide a foundation for mathematics. A methodological point, similar to the main point in the previous quotation, was made by Bernays (1923), where he emphasized:

> The possibility of a philosophical position that recognizes [natural] numbers as existent, non-sensory objects is not excluded by Hilbert's theory—but then, logically speaking, the same kind of ideal existence would have to be granted

also to transfinite numbers, in particular, to the numbers of the so-called second
number class. It is its [the theory's] goal, however, to make such a position
dispensable for the foundation of the exact sciences. (p. 163)

Within the finitist frame this ultimate goal of Hilbert's program could not be
achieved, due to Gödel's incompleteness theorems; the latter forced a re-
evaluation of the epistemological perspective that had been underlying Hilbert's
program.[17]

There is one point I would like to emphasize, namely: Hilbert's metamathematical way of precisely describing formalisms and of investigating them
by finitist means opened the way to the rigorous treatment of fascinating issues
that are still being pursued. This novel approach, going radically beyond Frege,
and its parallel to ordinary mathematical investigations were lucidly expressed
in Hilbert and Ackermann (1928): "Mathematical logic achieves more than a
sharpening of language by a symbolic representation of inferences. Once the
logical formalism is fixed, we can expect that a systematic, so-to-speak
calculatory treatment [rechnerische Behandlung] of logical formulas is possible
that corresponds roughly to the theory of equations in algebra. . . ." Herbrand,
as well as other young and quite brilliant mathematicians, was attracted by
Hilbert's approach and viewed mathematical logic as a new branch of
mathematics. He emphasized that it was independent of Hilbert's philosophical
opinions, but that the novel questions opened "a scarcely explored domain of
arithmetical investigations of the greatest interest, which may well contain
surprises" (Herbrand 1931b, 276). In particular, metamathematics allowed a
mathematical treatment of what Herbrand viewed "in a sense" as "the most
general problem of mathematics." Already at the end of his thesis he had
emphasized: "The solution of this problem would yield a general method in
mathematics and would enable mathematical logic to play with respect to
classical mathematics the role that analytic geometry plays with respect to
ordinary geometry."[18] We turn now to this problem.

1.3. Entscheidungsproblem

The problem Herbrand alluded to is closely related to the consistency problem;
it is the so-called *Entscheidungsproblem*, or decision problem, and was to be
subjected to a *rechnerische Behandlung*, that is, a calculatory treatment. Its
classical formulation is found in Hilbert and Ackermann (1928, 72–73): "The
Entscheidungsproblem is solved if one knows a procedure that allows one to
decide the validity (respectively, satisfiability) of a given logical expression by
a finite number of operations." Hilbert and Ackermann italicized this paragraph
and emphasized the fundamental importance of a solution to the decision
problem. Indeed, Herbrand viewed the decision problem as another route to
establishing consistency. Assume that **T** is a theory with finitely many axioms
$H_1, \ldots, H_n$[19]; if $\neg \phi$ is a theorem of **T**, then the validity (for Herbrand that
meant provability in predicate logic) of the formula $(H_1 \& \cdots \& H_n) \to \phi$ is
equivalent to the inconsistency of **T**. This connection was explained by

Herbrand (1930b, 213) after having described the decision problem most interestingly as follows:

> However, there is another viewpoint from which work can be done and in which encouraging results have already been obtained: the study of what the Germans call the *Entscheidungsproblem*, which consists of seeking a method allowing us to recognize with certainty (at the end of a number of operations which can be determined beforehand) whether or not a given proposition is an identity, and if it is to find a proof of the proposition.

Thus, a solution to the decision problem must consist of a method that effectively yields an answer (i.e., after finitely many steps) and of a finitist proof that establishes the termination of the method; such a proof would guarantee certainty and would also provide a bound on the number of required steps.[20] These additional requirements make it understandable why Herbrand reproved and extended partial results that had been obtained by Löwenheim and Behmann.[21] He emphasized that only his proof, not Löwenheim's, satisfied the stringent metamathematical or finitist requirements: "We could say that Löwenheim's proof was sufficient in mathematics; but, in the present work, we had to make it 'metamathematical'. . . so that it would be of some use to us."[22]

Researchers in the Hilbert school realized full well that a positive solution for predicate logic—together with the assumption of finite axiomatizability of theories and the quasi-empirical completeness of *Principia Mathematica*[23]—would allow the decision concerning the provability (truth) of any mathematical statement. For some that was a sufficient reason to expect a negative solution; von Neumann, for example, expressed his views (1927, 11–12) as follows:

> . . . it appears that there is no way of finding the general criterion for deciding whether or not a well-formed formula *a* is provable. (We cannot at the moment establish this. Indeed, we have no clue as to how such a proof of undecidability would go.) . . . the undecidability is even the *conditio sine qua non* for the contemporary practice of mathematics, using as it does heuristic methods, to make any sense. The very day on which the undecidability does not obtain any more, mathematics as we now understand it would cease to exist; it would be replaced by an absolutely mechanical prescription (eine absolut mechanische Vorschrift), by means of which anyone could decide the provability or unprovability of any given sentence.
>
> Thus we have to take the position: it is generally undecidable, whether a given well-formed formula is provable or not.

When claiming that we have no clue as to how a proof of undecidability would go, von Neumann pointed to the underlying conceptual problem. After all, there were well-known proofs for the unsolvability of certain mathematical problems; but these impossibility results were given relative to a determinate class of admissible means, for example, doubling the cube by using only straightedge and compass. Exactly here lies the problem: a negative solution to the *Entscheidungsproblem* required a mathematically precise answer to the question "What are *absolut mechanische Vorschriften*?"

It is almost a platitude to say that particular aspects of mathematical experience informed broad philosophical views on the nature of human knowledge; we just need to remind ourselves of Plato, Leibniz, Kant, or—closer to our own days—Frege and Husserl. On the other hand, epistemologically motivated concerns evolved, as I have shown, into normative requirements for the presentation of axiomatic mathematical theories. The resulting formal development of parts of mathematics seemed to give substance to the Hobbesian claim that mathematical reasoning is nothing but mechanical computation. This view came to the fore through the formalist and polemical side of Hilbert's Program: The whole "thought-content" of mathematics, so it was claimed, can be expressed in a comprehensive formal theory; mathematical activity can be reduced to the manipulation of symbolic expressions, and mathematics itself can be viewed as a formula game. Hilbert defended this playful view of classical mathematics against the intuitionists by remarking that

> The formula game that Brouwer so deprecates has, besides its mathematical value, an important general philosophical significance. For this formula game is carried out according to certain definite rules, in which the *technique of our thinking* is expressed. These rules form a closed system that can be discovered and definitively stated. The fundamental idea of my proof theory is none other than to describe the activity of our understanding, to make a protocol of the rules according to which our thinking actually proceeds. Thinking, it so happens, parallels speaking and writing: we form statements and place them one behind another. If any totality of observations and phenomena deserves to be made the object of serious and thorough investigation, it is this one—...[24]

Hilbert's last remark is undoubtedly correct. However, if we take the possibility of developing mathematics formally as a significant datum for reflection, we must keep in mind that the formality requirement expressed a philosophically motivated *restriction* on human cognitive capacities for particular purposes.[25] By addressing von Neumann's conceptual problem, we also will lay the basis for a characterization of these restricted cognitive capacities that are presupposed in formal presentations.

2. Church's Thesis

The background I just described—with its interweaving of mathematical, logical, and philosophical questions—should be kept in mind when we turn our attention to the central conceptual issue. I want to emphasize that in depicting the decision problem as *the* immediate context in which an analysis of effective calculability was needed I do not intend to neglect two other significant and closely related issues; namely, the *general formulation* (and thus applicability) of the incompleteness theorems and the *general characterization* of effective solvability for mathematical problems.[26] Indeed, it was the detailed examination of the incompleteness theorems and the notion of *Entscheidungsdefinitheit*, so pivotal for their proofs, that led the way to the (informal) understanding of effective calculability as rule-governed evaluation of number-theoretic functions in something like a formal calculus. This understanding underlies Gödel's proposal, is crucial for Church's early considerations and for his main argument (analyzed on pp. 85–87), and leads to a specially important class of Post's finitary processes.[27] It is this notion that is recognized by Gödel as *absolute* and was generalized, later on, by Hilbert and Bernays to their notion of *regelrechte Auswertbarkeit* (i.e., evaluation according to rules) in deductive formalisms. Technically, this understanding found its distinctive expression in Kleene's Normal Form Theorem. *Here we have a conceptual core that is associated, however, with a major stumbling block.* After all, this core does not provide a convincing analysis: steps taken in a calculus must be of a restricted character and they are assumed, for example by Church, without argument to be recursive. A related assumption is made by Hilbert and Bernays; the proof predicate of their deductive formalisms has to be primitive recursive. Finally, Post offers as a *working hypothesis* only that the primitive acts (steps) of his "formulation 1" are sufficient for a reduction of ever wider formulations. As to Gödel's dissatisfaction with his proposal, see the discussion in sections 2.1 and 2.4. In section 3, I will show that Turing's analysis removes exactly this stumbling block.

2.1. Gödel's General Recursion

Examples of effectively calculable functions were given by primitive recursive functions; they had been used in mathematical practice for a long time. The standard arithmetic operations like addition, multiplication, and exponentiation, but also the sequence of prime numbers and the Fibonacci numbers, are all primitive recursive. The schema of primitive recursion leads from primitive recursive functions g and h to a new primitive recursive function f satisfying the equations

$$f(x_1, \ldots, x_n, 0) = g(x_1, \ldots, x_n)$$

$$f(x_1, \ldots, x_n, y') = h(x_1, \ldots, x_n, y, f(x_1, \ldots, x_n, y))$$

The defining equations for f can be used as rules for determining the value of f for any particular set of arguments. Clearly, in order to recognize that this is a well-defined procedure one appeals to the buildup of the structure **N**. Dedekind gave a set-theoretic foundation of these functions,[28] whereas Skolem used them directly with their naive number-theoretic meaning in his development of elementary arithmetic through the recursive mode of thought. Hilbert and Bernays, finally, sharpened Skolem's mathematical frame to their Primitive Recursive Arithmetic (PRA). And it is most plausible that finitist mathematics, as intended by them, coincides with PRA—up to an elementary and unproblematic coding of finite mathematical objects as numbers.[29]

Primitive recursive functions and predicates were used in Gödel's classical paper (1931) to describe a simplified system of *Principia Mathematica*; obviously, syntactic structures had to be coded as numbers. From a finitist standpoint it was perfectly sensible to restrict the means for describing syntactic structures to primitive recursive functions; from a broader perspective, however, there was no reason to exclude other effective procedures in presenting "formal" theories.

Ackermann (1928) gave an effectively calculable, nonprimitive recursive function; that result had been mentioned already in 1925 by Hilbert. Thus, it made extremely good sense that in his 1934 Princeton lectures Gödel strove, as indicated by the title "On undecidable propositions of formal mathematical systems," to make his incompleteness results less dependent on particular formalisms. In the introductory section 1 he discussed the notion of "a formal mathematical system" in some generality and required that

> the rules of inference, and the definitions of meaningful formulas and axioms, be constructive; that is, for each rule of inference there shall be a finite procedure for determining whether a given formula B is an immediate consequence (by that rule) of given formulas $A_1, \ldots, A_n$, and there shall be a finite procedure for determining whether a given formula A is a meaningful formula or an axiom. (p. 346)

Again, he used primitive recursive functions and relations to present syntax, viewing the primitive recursive definability of formulas and proofs as a "precise condition which in practice suffices as a substitute for the unprecise requirement of section 1 that the class of axioms and the relation of immediate consequence be constructive."[30] But a notion that would suffice *in principle* was really needed, and Gödel attempted to arrive at a more general notion. He considered the fact that the value of a primitive recursive function can be computed by a "finite procedure" for each set of arguments as an "important property" and in footnote 3 added that "The converse seems to be true if, besides recursions according to the scheme (2) [i.e., primitive recursion as given above], recursions of other forms (e.g., with respect to two variables simultaneously) are admitted. This cannot be proved, since the notion of finite computation is not defined, but it can serve as a heuristic principle" (1986, 348).[31]

Other recursions that might be admitted are discussed in the last section of the lecture notes under the heading "General Recursive Functions." In it Gödel described a proposal for the definition of a general notion of recursive function that (he thought) had been suggested to him by Herbrand in a private communication of April 7, 1931: "If ϕ denotes an unknown function, and $\psi_1, \ldots, \psi_k$ are known functions, and if the ψ's and ϕ are substituted in one another in the most general fashions and certain pairs of resulting expressions are equated, then, if the resulting set of functional equations has one and only one solution for ϕ, ϕ is a recursive function" (Gödel 1986, 368).[32] He went on to make two restrictions on this definition and required, first of all, that the left-hand sides of the functional equations be in a standard form, with ϕ being the outermost symbol and, secondly, that "for each set of natural numbers $k_1, \ldots, k_l$ there shall be exactly one and only one m such that $\phi(k_1, \ldots, k_l) = m$ is a derived equation." The rules that were allowed in giving derivations are of a very simple character: variables in any derived equation can be replaced by numerals, and if the equation $\phi(k_1, \ldots, k_l) = m$ has been obtained, then occurrences of $\phi(k_1, \ldots, k_l)$ on the right-hand side of a derived equation can be replaced by m. So much about this proposal; it was taken up for systematic development by Kleene (1936).

What was important about Gödel's modifications? For Gödel himself the crucial point was the precise specification of *mechanical* rules for deriving equations or, to put it differently, for carrying out computations. That point of view was also expressed by Kleene, who wrote with respect to the definition of "general recursive function of natural numbers" that "it consists in specifying the form of the equations and the nature of the steps admissible in the computation of the values, and in requiring that for each given set of arguments the computation yield a unique number as value" (1936, 727). In a letter to van Heijenoort, dated August 14, 1964, Gödel asserted that "it was exactly by specifying the rules of computation that a mathematically workable and fruitful concept was obtained" (van Heijenoort 1985a, 115). When making this claim, Gödel took for granted what he had expressed in an earlier letter to van Heijenoort, namely, that Herbrand's suggestion had been "formulated *exactly* as on page 26 of my lecture notes, i.e., without reference to computability."[33] But Gödel had been unable to find Herbrand's letter among his papers and had to rely on his recollection, which, he said, "is very distinct and was still very fresh in 1934." However, Herbrand's letter was found by John W. Dawson in Gödel's *Nachlass*, and it reads like a preliminary version of parts of Herbrand (1931d). On the evidence of that letter it is clear that Gödel misremembered. As a matter of fact, describing a system of arithmetic and the introduction of recursively defined functions *into that system* with intuitionistic, that is, finitist, justification, Herbrand wrote:

> In arithmetic we have other functions as well, for example functions defined by recursion, which I will define by means of the following axioms. Let us assume that we want to define all the functions $f_n(x_1, x_2, \ldots, xp_n)$ of a certain finite or infinite set F. Each $f_n(x_1, \ldots)$ will have certain defining axioms; I will call these axioms (3F). These axioms will satisfy the following conditions:
>
> (i) The defining axioms for f_n contain, besides f_n, only functions of lesser index.
>
> (ii) These axioms contain only constants and free variables.
>
> (iii) We must be able to show, by means of intuitionistic proofs, that with these axioms it is possible to compute the value of the functions univocally for each specified system of values of their arguments.

It is most plausible that, in addition to the (intuitionistically interpreted) axioms, Herbrand admitted substitution rules of the sort formulated by Gödel as rules of computation. Indeed, he asserted (1931d)—as he had done in his letter to Gödel—that all intuitionistic computations can be carried out, for example, in the formal system **P** of *Principia Mathematica*. This is not to suggest that Gödel was wrong in his assessment, but rather to point to the most important step he had taken, namely, to *disassociate recursive functions from an epistemologically restricted notion of proof*. Later on, Gödel even dropped the regularity condition that guaranteed the totality of calculable functions. He emphasized then "that the precise notion of mechanical procedures is brought out clearly by Turing machines producing partial rather than general recursive functions" (Wang 1974, 84).[34] At this earlier historical juncture, however, the explicit introduction of an equational calculus with purely formal, mechanical rules for computing was important for the mathematical development of recursion theory and also for the conceptual analysis. After all, it brought out clearly what, according to Gödel, Herbrand had failed to see, namely, "that the computation (for all computable functions) proceeds by exactly the same rules" (van Heijenoort 1985a, 115).

2.2. Herbrand's Provably Recursive Functions

Before moving on to the further development, I want to make some additional remarks concerning Herbrand's proposals, emphasizing, in particular, the restrictive provability conditions he imposed. These remarks complement the discussion of the last subsection, but do constitute a digression: the main considerations are taken up again in section 2.3. A careful description and thoughtful interpretation of the proposals can be found in van Heijenoort's essay (1985a) on Herbrand's work. It should be noted, however, that this paper was written before Dawson's discovery of the Gödel–Herbrand correspondence. Van Heijenoort thus had to rely on Gödel's reports concerning the details of Herbrand's suggestion to him and its very framing, namely, that Herbrand was concerned with a general characterization of effective calculability. In any event, van Heijenoort distinguished three different occasions in 1931 on which Herbrand "proposed ... to introduce a class of computable functions that would be more general than that of primitive recursive functions" (1985a, 114).[35] The first proposal is found in Herbrand's note (1931b, 273), where he described the restricted means allowed in metamathematical arguments and required, in particular, that "all the functions introduced must be actually calculable for all values of their arguments by means of operations described wholly beforehand." The second proposal is the one reported in Gödel's lectures (without reference to computability), and the third suggestion was made in Herbrand's paper (1931d, 290, 291). It is formulated as follows, again in the context of a system for arithmetic:

> We can also introduce any number of functions $f_i(x_1, x_2, \ldots, xn_i)$ together with hypotheses such that
> (a) the hypotheses contain no apparent variables;
> (b) considered intuitionistically, they make the actual computation of the $f_n(x_1, x_2, \ldots, xp_n)$ possible for every given set of numbers, and it is possible to prove intuitionistically that we obtain a well-determined result.

To the first occurrence of "intuitionistically" in this quotation Herbrand attached the following footnote: "This expression means: when they are translated into ordinary language, considered as a property of integers and not as mere symbols." With van Heijenoort I assume that Herbrand used "intuitionistic" also here as synonymous with "finitist." (A more detailed description of intuitionistic arguments is given in Herbrand 1931d, note 5, 288–289.[36]) This third proposal is identical with the one made by Herbrand in his letter to Gödel that I quoted previously, except for clause (i) from the earlier definition; that clause is implicitly assumed, as is clear from the examples Herbrand discusses.

On the one hand, I view the first formulation as a preliminary, not fully elaborated, version of the second and third formulations; on the other hand, I view it as a more explicit description of the Kroneckerian elements in meta-mathematics that were pointed out in section 1. Thus, we can see the evolution of essentially one formulation!

Between these proposals there is certainly no conflict of the sort Gödel considered and that is reported by van Heijenoort (1985a, 115–117); that is, that Herbrand envisioned "unformalized and perhaps unformalizable computation methods" and indeed refused "to confine himself to formal rules of computation." This should become clear from the following discussion. Two features of Herbrand's schema have to be distinguished, namely, (1) that the defining axioms (plus suitable rules) must make the actual intuitionistic computation of the function value possible, and (2) that the termination of the computation with a unique value has to be provable intuitionistically. That is, in modern terminology, we are dealing with "intuitionistically provably total (or provably recursive) functions," where provability is, however, not a formal notion.

A connection to a formal notion is given by Herbrand in the fourth section of 1931d. Gödel's incompleteness theorems for the system **P** of *Principia Mathematica* are discussed there, and Herbrand asserts that any intuitionistic computation can be carried out in **P** and that any intuitionistic argument can be formalized in **P**. He concludes, after sketching Gödel's proof, that **P**'s consistency is not provable by arguments formalizable in **P** and thus is not provable intuitionistically. What is most interesting is his remark that Gödel's argument does not apply to the system of arithmetic that includes the above schema for introducing functions: the functions that are introducible cannot be described intuitionistically, because we could easily diagonalize and obtain additional functions. In two side remarks I want to mention that (1) Herbrand's last observation can be turned around so as to imply that the class of provably total functions of a formal theory cannot be enumerated by an element of that class, and (2) the aim of precisely characterizing the class of provably total functions for formal theories has been taken up in proof-theoretic research, starting with Georg Kreisel (1952); see also Gandy (1988, 74–75) and my "Herbrand analyses" (1991).

What is the extension of Herbrand's class of functions? According to Herbrand's discussion noted in the last three paragraphs, it properly includes the primitive recursive functions and is included in the class of provably recursive functions of **P**. Indeed, at the end of 1931d, Herbrand asserts that in the previous claims concerning the formalizability of intuitionistic computations and arguments ordinary analysis (I assume that means full second-order arithmetic) can take the place of **P**. Indeed, he conjectures that full first-order arithmetic, with recursion equations for addition and multiplication only, might be sufficient. If the latter conjecture were true, Herbrand's class would be included in the class of provably recursive functions of Peano arithmetic. Basic to this discussion is Herbrand's conviction that the system of arithmetic described in 1931d (even without the infinitary rule D) allows one to carry out all intuitionistic proofs. That paper was dated Göttingen, July 14, 1931; in the letter to Gödel sent from Berlin on April 7, 1931, the claim concerning intuitionistic proofs is explicitly stated for the much weaker system with only quantifier-free induction. As a matter of fact, Herbrand claims there also that "... each proof in this arithmetic, which has no bound variables, is intuitionistic—this fact rests on the definition of our functions and can be seen directly." If that were true, Herbrand's class would consist of only the primitive recursive functions.[37] In conclusion, it seems that Gödel was right—for stronger reasons than he put forward—when he cautioned that Herbrand had *foreshadowed*, but not *introduced*, the notion of general recursive function.[38]

2.3. Church's Main Argument

The concept introduced by Gödel characterized a wide class of calculable functions, a class that contained all known effectively calculable functions. Indeed, footnote 3 of the Princeton lectures that I quoted earlier seems to express a form of Church's Thesis. But in a letter to Martin Davis dated February 15, 1965, Gödel emphasized that no formulation of Church's Thesis is implicit in that footnote. He wrote:

> The conjecture stated there only refers to the equivalence of "finite (computation) procedure" and "recursive procedure." However, I was, at the time of these lectures, not at all convinced that my concept of recursion comprises all possible recursions; and in fact the equivalence between my definition and Kleene's ... is not quite trivial. (Davis 1982, 8)[39]

At the time Gödel was equally unconvinced by Church's proposal that effective calculability should be identified with λ-definability. In a conversation with Church early in 1934, he called the proposal "thoroughly unsatisfactory."[40] In spite of Gödel's not exactly encouraging reaction, Church announced his "thesis" in a talk given at the meeting of the American Mathematical Society in New York City on April 19, 1935. It was formulated in terms of recursiveness, not λ-definability.[41] I quote the abstract of the talk in full (Church 1935b):

> Following a suggestion of Herbrand, but modifying it in an important respect, Gödel has proposed (in a set of lectures at Princeton, N.J., 1934) a definition of the term *recursive function*, in a very general sense. In this paper a definition of *recursive function of positive integers* which is essentially Gödel's is adopted. And it is maintained that the notion of an effectively calculable function of positive integers should be identified with that of a recursive function, since other plausible definitions of effective calculability turn out to yield notions that are either equivalent to or weaker than recursiveness. There are many problems of elementary number theory in which it is required to find an effectively calculable function of positive integers satisfying certain conditions, as well as a large number of problems in other fields which are known to be reducible to problems in number theory of this type. A problem of this class is the problem to find a complete set of invariants of formulas under the operation of conversion (see abstract 41.5.204). It is proved that this problem is unsolvable, in the sense that there is no complete set of effectively calculable invariants.

In his famous 1936 paper, "An Unsolvable Problem of Elementary Number Theory," Church described the form of such number-theoretic problems and restated his proposal for identifying the class of effectively calculable functions with a precisely defined class:

> There is a class of problems of elementary number theory which can be stated in the form that it is required to find an effectively calculable function f of n positive integers, such that $f(x_1, x_2, \ldots, x_n) = 2$ is a necessary and sufficient condition for the truth of a certain proposition of elementary number theory involving $x_1, x_2, \ldots, x_n$ as free variables. ... The purpose of the present paper is to propose a definition of effective calculability which is thought to correspond satisfactorily to the somewhat vague intuitive notion in terms of which problems of this class are often stated, and to show, by means of an example, that not every problem of this class is solvable.[42]

Church's arguments in support of his proposal again used recursiveness. According to Church, the fact that λ-definability was an equivalent concept added "... to the strength of the reasons adduced below for believing that they [these precise concepts] constitute as general a characterization of this notion [i.e., effective calculability] as is consistent with the usual intuitive understanding of it."[43] Church claimed that those reasons, to be presented and examined in the next paragraph, justify the identification "so far as positive justification can ever be obtained for the selection of a formal definition to correspond to an intuitive notion."[44] Why was there a satisfactory correspondence for Church? What were his reasons for believing that the most general characterization of effective calculability had been found?

To give a deeper analysis, Church points out in section 7 of his paper that two methods to characterize effective calculability of number-theoretic functions suggest themselves. The first of these methods makes use of the notion of *algorithm*, and the second employs the notion of *calculability in a logic*. He argued that they do not lead to a definition that is more general than recursiveness; because these arguments have a similar structure, I discuss only the one pertaining to the second method.[45] Church considered a logic L, that is a system of symbolic logic whose language contains the equality symbol $=$, a symbol $\{\ \}(\ )$ for the application of a unary function symbol to its argument, and numerals for the positive integers. For unary functions F, he gave the definition: "F is *effectively calculable* if and only if there is an expression f in the logic L such that $\{f\}(\mu) = v$ is a theorem of L iff $F(m) = n$; here μ and v are expressions that stand for the positive integers m and n." Church claimed that such functions F are recursive, *assuming* that L satisfies certain conditions. And the conditions amount to requiring the theorem predicate of L to be recursively enumerable. Clearly (for us), the claim then follows immediately by an unbounded search. (The reason for the parenthetical addition in the last sentence is given in note 54.)

To argue for the recursive enumerability of L's theorem predicate, Church starts out by formulating conditions *any* system of logic has to satisfy if it is "to serve at all the purposes for which a system of symbolic logic is usually intended."[46] These conditions, Church notes in note 21, are "substantially" those from Gödel's Princeton lectures for a formal mathematical system, which I quoted previously (p. 81). They state that (i) each rule must be an effectively calculable operation, (ii) the set of rules and axioms (if infinite) must be effectively enumerable, and (iii) the relation between a positive integer and the expression which stands for it must be effectively determinable. Church supposed that these conditions can be, as he put it, "*interpreted*" to mean that, via a suitable Gödel numbering for the expressions of the logic, (i') each rule must be a recursive operation, (ii') the set of rules and axioms (if infinite) must be recursively enumerable, and (iii') the relation between a positive integer and the expression that stands for it must be recursive. The theorem predicate is then recursively enumerable; but the crucial *interpretative* step is not argued for at all and thus seems to depend on the very thesis that is to be supported!

Church's argument in support of the thesis may appear to be viciously circular; that would be too harsh a judgment. After all, the general concept of calculability is explicated by that of derivability in a logic, and Church used (i') to (iii') to sharpen the idea that within such a logical formalism one operates with an effective notion of immediate consequence.[47] In other words, the thesis is appealed to only in a very special case. It is precisely here that we encounter the major stumbling block for Church's analysis, and that stumbling block was quite clearly seen by Church. To substantiate the latter claim, let me modify a remark Church made with respect to the first method of characterizing effectively calculable functions: *If this interpretation* [what I called the "crucial interpretative step" in the preceding argument] *or some similar one is not allowed, it is difficult to see how the notion of a system of symbolic logic can be given any exact meaning at all.*[48] Given the crucial role this observation plays, it is appropriate to formulate the central thesis of Church as a normative requirement:

> *Church's Central Thesis:* The steps of any effective procedure (governing derivations of a symbolic logic) must be recursive.

If this central thesis is accepted and a function is *defined* to be effectively calculable if, and only if, it is calculable in a logic, then what Robin Gandy called Church's "step-by-step argument" *proves* that all effectively calculable functions are recursive.[49] All of these considerations can, for certain, be easily adapted to Church's first method of characterizing effectively calculable functions via algorithms. The detailed reconstruction of Church's justification for the "selection of a formal definition to correspond to an intuitive notion" and the pinpointing of the crucial difficulty show, first of all, the sophistication of Church's methodological attitude and, secondly, that at this point in 1936 there is no major opposition to Gödel's attitude. (A rather stark contrast is painted by Shapiro, in press, and is indeed quite commonly assumed.) These last points are supported by the directness with which Church recognized—in writing and already early in 1937—the importance of Turing's work as making the identification of effectiveness and (Turing) computability "immediately evident."

2.4. Absoluteness

The concept used in Church's argument is an extremely natural and fruitful one and is, of course, directly related to *Entscheidungsdefinitheit* for relations and classes introduced by Gödel in his 1931 paper and to representability of functions as used in his 1934 Princeton lectures.[50] Clearly, the equational calculus and the λ-calculus are two particular "logics" allowing the formal, mechanical computation of calculable functions in ways that are motivated by special circumstances. Gödel himself used the general notion "f is computable in a formal system S" in a brief note of 1936 entitled "On the Length of Proofs." He considered a hierarchy of systems S_i (of order i, $1 \leq i$), and observed in a "Remark" added to the note in proof that this notion of computability is independent of i in the following sense: If a function is computable in any of the systems S_i, possibly of transfinite order, then it is already computable in S_1. "Thus," Gödel (1986, 397) concluded, "the notion 'computable' is in a certain sense 'absolute', while almost all metamathematical notions otherwise known (for example, provable, definable, and so on) quite essentially depend upon the system adopted."[51] For someone who stressed the type-relativity of provability as strongly as Gödel did, this must have been a very surprising insight indeed. In his contribution to the Princeton Bicentennial Conference (1946), Gödel re-emphasized this absoluteness and took it as the main reason for the special importance of general recursiveness or Turing computability: Here, Gödel thought, we have the first interesting epistemological notion whose definition is not dependent on the chosen formalism. The significance of his discovery was described by Gödel to Kreisel in a letter of May 1, 1968: "That my [incompleteness] results were valid for all possible formal systems began to be plausible for me (that is since 1935[52]) only because of the *Remark* printed on p. 83 of 'The Undecidable'... But I was completely convinced only by Turing's paper" (Odifreddi 1990, 65).[53] And there was good reason not to be completely convinced. After all, the absoluteness was achieved, ironically, only relative to the description of the "formal" systems S_i; the stumbling block shows up exactly here.

Remark. If Gödel had been completely convinced of the adequacy of this notion, he could have established most easily the unsolvability of the decision problem for first-order logic: Given that mechanical procedures are exactly those that can be computed in the system S_1 (or any other system to which Gödel's incompleteness theorem applies) the unsolvability follows from Theorem IX of Gödel (1931). The theorem states that there are formally undecidable problems of predicate logic; it rests on the observation (made by Theorem X) that every sentence of the form $(\forall x)F(x)$, with F primitive recursive, can be shown in S_1 to be equivalent to the question of satisfiability for a formula of predicate logic. Historically, Theorem IX made a positive solution of the decision problem very unlikely. But, for the appendix to his paper on the fundamental problem of mathematical logic, Herbrand wrote in April 1931, when he already knew Gödel's results quite well (1931a, 259): "Note finally that, although at present it seems unlikely that the decision problem can be solved, it has not yet been proved that it is impossible to do so."

The absoluteness of the notion of computability in Gödel's sense follows from a marvelous and detailed example of conceptual analysis due to Hilbert and Bernays. They established independence from formalisms in an even stronger sense in *Grundlagen der Mathematik*; supplement 2 was entitled "Eine Präzisierung des Begriffs der berechenbaren Funktion und der Satz von Church über das Entscheidungsproblem." They made the core notion of *calculability in a logic* directly explicit and defined a number-theoretic function to be *regelrecht auswertbar* when it is computable (in the above sense) in *some* deductive formalism. Deductive formalisms must satisfy three *Rekursivitätsbedingungen* (recursiveness conditions); I will discuss only the crucial condition here, an analogue to Church's Central Thesis. That condition requires that the theorems of the formalism be enumerated by a primitive recursive function or, equivalently, that the proof predicate be primitive recursive. Then it is shown that (1) a special number-theoretic formalism (included in Gödel's S_1) suffices to compute the functions that are *regelrecht auswertbar*, and (2) the functions computable in this particular formalism are exactly the general recursive ones. Hilbert and Bernays' analysis is, in my view, a natural and most satisfactory capping of the development from *Entscheidungsdefinitheit* to an "absolute" notion of computability, because it captures directly the informal notion of rule-governed evaluation of effectively calculable number-theoretic functions and isolates the necessary restrictive conditions. But this analysis does *not* overcome the major stumbling block; rather, it puts it in plain view. Let me emphasize the main point of this subsection: the notion of rule-governed computation (in something like a logical calculus) provides a *conceptual core for the attempts to characterize effective calculability of number-theoretic functions; the core is associated, however, with a major stumbling block.* It is Turing's analysis, taking processes underlying computations in a "calculus" as a starting-point, that removes the stumbling block.

3. Turing's Analysis

Turing's notion of machine computability turned out to be equivalent to recursiveness and λ-definability, but it was hailed by Gödel as providing "a precise and unquestionably adequate definition of the general concept of formal system." In his review of Turing's paper, Church (1937a, 43) claimed when comparing Turing computability, recursiveness, and λ-definability: "Of these, the first has the advantage of making the identification with effectiveness in the ordinary (not explicitly defined) sense evident immediately—i.e., without the necessity of proving preliminary theorems."[54] What distinguished Turing's proposal so dramatically from Church's, at least for Gödel and Church? One has to find an answer to this question, because the naive examination of Turing machines hardly produces the conviction formulated by Gödel and hardly carries the immediate evidence asserted by Church. (The key to the answer to the question is offered at the end of section 3.1; the answer is formulated in sections 3.2 and 3.3.)

3.1. Turing's Machines and Post's Workers

Let me describe Turing machines very briefly, following Davis (1958), rather than Turing's original presentation.[55] A Turing machine consists of a finite but potentially infinite tape; the tape is divided into squares, and each square may carry a symbol from a finite alphabet, say, just the two-letter alphabet consisting of 0 and 1, or B(lank) and |. The machine is able to scan one square at a time and perform, depending on the content of the observed square and its own internal state, one of four operations: print 0, print 1, or shift attention to one of the two immediately adjacent squares. The operation of the machine is given by a finite list of commands in the form of quadruples $q_i s_k c_l q_m$ that express the following: If the machine is in internal state q_i and finds symbol s_k on the square it is scanning, then it is to carry out operation c_l and change its state to q_m. The deterministic character of the machine operation is guaranteed by the requirement that a program must not contain two different quadruples with the same first two components. Gandy (1988, 88) gave a lucid description of a Turing machine computation in very general terms without using internal states or, as Turing called them, states of mind: "The computation proceeds by discrete steps and produces a record consisting of a finite (but unbounded) number of cells, each of which is either blank or contains a symbol from a finite alphabet. At each step the action is local and is locally determined, according to a finite table of instructions." How the reference to internal states can be avoided should be clear from the following discussion of Post's worker, and why such a general formulation is appropriate will be seen in section 3.2.

For the moment, however, let me consider the special Turing machines I just described. Taking for granted a representation of natural numbers in the two-letter alphabet and a straightforward definition of when to call a number-theoretic function Turing computable, I turn the earlier remark into a question: Does this notion provide (via some Gödel numbering) "an unquestionably adequate definition of the general concept of formal system?" Is it at all plausible that every effectively calculable function is Turing computable? It seems to me that a naive inspection of the seemingly very restricted notion of Turing computability should lead to "no" as a tentative answer to the second question and, thus, to the first one. However, a systematic development of the theory of Turing computability quickly convinces one that it is indeed a powerful notion. One almost immediately goes beyond the examination of particular functions and the writing of programs for machines computing them; instead, one considers machines that correspond to operations that yield, when applied to computable functions, other functions that are again computable.[56] Two such functional operations are crucial, namely, composition and minimalization. Given those operations and the Turing computability of a few simple initial functions, the computability of *all* recursive functions follows. (This claim takes for granted Kleene's 1936 proof of the equivalence between general recursiveness in Gödel's sense and μ-recursiveness.) Because Turing computable functions are readily shown to be among the recursive ones, it seems that we are now in exactly the same position as before with respect to the evidence for

Church's Thesis. This remark holds also for Post's model of computation, which is so strikingly similar to Turing's.

In 1936, the very year in which Turing's paper appeared, Post published a brief note in *The Journal of Symbolic Logic* with the title "Finite Combinatory Processes—Formulation 1." Here we have a worker who operates in a *symbol space* consisting of

> a two-way infinite sequence of spaces or boxes, i.e., ordinally similar to the series of integers .... The problem solver or worker is to move and work in this symbol space, being capable of being in, and operating in but one box at a time. And apart from the presence of the worker, a box is to admit of but two possible conditions, i.e., being empty or unmarked, and having a single mark in it, say a vertical stroke.[57]

The worker can perform a number of *primitive acts*, namely, make a vertical stroke $[V]$, erase a vertical stroke $[E]$, move to the box immediately to the right $[M_r]$ or to the left $[M_l]$ (of the box he is in), and determine whether that box is marked or not $[D]$. In carrying out a particular combinatory process, the worker begins in a special box (the *starting point*) and then follows directions from a finite, numbered sequence of instructions. The ith direction, i between 1 and n, is in one of the following forms: (1) carry out act V, E, M_r, or M_l and then follow direction j_i; (2) carry out act D and then, depending on whether the answer was positive or negative, follow direction j_i' or j_i''. (Post has a special stop instruction, but that can be replaced by stopping, conventionally, in case the number of the next direction is greater than n.) Are there intrinsic reasons for choosing formulation 1, except for its simplicity and Post's expectation that it will turn out to be equivalent to recursiveness? An answer to this question is not clear (from Post's paper), and the claim that psychological fidelity is the aim seems quite opaque. At the very end of his paper Post wrote:

> The writer expects the present formulation to turn out to be equivalent to recursiveness in the sense of the Gödel–Church development. Its purpose, however, is not only to present a system of a certain logical potency but also, in its restricted field, of psychological fidelity. In the latter sense wider and wider formulations are contemplated. On the other hand, our aim will be to show that all such are logically reducible to formulation 1. We offer this conclusion at the present moment as a *working hypothesis*. And to our mind such is Church's identification of effective calculability with recursiveness. (Davis 1965, 291)[58]

For Post, investigating wider and wider formulations and reducing them to formulation 1 would change this "hypothesis not so much to a definition or to an axiom but to a *natural law*."[59]

It is methodologically remarkable that Turing proceeded in exactly the opposite way when trying to support the claim that all computable numbers are machine computable or, in our way of speaking, that all effectively calculable functions are Turing computable: He did not try to extend a narrow notion reducibly and obtain in this way additional quasi-empirical support; rather, he analyzed the intended broad concept and reduced it to a narrow one—once and for all. (I would like to emphasize this, as it is claimed over and over that Post provided in his 1936 paper "much the same analysis as Turing."[60]) By examining Turing's analysis and reduction we can find the key to answering the question I raised about the difference between Church's and Turing's proposals. Very briefly put, it is this: Turing deepened Church's step-by-step argument by focusing on the mechanical operations underlying the steps and by formulating finiteness conditions that *guarantee* their recursiveness. Let me now present Turing's considerations in systematic detail, with simplifications and added structure.

3.2. Mechanical Computer

Turing's classical paper (1936) opens with a brief description of what is ostensibly its subject, namely, "computable numbers" or "the real numbers whose expressions as a decimal are calculable by finite means" (Davis 1965, 116). Turing is quick to point out that the fundamental problem of explicating "calculable by finite means" is the same when considering computable functions of an integral variable, computable predicates, and so forth. So it is sufficient to address the question: What does it mean for a real number to be calculable by finite means? Turing admits that "this requires rather more explicit definition. No real attempt will be made to justify the definitions given until we reach §9. For the present I shall only say that *the justification lies in the fact that the human memory is necessarily limited*" (Davis 1965, 117).[61] In section 9 he argues that the operations of his machines "include all those which are used in the computation of a number." (Clearly, the operations need not be available as basic ones; it suffices that they can be mimicked by suitably complex sub-routines.) He does not try to establish the claim directly; rather, he attempts to answer "the real question at issue," that is, "What are the possible processes which can be carried out [implicitly: by a human computor[62]] in computing a number?" Given the systematic context that reaches back to Leibniz's "Calculemus!", this is exactly the pertinent question to ask, because the general problematic *requires* an analysis of the possibilities of a mechanical computor. Gandy (1988, 83–84) emphasizes, absolutely correctly, as we will see, that "Turing's analysis makes no reference whatsoever to calculating machines. Turing machines appear as a result, as a codification, of his analysis of calculations by humans."

Turing imagines a mechanical computor writing symbols on paper that is divided into squares "like a child's arithmetic book." Since the two-dimensional character of this computing space is taken not to be an "essential of computation,"[63] Turing takes a one-dimensional tape divided into squares as the basic computing space.[64] What determines the steps of the computor? And what kind of elementary operations can he carry out? Before turning to these questions, let me formulate one important restriction. It is motivated by definite limits of our sensory apparatus to distinguish—*at one glance*—between symbolic configurations of sufficient complexity; it states that only finitely many distinct symbols can be written on a square. This restriction will be part of condition

(1.1). Turing suggests a reason for this restriction by remarking,[65] "If we were to allow an infinity of symbols, then there would be symbols differing to an arbitrarily small extent." There is a second but closely related way of arguing for this restriction: If, for example, Arabic numerals like 17 or 9999999 are considered as one symbol, then it is not possible for us to determine at one glance whether or not 9889995496789998769 is identical with 98899954967899998769.

The behavior of a computor is determined *uniquely* at any moment by two factors: (1) the symbols or symbolic configuration he observes, and (2) his "state of mind" or "internal state." This uniqueness requirement may be called the *determinacy condition* (D) and guarantees that computations are deterministic. Internal states are introduced in order to have the computor's behavior depend possibly on earlier observations, that is, to reflect the computor's experience.[66] Turing wants to isolate operations of the computor that are "so elementary that it is not easy to imagine them further divided" (Davis 1965, 136). Thus, it is crucial that symbolic configurations relevant for fixing the circumstances for the actions of a computor are *immediately recognizable*, and we are led to postulate that a computor has to satisfy two *finiteness conditions*:

(1.1) There is a fixed finite number of symbolic configurations a computor can immediately recognize.

(1.2) There is a fixed finite number of states of mind that need to be taken into account.

For a given computor there are only finitely many different relevant combinations of symbolic configurations and internal states. Because the computor's behavior is—according to (D)—uniquely determined by such combinations and associated operations, the computor can carry out at most finitely many different operations and, *consequently*, his behavior is fixed by a finite list of commands. The operations a mechanical computor can carry out are restricted as follows:

(2.1) Only elements of observed symbolic configurations can be changed.[67]

(2.2) The distribution of observed squares can be changed, but each of the new observed squares must be within a bounded distance L of an immediately previously observed square.[68]

Turing emphasizes that "the new observed squares must be immediately recognizable by the computor," and that means the distributions of the new observed squares arising from changes according to (2.2) must be among the finitely many ones of (1.1). Clearly, the same must hold for the symbolic configurations resulting from changes according to (2.1). Because some of the operations may involve a change of state of mind, Turing concludes:

The most general single operation must therefore be taken to be one of the following: (A) A possible change (a) of symbol [as in (2.1)] together with a possible change of state of mind. (B) A possible change (b) of observed squares [as in (2.2)] together with a possible change of state of mind.[69]

With this restrictive analysis of the steps a mechanical computor can take, the proposition that his computations can be carried out by a Turing machine is established rather easily. Indeed, Turing first "constructs" machines that mimic the work of the computor directly and then observes:

> The machines just described do not differ very essentially from computing machines as defined in §2, and corresponding to any machine of this type a computing machine can be constructed to compute the same sequence, that is to say the sequence computed by the computer [in my terminology: computor].[70]

Thus, shifting back to computations of number-theoretic functions, we have *Turing's Theorem*: Any number-theoretic function F that can be computed by a computor, satisfying the determinacy condition (D) and the conditions (1.1)–(2.2), can be computed by a Turing machine.

Both Gödel and Church state they were convinced by Turing's analysis that the identification of effective calculability with Turing computability (thus also with recursiveness and λ-definability) is correct. Church expressed his views in the 1937 review of Turing's paper, from which I quoted in the introduction: On account of Turing's work the identification is "immediately evident." As to Gödel, I have not been able to find in his papers any reference to Turing's analysis before 1946; that paper was discussed in section 2.4. But what did convince them? Gödel gave some indication in the postscriptum to his Princeton lectures, where he is perfectly clear about the *structure* of Turing's argument. "Turing's work," he writes, "gives an analysis of the concept 'mechanical procedure' (alias 'algorithm' or 'computation procedure' or 'finite combinatorial procedure'). This concept is *shown* [my emphasis] to be equivalent with that of a 'Turing machine'." In a footnote attached to this observation he calls "previous equivalent definitions of computability"—referring to λ-definability and recursiveness—"much less suitable for our purpose." What is not elucidated by any remark of Gödel, as far as I know, is the *result* of Turing's analysis, that is, the axiomatic formulation of restrictive conditions. And there is consequently no discussion of the *reasons* for the correctness of these conditions or, for that matter, of the analysis.

Church was very much on target in his review, though there is a misunderstanding as to the relative role of the human computor and machine computability in Turing's argument. For Church, computability by a machine "occupying a finite space and with working parts of finite size" is analyzed by Turing; one then can observe that "in particular, a human calculator, provided with pencil and paper and explicit instructions, can be regarded as a kind of Turing machine" (Church 1937a). On account of the analysis and this observation for Church it is then "immediately clear" that (Turing) machine computability can be identified with effectiveness. This is reemphasized in the rather critical review of Post's 1936 paper in which Church points to the essential finiteness requirements in Turing's analysis: "To define effectiveness as computability by an arbitrary machine, subject to restrictions of finiteness, would seem to be an adequate representation of the ordinary notion, and if this is done the need for a working hypothesis disappears" (1937b). This is right, as far as emphasis on finiteness restrictions is concerned. But Turing analyzed, as we saw, a mechanical computor, and *that* provides the basis for judging the correctness of the finiteness conditions.

Church's apparent misunderstanding is rather common; cf. note 4 on Mendelson (1990). So it is worthwhile to point out that machine computability was analyzed only much later, by Gandy (1980). Turing's three-step procedure of analysis, axiomatic formulation of general principles, and proof of a "reduction theorem" is followed there, but for "discrete deterministic mechanical devices." Gandy showed that everything computable by a device satisfying the principles—a "Gandy machine"—can already be computed by a Turing machine; cf. Sieg (1989). To see clearly the difference between Turing's and Gandy's analysis, note that Gandy machines incorporate parallelism. They compute directly, for example, Conway's Game of Life, and thus violate the basic assumption that mechanical computors operate only on symbolic configurations of bounded size. Furthermore, the different boundedness conditions for Gandy machines (in particular, the principle of local causation) are motivated not by limitations of the human sensory apparatus, but by physical considerations.

3.3. Turing's Thesis

Turing's analysis and his theorem can be generalized by making an observation concerning the determinacy condition: (D) is not needed to guarantee the Turing computability of F in the theorem. More precisely, (D) was used in conjunction with (1.1) and (1.2) to argue that computors can carry out only finitely many operations; this claim follows already from conditions (1.1)–(2.2) *without* appealing to (D). Thus, the behavior of computors can still be fixed by a finite list of commands, but it may exhibit nondeterminism. Such computors can be mimicked by nondeterministic Turing machines and thus, exploiting the reducibility of nondeterministic to deterministic machines, by deterministic Turing machines.

This observation is by no means difficult, but it is intellectually pleasing that it allows one to connect in a straightforward way Turing's considerations with those of Church discussed in section 2.3. Consider an effectively calculable function F and a nondeterministic computor who calculates—in Church's sense—the value of F in a logic **L**. Using the generalized theorem and the fact that Turing computable functions are recursive, F is then recursive. This argument for F's recursiveness does no longer appeal to Church's Thesis, not even to the more restricted Central Thesis; rather, such an appeal is replaced by the assumption that the calculation in the logic is done by a computor satisfying conditions (1.1)–(2.2). Indeed, any system satisfying these axiomatic conditions would do. Turing's analysis thus leads to a result that is in line with Gödel's general methodological expectations expressed to Church in 1934 (and reported by Church to Kleene in 1935): "His [i.e. Gödel's] only idea at the time was that it might be possible, in terms of effective calculability as an undefined notion, to state a set of axioms which would embody the generally accepted properties of this notion, and to do something on that basis."[71]

If the assumption in the argument for the recursiveness of F is to be discharged, then a substantive thesis is needed. And it is this thesis that I want to call *Turing's Thesis*. It says that a mechanical computor satisfies the finiteness conditions (1.1) and (1.2), and that the elementary operations the computor can carry out are restricted as conditions (2.1) and (2.2) require. In short, if the clarification of effective calculability as meaning computability by a mechanical computor is accepted, then Turing's Thesis is the final piece to guarantee the equivalence of that notion and recursiveness. And *if* Turing's Thesis is correct, then the conceptual problem of von Neumann is resolved, because we have a precise and—via Turing's Theorem—mathematically handy characterization of *absolut mechanische Vorschriften*. Gödel, then, was also right when concluding that Turing computability captures the "essence" of formal systems, namely, "that reasoning is completely replaced by mechanical operations on formulas."[72]

The first section of this chapter had the explicit purpose of describing the context for the investigations of Herbrand, Gödel, Church, Kleene, and Turing. There is no doubt, it seems to me, that an analysis of human computability on finite (symbolic) configurations was called for, and that the epistemological restrictions were cast in "mechanical" terms; see the remarks of Frege and Gödel quoted in section 1.1 as striking examples. Thus, Turing's clarification of effective calculability as *calculability by a mechanical computor* should be accepted. Two related issues remain: first, the question whether the thesis is correct and, second, Turing's claim that its ultimate justification lies in the necessary limitation of human memory. As to the first issue, we have to ask ourselves whether the restrictive conditions do in fact apply to mechanical computors. According to Gandy, Turing arrives at the restrictions "by consider-ing the limitations of our sensory and mental apparatus." However, only limitations of our sensory apparatus seem to be involved, unless "state of mind" is given a mental touch. That is technically unnecessary, as I pointed out in section 3.1, *and* is not central to Turing: In section 9(III) of his paper he describes a modified computor and avoids introducing "state of mind," considering instead "a more physical and definite counterpart of it."[73] Without discussing this modification, whose context is a little complex, the analysis appeals only to sensory limitations of the type I discussed at the beginning of section 3.2. Such limitations are operative when we work as purely mechanical computors.[74]

Turing sees memory limitations as ultimately justifying the restrictive con-ditions. But none of the conditions is motivated by such a limitation; so how are we to understand his claim? I suggest the following: If our memory were not subject to limitations of the same character as our sensory apparatus, we could scan (with the limited sensory apparatus) a symbolic configuration that is not immediately recognizable, read in sufficiently small parts so that their representations could be assembled in a unique way to a representation of the given symbolic configuration, and, finally, carry out (generalized) operations on that representation in memory. Is one driven to accept Turing's assertion as to the limitation of memory? I suppose so, if one thinks that information concerning symbolic structures is physically encoded and that there is a bound on the number of available codes.

Turing viewed his argument for the identification of effectively calculable functions with functions computable by his machines as being basically "a direct appeal to intuition." Indeed, he claimed more strongly, "All arguments which can be given [for this identification] are bound to be, fundamentally, appeals to intuition, and for that reason rather unsatisfactory mathematically."[75] If we look at his paper on ordinal logics (Turing 1939), the claim that such arguments are "unsatisfactory mathematically" becomes at first rather puzzling, because he observed that intuition is inextricable from mathematical reasoning. Turing's concept of intuition is much more general than that ordinarily used in the philosophy of mathematics. It was introduced in Turing's 1939 paper explicitly to address the general issues raised by Gödel's first incompleteness theorem in the context of work on ordinal logics or what was later called progressions of theories; the discussion is in Davis (1965, section 11, 208–210):

> Mathematical reasoning may be regarded rather schematically as the exercise of a combination of two faculties, which we may call *intuition* and *ingenuity*. The activity of the intuition consists in making spontaneous judgements which are not the result of conscious trains of reasoning. These judgements are often but by no means invariably correct (leaving aside the question of what is meant by "correct").... The exercise of ingenuity in mathematics consists in aiding the intuition through suitable arrangements of propositions, and perhaps geometrical figures or drawings. It is intended that when these are really well arranged the validity of the intuitive steps which are required cannot seriously be doubted.

It seems to me that the propositions in Turing's argument are arranged with sufficient ingenuity so that "the validity of the intuitive steps which are required cannot seriously be doubted"; or, at least, their arrangement allows us to point to the central conditions with clearer, adjudicable content than Church's normative Central Thesis.

4. Aspects of Mathematical Experience

Let me move from the details of the conceptual analysis to its use for an interpretation of the incompleteness theorems. If their formulation and their interpretation are to be general, the relation of Turing computability to effective calculability, and the informal understanding of the latter notion, have to come to the fore. I argued that historically the insistence on formality was motivated by epistemological concerns; it is quite clear that a genuine restriction on our cognitive, more particularly, mathematical capacities was intended. Thus, it may be surprising that some of the pioneers interpreted these results, prima facie, in a quite dramatic way. For example, Post (1936) emphasized that the theorems I mentioned exemplify "a fundamental discovery in the limitations of the mathematizing power of Homo Sapiens." Later he remarked with respect to these results: "Like the classical unsolvability proofs, these proofs are of unsolvability by means of given instruments. What is new is that in the present case these instruments, in effect, seem to be the only instruments at man's disposal."[76]

The last part of this chapter will start out with reflections of Gödel on these issues. His considerations will lead me to look at two aspects of mathematical experience. The first, the *quasi-constructive* aspect, has to do with the recognition of laws for "accessible domains"; this includes, in particular, our recognition of set-theoretic axioms and their extendability by suitable axioms of infinity. The second, the *conceptional* aspect, deals with the uncovering of abstract, axiomatically characterized notions. Turing's analysis shows, it seems to me, that calculability exemplifies the second aspect.

4.1. Gödel's Consequences

Turing's work provides "a precise and unquestionably adequate definition of the general concept of formal system"; consequently, the incompleteness theorems hold for *arbitrary formal* systems (satisfying the usual conditions). But, in contrast to Post, for Gödel they do not establish "any bounds for the powers of human reason, but rather for the potentialities of pure formalism in mathematics" (Davis 1965, 72–73). In Gödel (1972b) there is a discussion of a "philosophical error in Turing's work" that can, according to Gödel, be regarded as a footnote to the word "mathematics" in this very quotation. Gödel claims that Turing gives an argument, on page 136 of Davis (1965), to show that "mental procedures cannot go beyond mechanical procedures". But Turing sketches there only an argument showing that "the number of states of mind that need be taken into account is finite." The context makes it crystal clear that mechanical procedures are being analyzed. Thus, I cannot see a philosophical error in Turing's work, but rather in Gödel's interpretation.[77] However, the further remarks in Gödel's note are of interest independent of Gödel's error; they summarize points he had made more extensively in his Gibbs Lecture of 1951.

In that lecture Gödel stated that if mathematics is viewed as a body of propositions that "hold in an absolute sense," then the incompleteness theorems express the fact that mathematics is not exhaustible by a mechanical enumeration of its theorems. After all, the first theorem yields, for any consistent formal system S containing a modicum of number theory, a simple arithmetic sentence that is independent of S. But Gödel (1951, 5–6) emphasized that it is the second theorem that makes this phenomenon of inexhaustibility particularly evident:

> For it makes it impossible that someone should set up a certain well-defined system of axioms and rules and consistently make the following assertion about it: All of these axioms and rules I perceive (with mathematical certitude) to be correct, and moreover I believe that they contain all of mathematics.

It someone claims this, he contradicts himself: Recognizing the correctness of all axioms and rules means recognizing the consistency of the system. Thus, a mathematical insight has been gained that does not follow from the axioms. To explain the meaning of this situation Gödel carefully distinguished between "objective" and "subjective" mathematics: objective mathematics is viewed as the body of true mathematical propositions; subjective mathematics is conceived of as consisting of all humanly provable mathematical propositions.

There clearly cannot be a complete formal system for objective mathematics, but it is not excluded that for mathematics in the subjective sense there might be a finite procedure yielding all of its evident axioms. Clearly, we could never be certain that all of these axioms are correct; but if there were such a procedure, then—at least as far as mathematics is concerned—the human mind would be equivalent to a Turing machine. Furthermore, there would be simple arithmetic problems that could not be decided by any mathematical proof intelligible to the human mind. If, according to Gödel (1951, 7), we call such a problem *absolutely undecidable* we have established with full mathematical rigor that *either* mathematics is inexhaustible in the sense that its evident axioms cannot be generated by a finite procedure *or* there are absolutely undecidable arithmetic problems.

This fact appears to Gödel to be of "great philosophical interest." That is not surprising, as he explicates the first alternative in the following way: ". . . that is to say, the human mind (even within the realm of pure mathematics) infinitely surpasses the powers of any finite machine." The further philosophical consequences Gödel tries to draw are concerned with his Platonism, familiar from some of his published writings. In 1933 Gödel already claimed that the axioms of set theory, "if interpreted as meaningful statements, necessarily presuppose a kind of Platonism." But at that time he added the relative clause "which cannot satisfy any critical mind and which does not even produce the conviction that they are consistent" (p. 7). I would go too far afield if I tried to present the reasons why I do not find Gödel's general considerations (in the Gibbs Lecture) convincing. My criticism would not start with his Platonism for set theory, but at the point where he contrasts the objects of finitist and intuitionistic mathematics in his *Dialectica* paper. There he tried to draw an extremely sharp distinction within constructive mathematics that seems to me to be mistaken (and to parallel his equally mistaken radical opposition of classical and constructive mathematics). According to Gödel (1958, 240), the specifically finitist character of mathematical objects requires them to be "finite space-time configurations whose nature is irrelevant except for equality and difference"; furthermore, in proofs of propositions concerning them, one uses only insights that derive from the combinatorial space-time properties of sign combinations representing them.[78] These remarks stand in conflict with Bernays' position, to which Gödel appealed in his *Dialectica* paper. Bernays stressed the uniform character of the generation of natural numbers, the local structure of the schematic "iteration figure," and the need to "*reflect* on the general features (allgemeine Charakterzüge) of intuitive objects" (1930). Indeed, our understanding of natural numbers as being generated in such a uniform way allows us to grasp laws concerning them. It seems to me that this observation is correct also for more general inductively generated classes, and it points to the first of two critical aspects of mathematical experience I want to describe now.

4.2. Accessibility and Conception

If one takes seriously the reformulation of the first alternative in Gödel's Main Theorem, then one certainly should try to see ways in which the human mind "transcends" the limits of mechanical computors. Gödel (1972b) suggested that there may be (humanly) effective but nonmechanical procedures. But even the most specific of his proposals, Gödel admitted, "would require a substantial advance in our understanding of the basic concepts of mathematics." That proposal concerned the extension of systems of axiomatic set theory by axioms of infinity, that is, extending segments of the cumulative hierarchy. The problem of extending what I call *accessible domains* is not special to the case of set theory (and Platonism); rather, there are completely analogous issues for the theory of primitive recursive functionals (and finitism) and for the theory of constructive ordinals in the second number class (and intuitionism). This is the first of the two aspects of mathematical experience on which I want to focus; both are related to features of "mental procedures" Gödel discussed, but their interest is quite independent of Gödel's speculations.

Accessible domains, constituted by inductively generated elements, are most familiar from mathematics and logic. In proof theory, for example, inductively defined higher constructive number classes have been used in consistency proofs for impredicative subsystems of analysis. These and other classes provide special cases in which generating procedures allow us to grasp the intrinsic buildup of mathematical objects. Such an understanding is a fundamental source of our knowledge of mathematical principles for the domains constituted by them; for it is the case, I suppose, that the definition and proof principles for such domains follow directly from the comprehended buildup. A broad framework for the "inductive or rule-governed generation" of mathematical objects is described by Aczel (1977); it is indeed so general that it encompasses not only finitary i.d. classes, higher number classes, and models of a variety of constructive theories, but also segments of the cumulative hierarchy. It provides a uniform framework in which the difficulties (in our understanding) of generating procedures can be compared and explicated. If we understand the set-theoretic generation procedure for a segment of the cumulative hierarchy, then it is indeed the case that the axioms of ZF^- (i.e., ZF without the postulate for the existence of the first infinite ordinal), together with a suitable axiom of infinity, "force themselves upon us as being true" in Gödel's famous phrase; they simply formulate the principles underlying the "construction" of the objects in this segment.[79]

The sketch of this quasi-constructive aspect of mathematical experience is extremely schematic and yet, I think, helpful for further orientation. Recall that for Dedekind consistency proofs were intended to ensure that axiomatically characterized notions (like that of a complete ordered field) were free from "internal contradictions." Here we are dealing with *abstract* notions without an "intended model" constituted by *inductively generated* elements.[80] These notions are distilled from mathematical practice for the purpose of comprehending complex connections, of making analogies precise, and of obtaining a more profound understanding. It is in this way that the axiomatic method teaches us, as Bourbaki (1950) expressed it in Dedekind's spirit,

> to look for the deep-lying reasons for such a discovery [that two, or several, quite distinct theories lend each other "unexpected support"], to find the

common ideas of these theories, ... to bring these ideas forward and to put them in their proper light. (p. 223)

Notions like group, field, topological space, and differentiable manifold are abstract in this sense: They are properly and in full generality investigated in category theory. Another example of such a notion is that of Turing's mechanical computor. Although Gödel used "abstract" in a more inclusive way than I do here, it seems that the notion of computability exemplifies his broad claim (1972b, 306), "that we understand abstract terms more and more precisely as we go on using them, and that more and more abstract terms enter the sphere of our understanding."

This conceptional aspect of mathematical experience and its profound function in mathematics has been entirely neglected in the logico-philosophical literature on the foundations of mathematics—except in the writings of Paul Bernays. Indeed, detailed investigations of these two aspects of mathematical experience can be viewed as addressing the central problem expressed by Bernays in the quotation from his 1922 work given in section 1.2: Which principled position can we take regarding the "transcendent assumptions" of mathematics? Those assumptions are reflected through accessible domains, relative to which abstract notions can be shown to be consistent via structural reductions. Here we have a generalized and redirected Hilbert program that mediates between Richard Dedekind and a liberalized version of Leopold Kronecker! The traditional contrast between "Platonist" and "constructivist" tendencies in mathematics comes to light here in refined distinctions concerning the admissibility of operations, of their iteration, and of deductive principles. The considerations on the quasi-constructive aspect of mathematical experience cut across traditional "school" boundaries; so do those on its conceptional aspect.

5. Final Remarks

I argued that the sharpening of axiomatic theories to formal ones was motivated by epistemological concerns. A central point was the requirement that the checking of proofs ought to be done in a radically intersubjective way; it should involve only operations similar to those used by a computor when carrying out an arithmetic calculation. Turing analyzed the processes underlying such operations and formulated a notion of computability by means of his machines; that was in 1936. In a paper written about ten years later and entitled "Intelligent Machinery" Turing (1948, 21) stated what really is the central problem of cognitive psychology:

> If the untrained infant's mind is to become an intelligent one, it must acquire both discipline and initiative. So far we have been considering only discipline [via the universal machine, W.S.]. ... But discipline is certainly not enough in itself to produce intelligence. That which is required in addition we call initiative. This statement will have to serve as a definition. Our task is to discover the nature of this residue as it occurs in man, and to try to copy it in machines.

The task of copying is difficult, some would argue impossible, in the case of mathematical thinking. But before we can start copying, we have to discover— at least partially—"the nature of the residue." As you may recall, Turing distinguished between ingenuity and intuition in his 1939 paper, and he argued that in formal logics their respective roles take on a greater definiteness: intuition is used for "setting down formal rules for inferences which are always intuitively valid"; ingenuity, to "determine which steps are the more profitable for the purpose of proving a particular proposition." He noted, "In pre-Gödel times it was thought by some that it would be possible to carry this programme to such a point that all the intuitive judgements of mathematics could be replaced by a finite number of these rules. The necessity for intuition would then be entirely eliminated" (1939, 209).

Proofs in a formal logic can be obtained uniformly by a (patient) search through an enumeration of all theorems, but additional nonmechanical, intuitive steps remain necessary because of the incompleteness theorems. Turing suggested particular kinds of intuitive steps in his ordinal logics; his arguments are utterly theoretical, but connect directly to the discussion of actual or projected computing devices that appear in his "Lecture to London Mathematical Society" (1986) and in "Intelligent Machinery" (1948). In these papers he calls for "intellectual searches" (i.e., heuristically guided searches) and "initiative" (that includes, in the context of mathematics, proposing intuitive steps). However, Turing (1986, 122) emphasizes that "As regards mathematical philosophy, since the machines will be doing more and more mathematics themselves, the centre of gravity of the human interest will be driven further and further into philosophical questions of what can in principle be done etc." Thus we are straightforwardly led back to the questions: What are essential aspects of mathematical experience? Are they mechanizable?

I have tried to give a very tentative and partial answer to the first question. As far as the second question is concerned, I don't have even a conjecture on how it will be answered. Is Gödel's search for humanly effective but non-mechanical procedures in mathematics more than searching for a "pie in the sky" (as Kleene thinks)? Or is Post, drawing on similar mathematical facts, right when making the observation:

> The creative germ ... can be stated as consisting in constructing ever higher types. These are as transfinite ordinals and the creative process consists in continually transcending them by seeing previously unseen laws which give a sequence of such numbers. Now it seems that this complete seeing is a complicated process mostly subconscious. But it is not given till it is made completely conscious. But then it ought to be constructable [sic] purely mechanically.[81]

Whatever the right answers may be, mathematical experience represents an extremely important component of Turing's problem, and we should investigate crucial aspects vigorously: by historical case studies, theoretical analysis, psychological experimentation, and—quite in Turing's open spirit—by machine simulation.

Appendix

This appendix uses some new documents to further elucidate significant conceptual issues and to support conjectural remarks pertaining to the impact of (the proof of) Gödel's incompleteness theorems on Herbrand and Church. Incidentally, both men got to know Gödel's results through Johan von Neumann; Herbrand in November 1930 in Berlin, Church about a year later in Princeton. With respect to Herbrand I want to emphasize, as I did in section 2.2, that he was concerned with the notion of *provably* recursive function; as to Church, I want to stress that his belief in the correctness of his thesis hardly rested on any particular "motivation" for λ-definability, but rather on general facts concerning the notion of "calculability in a logic" and on his Central Thesis. In any event, there still is extremely interesting material to be uncovered and evaluated; there also remains a great deal of important analytical work to be done. Gödel's proof provided the seminal idea of representing number-theoretic functions in a formal system; his results provided the stimulus for investigations concerning their proper applicability and the precise extension of effectiveness. How surprising his results were (for logicians) is sometimes no longer appreciated; consider Herbrand's reaction, described in his letter of December 3, 1930, to his friend Claude Chevalley:

> Les mathématiciens sont une bizarre chose; voici une quinzaine de jours que chaque fois que je vois [von] Neumann nous causons d'un travail d'un certain Gödel, qui a fabriqué de bien curieuses fonctions; et tout cela détruit quelques notions solidement ancreés.

This sentence opens the letter; after having sketched Gödel's arguments and reflected on the results Herbrand concludes it with: "*Excuse ce long début; mais tout cela me poursuit, et de l'écrire m'en exorcise un peu.*"

1. If, as I described in sections 2.1 and 2.2, Gödel took off in a generalizing mood from Herbrand's schema for the introduction of "recursive" functions, and if Herbrand was not attempting to characterize a general notion of effectively calculable function, what did motivate Herbrand to formulate the schema? First recall the widely shared assumptions, namely: (1) the general notion of recursive function was captured by Herbrand's schema, and (2) the schema emerged from Herbrand's general reflections on intuitionistic methods. These assumptions are formulated, for example, by van Heijenoort (1971, 283), but also by Dawson (1991):

> The functions [characterized by the schema formulated in Herbrand (1931d), W.S.] are, in fact, (general) recursive functions, and here is the first appearance of the notion of recursive (as opposed to primitive recursive) function. It is interesting to see how, a few months earlier, Herbrand had been led to this notion by his conception of "intuitionism."

For the earlier discussion van Heijenoort refers to Herbrand's note (1931b), and, with respect to Herbrand (1931d), he writes:

> Herbrand's consistency proof for a fragment of arithmetic still belongs to the
> period that preceded Gödel's famous result (1931). He probably started to
> write his paper before Gödel's paper reached him. But he had ample oppor-
> tunity to examine Gödel's result and he wrote a last section dealing with it.

This scenario is incorrect: The notes (1931b and c) and the paper (1931d)
were all written *after* Herbrand knew quite well about the incompleteness theorems. This seems to be clear from internal evidence, but Herbrand's letter to
Chevalley puts it beyond any doubt. In it Herbrand tells us (1) that it was
von Neumann from whom he learned of Gödel's theorems, and (2) that the
encounters with von Neumann took place in the second half of November 1930.
That new information also puts into sharper focus the remark in Herbrand
(1931c, 279) that was submitted, according to the introduction by Goldfarb,
to Hadamard "at the beginning of 1931":

> Recent results (not mine) show that we can hardly go any further: it has been
> shown that the problem of consistency of a theory containing all of arithmetic
> (for example, classical analysis) is a problem whose solution is impossible.
> [Herbrand is here alluding to Gödel 1931.] In fact, I am at the present time
> preparing an article in which I will explain the relationships between these
> results and mine [this article is 1931d].[82]

Thus, it is Herbrand's attempt to come to a thorough understanding of the
relationship between Gödel's incompleteness theorems and his own work that
seems to have prompted the specific details in his letter to Gödel and his paper
(1931d). Indeed, I think that Herbrand's proposal for the introduction of
functions is a natural generalization of the definition schemata for effectively
calculable functions known to him and that it emerges quite directly from his
way of proving consistency of (weak) systems of arithmetic already in his thesis.
In the note to Bernays that accompanied the copy of his letter to Gödel,
Herbrand contrasts his consistency proof with that of Ackermann:

> In my arithmetic the axiom of complete induction is restricted, but one may use
> a variety of other functions than those that are defined by simple recursion: in
> this direction, it seems to me, that my theorem goes a little farther than yours.[83]

This is hardly a description of a class of functions that is deemed to be of fundamental significance! However, a detailed account of the evolution of Herbrand's
schema, as well as the precise characterization of the provably total functions
of Herbrand's system of arithmetic (1931d), has to wait for another occasion.

2. Kleene (1987a, 491) emphasized that the approach to effective calculability
through λ-definability had "quite independent roots (motivations)" and would
have led Church to his main results "even if Gödel's paper (1931) had not
already appeared." Perhaps Kleene is right, but I doubt it. The flurry of activity
surrounding Church's *A Set of Postulates for the Foundation of Logic* (published
in 1932 and 1933) is hardly imaginable without knowledge of Gödel's work, in
particular, not without the central notion of representability and, as Kleene
pointed out, the arithmetization of metamathematics. Since the fall of 1931 the
Princeton group of Church, Kleene, and Rosser knew of Gödel's theorems

through a lecture of von Neumann: Kleene (1987a, 491) reports that through this lecture "Church and the rest of us first learned of Gödel's results" (cf. also Rosser 1984). The centrality of representability for Church's considerations comes out quite clearly in his lecture on Richard's Paradox given in December 1933 and published in 1934. According to Kleene (1981, 59), Church already had formulated his thesis for λ-definability in the fall of 1933, so it is not difficult to read the following statement as an extremely cautious statement of the thesis (Church 1934, 358):

> ... it appears to be possible that there should be a system of symbolic logic containing a formula to stand for every definable function of positive integers, and I fully believe that such systems exist.[84]

One has only to realize from the context that (1) "definable" means "constructively definable," so that the value of the function can be calculated, and (2) that "to stand for" means "to represent." In a letter to Bernays dated January 23, 1935, Church claims explicitly that the λ-calculus may be a system that allows the representability of all constructively defined functions:

> The most important results of Kleene's thesis concern the problem of finding a formula to represent a given intuitively defined function of positive integers (it is required that the formula shall contain no other symbols than λ, variables, and parentheses). The results of Kleene are so general and the possibilities of extending them apparently so unlimited that one is led to conjecture that a formula can be found to represent any particular constructively defined function of positive integers whatever. It is difficult to prove this conjecture, however, or even to state it accurately, because of the difficulty in saying precisely what is meant by "constructively defined." A vague description can be given by saying that a function is constructively defined if a method can be given by which its values could be actually calculated for any particular positive integer whatever. Every recursive definition, of no matter how high an order, is constructive, and as far as I know, every constructive definition is recursive.

One and a half years later, Church sent Bernays a copy of a letter he had written on June 8, 1937, to the Polish logician Jozef Pepis. Pepis earlier had informed Church about his project of constructing a numerical function that is effectively calculable, but not general recursive. In his response, Church confessed himself to be "extremely skeptical—although this attitude is of course subject to the reservation that I may be induced to change my opinion after seeing your work." Church stated his impression that Pepis might "not fully appreciate the consequences which would follow from the construction of an effectively calculable non-recursive function" and went on to formulate such consequences— giving a most sophisticated defense of Church's Thesis by an argument that makes implicit use of a concept close to Gödel's notion of absoluteness:

> For instance, I think we may assume that we are agreed that *if a numerical function* f *is effectively calculable then for every positive integer* a *there must be a positive integer* b *such that a valid proof can be given of the proposition* f(a) = b (at least *if we are not agreed on this then our ideas of effective calculability are so*

different as to leave no common ground for discussion) [my emphasis]. But it is proved in my paper in the *American Journal of Mathematics*[85] that if the system of *Principia Mathematica* is omega-consistent, and if the numerical function f is not general recursive, then, whatever permissible choice is made of a formal definition of f within the system of *Principia*, there must exist a positive integer a such that for no positive integer b is the proposition $f(a) = b$ provable within the system of *Principia*. Moreover, this remains true if instead of the system of *Principia* we substitute any one of the extensions of *Principia* which have been proposed (e.g., allowing transfinite types), or any one of the forms of the Zermelo set theory, or indeed any system of symbolic logic whatsoever which to my knowledge has ever been proposed.

Because of the metamathematical facts and the assumed minimal agreement on effective calculability, Church concludes that to discover an effectively calculable nonrecursive function "would imply discovery of an utterly new principle of logic, not only never before formulated, but never before actually used in a mathematical proof—since all extant mathematics is formalizable within the system of *Principia*, or at least within one of its known extensions." Yet the final line of defense is what I called Church's Central Thesis:

> Moreover, this new principle of logic must be of so strange, and presumably complicated, a kind that its metamathematical expression as a rule of inference was [sic!] not general recursive (for this reason, if such a proposal of a new principle of logic were ever actually made, I should be inclined to scrutinize the alleged effective applicability of the principle with considerable care).

Substantiating my claim of the "dependent" development in Princeton requires further detailed (historical) work I am not going to pursue here; but I add that this is not an issue of settling priorities, but of elucidating the role of central informal notions.

Notes

Acknowledgements—It is a pleasure to acknowledge that the considerations in parts 2 and 3 have profited from discussions with Guglielmo Tamburrini and Robin Gandy. As to the published literature, the original papers of Gödel, Church, Turing, Post, and Kleene, and the essays of Gandy (1980, 1988), were particularly important to me; I also learned a great deal from the historical papers of Davis (1982) and Kleene (1981, 1988). To Clark Glymour I owe thanks for bringing Herbrand's remarkable letter to Claude Chevalley to my attention, and to Catherine Chevalley for permission to quote from it. Thanks for improvements are due to C. Bartusis, A. Behboud, J. Byrnes, A. Ignjatovic, G. H. Müller, P. Odifreddi, T. Seidenfeld, and, especially, to J. W. Dawson. Finally, I am grateful to the editors of Gödel's *Collected Works* (Solomon Feferman, John W. Dawson, Warren Goldfarb, and Charles D. Parsons) for access to the correspondence between Herbrand and Gödel, Bernays and Gödel, and to Gödel's as yet unpublished lectures of 1933 and 1951. The Institute for Advanced Studies at Princeton gave me permission to quote from this unpublished material; similarly, the Bibliothek der ETH, Zürich, allowed me to use Bernays' correspondence with Church, Herbrand, and Turing.

1. From Wittgenstein (1980), section 1096. I first read this remark in Shanker (1987), where it is described as a "mystifying reference to Turing machines."

2. The speculation is taken up briefly in the last section of this chapter and, in detail, in my paper with Tamburrini, "Does Turing's Thesis Matter?"

3. But see Tamburrini (1988), and the critical survey of the literature given there. The present paper is part of a book project Tamburrini and I have been pursuing for a number of years. A detailed review of the classical arguments is in Kleene (1954), sections 62, 63, and 70; section 6.4 of Shoenfield (1967) also contains a careful discussion of Church's Thesis; and, finally, the first chapter of Odifreddi (1989) provides a broad perspective for the whole discussion.

4. Mendelson (1990) intends "to renounce the standard views concerning the nature of Church's thesis" and concludes that the thesis is *true* on account of "Turing's analysis of the essential elements involved in computation" (p. 233). Very standardly, however, he emphasizes (1) that the "independently proposed" explications of Church, Post, and Turing are "quite different," and (2) that Turing used his machines directly as mathematical models "to capture the essence of computability." (The real target of) Turing's analysis and the source of the restrictive, "normalizing assumptions" for Turing machine computations are not mentioned at all; see section 3.2.

5. Turing (1939); see the reprint in Davis (1965, 160). I want to warn the reader against misinterpretations of Turing's Thesis by "mechanists"—as in Webb (1980, 9), where it is claimed that it is a very strong thesis indeed, "for it says that *any* effective procedure whatever, using whatever 'higher cognitive processes' you like, is after all mechanizable"—but also against the misunderstanding of the thesis and an emphasis on absolutely misleading issues by "anti-mechanists"—as in Searle (1990), in particular pp. 24–28. On p. 26, for example, Searle claims that the standard definition of "digital computer", which he traces back to Turing, seems to imply: "For any object there is some description of that object such that under that description the object is a digital computer."

6. Here and in section 4.2 I draw on my paper (1990a) and refer to it for additional and relevant details. For a comprehensive discussion of Leibniz's views, see Spruit and Tamburrini (1991); Krämer (1988) traces the historical development of calculi in a very informative way. Note that I focus here on the—for my purposes—most relevant background and do not discuss, for example, Babbage's (theoretical) work; for that see Gandy (1988).

7. There is much mathematical work, partly related to proof theory, that started with Weyl's "Das Kontinuum" and early lectures of Hilbert's presented in the second volume of *Grundlagen der Mathematik*. During the last decade important and most relevant work was done in "reverse mathematics"; see my review (1990b).

8. Van Heijenoort (1967, 101).

9. P. 237. But he was careful to emphasize (in other writings) that all of thinking "can never be carried out by a machine or be replaced by a purely mechanical activity," Frege (1969, 39). He went on to claim: "Wohl läßt sich der Syllogismus in die Form einer Rechnung bringen, die freilich auch nicht ohne Denken vollzogen werden kann, aber doch durch die wenigen festen und anschaulichen Formen, in denen sie sich bewegt, eine grosse Sicherheit gewährt."

10. He added parenthetically: "This has the consequence that there can never be any doubt [as] to what cases the rules of inference apply, and thus the highest possible degree of exactness is obtained."

11. Another significant influence was the sharpening of the "hypothetico-deductive method" within mathematics; a sharpening that brought about a separation of syntax

and semantics for mathematical theories. This separation was clear to Dedekind, for example. Wiener's talk at the meeting of the Deutsche Mathematiker Vereinigung in Halle, succinctly summarized in his Wiener (1891), made this methodological point very forcefully and impressed Hilbert strongly. For this development compare Guillaume (1985, 766–777).

12. Clearly, an adequate representation of content was taken for granted. Cf. Kreisel (1968) for the following discussion.

13. I assume that Herbrand had in mind Dirichlet's theorem mentioned previously. See also Herbrand (1930, 187), where he hopes that his approach will allow the elimination of "transcendental methods" from proofs of arithmetic theorems.

14. Support for this claim is given in Sieg (1990a, 271–272). The "mediating" role of the program was not only described by the immediate members of the Göttingen school, but also, for example, by Herbrand; see Herbrand (1971, 211–212).

15. These connections are elaborated in Sieg (1984); as to the lively interest in Kronecker's ideas in Germany in the twenties, see Pasch (1918) and Kneser (1925). When describing the central features of "intuitionist" mathematics, for example in 1931a and c, Herbrand emphasized exactly Kronecker's points; see Herbrand (1971, 273, and footnote 5, 288–289).

16. I will come back to these remarks in section 4.2.

17. That is expressed in the Nachtrag to Bernays (1930), reprinted in Bernays (1976, 61). In a letter to Gödel, written on September 7, 1942, Bernays emphasized that the methodological points of the above character do not correspond to a "strict *formalist* standpoint"; he continued: "... aber einen solchen habe ich niemals eingenommen, insbesondere habe ich mich in meinem (Sommer 1930 geschriebenen) Aufsatz 'Die Philosophie der Mathematik und die Hilbertsche Beweistheorie' deutlich davon distanziert, und noch mehr dann in dem (Ihnen wohl bekannten) Vortrag 'Sur le platonisme dans les mathématiques'."

18. Herbrand (1930a, 188); the same point is made in (1930b, 214).

19. Herbrand thought that this assumption was not restrictive: "And in general," he wrote (1930b, 213), "we can contrive so as to make all usual mathematical arguments in theories that have only a determinate finite number of hypotheses. Thus we can see the importance of this problem, whose solution would allow us to decide with certainty with regard to the truth of a proposition in a determinate theory."

20. In Gandy (1988, 64–65), one finds the remark that this idea of requiring bounds turns up over and over "like a bad penny"; but in the context of the issues Herbrand and others were working on it is a most natural constructivity requirement. However, and here I agree with Gandy, in a general theory of computability there is no good reason to "mix together constructive and nonconstructive notions of existence." This point will come up again in the discussion of Gödel's notion of general recursive function that was based, as Gödel put it, on a suggestion of Herbrand.

21. Löwenheim's work on the decision problem was done in the Boole–Schröder tradition of algebraic logic. He had established results that could be used to obtain (partial) answers to the decision problem also for Frege's *Begriffsschrift*; namely, he solved the problem for monadic predicate logic and reduced that for full predicate logic to the fragment with just binary predicates. Independently, Behmann (1922) proved these results directly for a system of symbolic logic building on the work of Frege, and Whitehead and Russell.

22. Herbrand (1930a, 176), compare also Herbrand (1929b, 42).

23. That was already explicit in Löwenheim (1915); see van Heijenoort (1967, 246). Cf. also Herbrand (1930b, 207), where Herbrand speaks of an "experimental certainty"

that *Principia Mathematica* allows the representation of all mathematical statements and arguments. That point was made forcefully also in Herbrand (1930a, 48).

24. Hilbert (1927), translated in van Heijenoort (1967, 475).

25. This observation extends to the interpretation of the incompleteness and undecidability theorems of Gödel, Church, and Turing. The most striking and contentious "consequence" of these particular metamathematical results is briefly formulated as: Minds are (not) machines. As to the unnegated statement, see Myhill (1952) and Webb (1980, 1990); the negated statement has been defended in, for example, Löb (1959) and Lucas (1961).

26. Herbrand and Church reacted to the incompleteness theorems in the same way: "They can't apply to my formalism!" As to Gödel's interest in the first issue, see section 2.4. That the second issue was central for Gödel should be clear from the following text. I thus agree with Shapiro (1983), who emphasized that the problem of generalizing Gödel's incompleteness theorems was a "central item" in the development of a theory of computability. Gödel was also concerned about the third problem as evidenced by his discussion of Diophantine problems (1931, 1934). That naturally connects to Hilbert's Tenth Problem and other mathematical problems requiring decision procedures, like Thue's word problem for semigroups; see Gandy (1988, 60–61).   27. See footnote 7 of Post (1936), reprinted in Davis (1965, 291). Post's proposal is discussed in section 3.1, where I also describe the major difference with Turing's.

28. In section 9 of his 1888 work; see, in particular, theorem 126 and its applications in sections 11–13.

29. Tait (1981) argues for this claim. Gödel's system *A* (1933) seems to be just *PRA* and is claimed to contain all of finitist mathematics (actually used by "Hilbert and his disciples").

30. Gödel (1934), reprinted in Davis (1965, 61).

31. Gödel added for the publication of the lecture notes in Davis (1965): "This statement is now outdated; see the Postscriptum, pp. 369–371." He refers to the postscriptum appended to the lectures for Davis' volume.

32. As to the background for Herbrand's proposal, see section 2.2. Kalmar (1955) pointed out that the class of functions satisfying such functional equations is strictly greater than the class of (general) recursive functions.

33. In a letter to van Heijenoort of April 23, 1963, excerpted in the introductory note to Herbrand (1931d); see Herbrand (1971, 283). (Gödel refers to his 1934 lectures.) The background for, and content of, the Herbrand–Gödel correspondence is described in Dawson (1991).

34. The very notion of partial recursive function had been introduced in Kleene (1938).

35. The connection between the "different" proposals is also discussed by Gödel in correspondence with van Heijenoort, partially contained in van Heijenoort (1971) and in footnote 34 of Gödel (1934); that note was expanded in 1964. An earlier discussion of this issue is found in a letter to J. R. Büchi that was written by Gödel on November 26, 1957.

36. Herbrand considered the Ackermann function to be a finitist function, as he asserts—without giving a hint of an argument why (b) is satisfied—that it can be introduced according to the above schema; cf. n. 37.

37. This holds in spite of the explicit (but in this case definitely false) claim that the Ackermann function is among those that can be introduced intuitionistically. How is this confusing state of affairs to be understood? The discrepancy between Herbrand's conjecture in April and that in July is elucidated, it seems to me, by letters of Bernays

to Gödel from this period. Bernays and Herbrand had been in contact, in Berlin and also in Göttingen; Herbrand even sent Bernays a copy of his letter to Gödel—with an interesting accompanying letter dated, as the letter to Gödel was, April 7, 1931. In his letter of April 20, 1931, Bernays asked Gödel why the recursive definition of arithmetic truth could not be formalized in Z and why Ackermann's consistency proof could not be carried out in Z. Without waiting for Gödel's response, Bernays conjectured in his next letter to Gödel of May 3, 1931, that the answer to his questions lay in the unformalizability of certain types of recursive definitions in Z, the definition of truth and that of the Ackermann function being among them. (As to the Ackermann function, Bernays is still not right: it cannot be introduced in the fragment of arithmetic with induction for Σ_1^0 formulas, but in the fragment with Π_2^0 induction it can be introduced.)

38. In a letter to van Heijenoort of August 14, 1964; see van Heijenoort (1985a, 115–116).

39. In the postscriptum, Davis (1965, 73), Gödel asserts that the question raised in footnote 3 of the lectures can be "answered affirmatively" for recursiveness as given in section 9, "which is equivalent with general recursiveness as defined today." As to the contemporary definition, he seems to point to μ-recursiveness. But I do not understand how that definition could have convinced Gödel that "all possible recursions" are captured; nor do I understand how the Normal Form Theorem—as Davis (1981, 11) indicates—could do so without assuming some version of Church's Central Thesis. Indeed, such arguments seem to me crucially to require an appeal to that thesis and are, essentially, reformulations of Church's argument analyzed in the following text. That holds also for the appeal to the recursion theorem in (1954, 352), when Kleene argues that "Our methods ... are now developed to the point where they seem adequate for handling any effective definition of a function which might be proposed."

40. Church, in a letter to Kleene, dated November 29, 1935, and quoted in Davis (1982, 9).

41. As to the evolution of the concept of λ-definability and an earlier formulation of the thesis, see Appendix.

42. Church (1936a), reprinted in Davis (1965, 89–90). f is the characteristic function of the proposition; that 2 is chosen to indicate "truth" is, as Church remarked, accidental and nonessential.

43. Church (1936a, footnote 3), reprinted in Davis (1965, 90).

44. Ibid., 100.

45. An argument pertaining quite closely to the first method is given in Shoenfield (1967, 120). Church grappled with the connection of intuitive (effective) definability and representability in a system of symbolic logic already in Church (1934).

46. Church (1936a), reprinted in Davis (1965, 101). As to what is intended, namely for L to satisfy epistemologically motivated restrictions of the sort mentioned previously, see Church (1956, section 07, in particular pp. 52–53).

47. Compare footnote 20 in Davis (1965, 101), where Church remarks: "In any case where the relation of immediate consequence is recursive it is possible to find a set of rules of procedure, equivalent to the original ones, such that each rule is a (one-valued) recursive operation, and the complete set of rules is recursively enumerable."

48. The remark is obtained from footnote 19 of Church (1936a), reprinted in Davis (1965, 101), by replacing "an algorithm" by "a system of symbolic logic." Cf. Church's letter to Jozef Pepis quoted in part 2 of Appendix.

49. It is most natural and general to take the underlying generating procedures directly as finitary inductive definitions. That is Post's approach via his production systems; using Church's Central Thesis to fix the restricted character of the generating

steps guarantees the recursive enumerability of the generated set. Cf. Kleene's discussion of Church's argument in (1954, 322–323). To see how pervasive this kind of argument is, compare note 39 and part 2 of Appendix.

50. As to the former, compare Gödel (1986, 170 and 176); as to the latter, see Davis (1965, 58).

51. There is no indication of an argument for the absoluteness of computability; I can think only of proofs of the Normal Form Theorem type. Also, Gödel did not compare the class of computable functions with other classes of functions, except for remarking that, "In particular, all recursively defined functions, for example, are already computable in classical arithmetic, that is, the system S_1." But here, I assume, he used "recursive" either in the sense of "primitive recursive" or "recursive of arbitrarily high order," but not "general recursive." The concept of recursion of arbitrarily high order is used in Gödel (1936b), a review of Church (1935a), in the context of λ-definability.

52. The content of Gödel's note was presented in a talk on June 19, 1935. See Davis (1982, 15, footnote 17) and Dawson (1986, 39).

53. "Remark printed on p. 83" of Davis (1965) refers to the remark concerning absoluteness that Gödel added in proof to the original German publication.

54. Church's remark about the "necessity of proving preliminary theorems" can be easily clarified: in my description of his argument for the recursiveness of the function F that is calculable in a logic I glossed over the very last step; to take it, Church refers to an earlier theorem (IV) in his paper, asserting that the class of recursive functions is closed under the μ-operator—in the "normal case."

55. As to the crucial points of difference, see Kleene's discussion in (1954, 361), where it is also stated that this treatment "is closer in some respects to Post 1936."

56. In Feferman (1991, 1–2) the case is made "for the primary significance for practice of the various notions of relative (rather than absolute) computability, . . ." Indeed, Feferman argues later (p. 25) that "notions of *relative* computability have a much greater significance for practice than those of *absolute* computability." The reason given is that the organization and control of computational devices have to be structured into "*conceptual levels* and at each level into interconnected *components*." Although I can hardly disagree with that remark, it is heeded in the theory of absolute computability and, furthermore, if some process carried out by a device is to be called a "computation," it will certainly have to satisfy the general conditions formulated for absolute computability.

57. Post (1936), reprinted in Davis (1965, 289). Post remarks that the infinite sequence of boxes can be replaced by a potentially infinite one, expanding the finite sequence as necessary.

58. The emphasis is mine. To clarify some of the difficulties here, one has to consider other papers of Post's. A good starting point might be the discussion in Davis (1982, 21–22) and Post's remarks on finite methods in Davis (1965, 426–428).

59. Post (1936), reprinted in Davis (1965, 291).

60. This is from Kleene (1988, 34). In Gandy (1988, 98), one finds the pertinent and correct remark on Post's 1936 paper: "Post does not analyze nor justify his formulation, nor does he indicate any chain of ideas leading to it." In his review of that paper Church is also quite critical. But compare the second part of note 58.

61. My emphasis. This justification is discussed in section 3.3.

62. I am following the useful convention of Gandy's whereby a human carrying out a computation is a *computor*, whereas *computer* refers to some machine or other. In the *Oxford English Dictionary* the meaning of "mechanical" as applied to a person is given by: "resembling (inanimate) machines or their operations; acting or performed without the exercise of thought or volition; . . ."

63. Turing (1936), reprinted in Davis (1965, 135).

64. A formulation of a computor operating in a two-dimensional computing space will be given in Sieg (forthcoming); such a computor satisfies appropriately generalized finiteness conditions, and it can be shown that his computations can be carried out by a "linear" computor. So this step is indeed without theoretical consequence. This analysis is of a significantly more general character than the investigations of generalized Turing machines in Kleene (1954).

65. In Davis (1965, 135) a very similar reason is given for restricting the number of states of mind. My account here is not a pure reconstruction, but joins Turing's considerations for restricting the number of symbols and states of mind with the (later) ones on immediate recognizability.

66. Turing relates state of mind to memory in section 1, p. 117, for his machines: "By altering its *m*-configuration [i.e., its state of mind] the machine can effectively remember some of the symbols which it has 'seen' (scanned) previously." This point is also emphasized by Kleene (1988, 22): "A person computing is not constrained to working from just what he sees on the square he is momentarily observing. He can remember information he previously read from other squares. This memory consists in a state of mind, his mind being in a different state at a given moment of time depending on what he remembers from before."

67. Turing actually argues that the changed squares must satisfy similar conditions as the observed squares and, for that reason, can be taken as being among them; in addition, the changes can be carried out one square at a time.

68. This last condition is specific for a "linear" computor; in general, one would have to require that there is a fixed finite number of configurations that can serve as "paths" from one observed symbolic configuration to the next. (Cf. n. 64.)

69. Turing (1936), reprinted in Davis (1965, 137).

70. Ibid., 138.

71. Church, in the letter to Kleene of November 29, 1935, quoted in Davis (1982, 9).

72. Postscriptum to Gödel (1934), reprinted in Davis (1965, 72). Cf. also Turing's remark in which formal systems are characterized as "mechanical" ones: Turing (1939), reprinted in Davis (1965, 194).

73. Turing (1936), reprinted in Davis (1965, 139).

74. It should be possible to present counterexamples that would show—as those in Gandy (1980)—that weakening of the conditions (1.1)–(2.2) leads to "omniscient computors."

75. Turing (1936), reprinted in Davis (1965, 135).

76. Post (1944), reprinted in Davis (1965, 310). See also footnote 1 of Post (1965).

77. Compare Webb (1990) for a detailed discussion that in my view is mistaken—mainly because Webb accepts the premise of Gödel's argument; that premise is clearly congenial to Webb's understanding of Turing's Thesis. (For the latter, see my note 5.)

78. It is informative to compare this statement of Gödel's with the (incorrect) translation on p. 241 *and*, most significantly, with the corresponding remark in Gödel (1972a, 273). In the latter, Gödel in effect added "from a reflection upon" to "insights that derive" in this remark.

79. There is a rich literature dealing with the "iterative conception of set," including papers by Parsons and Wang; this literature cannot be discussed here. For references to it, see the second edition of *Philosophy of Mathematics*, edited by P. Benacerraf and H. Putnam and published by Cambridge University Press in 1983, and also Parsons (1990).

80. The categoricity of the second-order theory of complete ordered fields does not

argue against this point; as another example of a theory exhibiting similar features, consider the theory of dense linear orderings without end points.

81. Post (1965), reprinted in Davis (1965, 423).

82. The remarks in brackets are due to Goldfarb, the editor of Herbrand (1971).

83. This is a literal rendition of Herbrand's remark. Bernays, in his letter to Gödel of April 20, 1931, pointed out that Herbrand had misunderstood him in an earlier discussion: he, Bernays, had not talked about a result of his, but rather about Ackermann's consistency proof.

84. Clearly, Church assumed the converse of this claim.

85. Church alluded to the last page (1936a), that is, to Davis (1965, 107).

References

Ackermann, Wilhelm. 1928. Zum Hilbertschen Aufbau der reellen Zahlen. *Mathematische Annalen* 99, 118–133.

Aczel, Peter. 1977. An introduction to inductive definitions. In J. Barwise, ed., *Handbook of Mathematical Logic*. Amsterdam, 739–782.

Behmann, Heinrich. 1922. Beiträge zur Algebra der Logik, insbesondere zum Entscheidungsproblem. *Mathematische Annalen* 86, 163–229.

Bernays, Paul. 1922. Über Hilberts Gedanken zur Grundlegung der Arithmetik. *Jahresbericht der Deutschen Mathematiker Vereinigung* 31, 10–19.

———. 1923. Erwiderung auf die Note von Herrn Aloys Müller: "Über Zahlen als Zeichen." *Mathematische Annalen* 90, 159–163.

———. 1930. Die Philosophie der Mathematik und die Hilbertsche Beweistheorie; Blätter für Deutsche Philosophie 4, 326–367; reprinted in Bernays (1976), 17–61.

———. 1936. Review of Church (1936a and b). *Journal of Symbolic Logic* 1(2), 73–74.

———. 1976. *Abhandlungen zur Philosophie der Mathematik*. Darmstadt.

Bourbaki, Nicolas. 1950. The architecture of mathematics. *Mathematical Monthly* 57, 221–232.

Church, Alonzo. 1932. A set of postulates for the foundation of logic. *Annals of Mathematics* 33(2), 346–366.

———. 1933. A set of postulates for the foundation of logic, second paper. *Annals of Mathematics* 34(2), 839–864.

———. 1934. The Richard Paradox. *American Mathematical Monthly* 41, 356–361.

———. 1935a. A proof of freedom from contradiction. *Proceedings of the National Academy of Sciences, U.S.A.* 21, 275–281.

———. 1935b. An unsolvable problem of elementary number theory. Preliminary report (abstract). *Bulletin of the American Mathematical Society* 41, 332–333.

———. 1936a. An unsolvable problem of elementary number theory. *American Journal of Mathematics* 58, 345–363; reprinted in Davis (1965), 89–107.

———. 1936b. A note on the Entscheidungsproblem. *Journal of Symbolic Logic* 1(1), 40–41.

———. 1937a. Review of Turing (1936). *Journal of Symbolic Logic* 2(1), 42–43.

———. 1937b. Review of Post (1936). *Journal of Symbolic Logic* 2(1), 43.

———. 1956. *Introduction to Mathematical Logic*. Princeton, University Press.

Davis, Martin. 1958. *Computability and Unsolvability*. New York, McGraw-Hill.

———. 1965. *The Undecidable*. New York, Raven Press.

———. 1982. Why Gödel didn't have Church's Thesis. *Information and Control* 54, 3–24.

Dawson, John W. 1986. A Gödel chronology. In Gödel (1986), 37–43.

———. 1991. Prelude to recursion theory: the Gödel–Herbrand correspondence. Manuscript.

Dedekind, Richard. 1888. *Was sind und was sollen die Zahlen.* Braunschweig.

———. 1890. Letter to Keferstein. In van Heijenoort (1967), 98–103.

Feferman, Solomon. 1988. Turing in the land of $O(z)$. In Herken (1988), 113–147.

———. 1991. Turing's "Oracle": From absolute to relative computability—and back. Forthcoming in *Proceedings of the Symposium on Structures in Mathematical Theories* (held in San Sebastian, Spain, September 25–29, 1990).

Frege, Gottlob. 1879. *Begriffsschrift, eine der arithmetischen nachgebildete Formelsprache des reinen Denkens.* Halle, Verlag Louis Nebert.

———. 1893. *Grundgesetze der Arithmetik, begriffsschriftlich abgeleitet.* Jena, Verlag H. Pohle.

———. 1969. *Nachgelassene Schriften.* H. Hermes, F. Kambartel, and F. Kaulbach, eds. Hamburg, Felix Meiner Verlag.

———. 1984. *Collected Papers on Mathematics, Logic, and Philosophy.* B. McGuinness, ed. Oxford, Oxford University Press.

Gandy, Robin. 1980. Church's Thesis and principles for mechanisms. In Barwise, Keisler, and Kunen, eds. *The Kleene Symposium.* Amsterdam, 123–148.

———. 1988. The confluence of ideas in 1936. In Herken (1988), 55–111.

Gödel, Kurt. 1931. Über formal unentscheidbare Sätze der Principia Mathematica und verwandter Systeme. *Monatshefte für Mathematik und Physik* 38, 173–198.

———. 1933. The present situation in the foundations of mathematics. Lecture delivered at the meeting of the Mathematical Association of America in Cambridge, Massachusetts, December 29–30, 1933, to appear in Gödel's *Collected Works*, Vol. III.

———. 1934. On undecidable propositions of formal mathematical systems; lecture notes, Princeton; reprinted in Davis (1965), 39–71, and *Collected Works*, Vol. I, 346–371.

———. 1936a. Über die Länge von Beweisen. *Ergebnisse eines mathematischen Kolloquiums* 7, 23–24.

———. 1936b. Review of Church (1935a): A proof of freedom from contradiction. in Gödel (1986), 398–401.

———. 1946. Remarks before the Princeton bicentennial conference on problems in mathematics; reprinted in Davis (1965), 84–88, and *Collected Works*, Vol. II, 150–153.

———. 1951. Some basic theorems on the foundations of mathematics and their implications. Unpublished Gibbs Lecture, to appear in Gödel's *Collected Works*, Vol. III.

———. 1958. Über eine bisher noch nicht benützte Erweiterung des finiten Standpunktes. *Dialectica* 12, 280–287; reprinted in *Collected Works*, Vol. II, 240–250.

———. 1972a. On an extension of finitary mathematics which has not yet been used; reprinted in *Collected Works*, Vol. II, 271–280.

———. 1972b. Some remarks on the undecidability results. In *Collected Works*, Vol. II, 305–306.

———. 1986. *Collected Works*, Vol. I. Oxford, Oxford University Press.

———. 1990. *Collected Works*, Vol. II. Oxford, Oxford University Press.

Guillaume, Marcel. 1985. Axiomatik und Logik. In Jean Dieudonné, ed., *Geschichte der Mathematik, 1700–1900.* Braunschweig, 748–881.

Herbrand, Jacques. 1928. On proof theory. In Herbrand (1971), 29–34.

————. 1929a. The consistency of the axioms of arithmetic. In Herbrand (1971), 35–37.

————. 1929b. On the fundamental problem of mathematics. In Herbrand (1971), 41–43.

————. 1930a. Investigations in proof theory. In Herbrand (1971), 44–202.

————. 1930b. The principles of Hilbert's logic. In Herbrand (1971), 202–214.

————. 1931a. On the fundamental problem of mathematical logic. In Herbrand (1971), 215–259.

————. 1931b. Unsigned note on Herbrand's thesis, written by Herbrand himself. In Herbrand (1971), 272–276.

————. 1931c. Note for Jacques Hadamard. In Herbrand (1971), 277–281.

————. 1931d. On the consistency of arithmetic. In Herbrand (1971), 282–298.

————. 1971. *Logical Writings*. Warren Goldfarb, ed. Cambridge, Mass., Harvard University Press.

Herken, Rolf, ed. 1988. *The Universal Turing Machine—a Half-century Survey*. Oxford, Oxford University Press.

Hilbert, David. 1900a. Über den Zahlbegriff. *Jahresbericht der Deutschen Mathematiker Vereinigung* 8, 180–194.

————. 1900b. Mathematische Probleme. *Archiv der Mathematik und Physik* 1(1901), 44–63, 213–237.

————. 1904. Über die Grundlagen der Logik und der Arithmetik; reprinted in van Heijenoort (1967), 129–138.

————. 1925. Über das Unendliche; reprinted in van Heijenoort (1967), 367–392.

————. 1927. Die Grundlagen der Mathematik; reprinted in van Heijenoort (1967), 464–479.

Hilbert, David, and Wilhelm Ackermann. 1928. *Grundzüge der theoretischen Logik*. Berlin.

Hilbert, David, and Paul Bernays. 1935. *Grundlagen der Mathematik*, Vol. I. Berlin, Springer.

————. 1939. *Grundlagen der Mathematik*, Vol. II. Berlin, Springer.

Kalmar, Laszlo. 1955. Über ein Problem, betreffend die Definition des Begriffes der allgemein-rekursiven Funktion. *Zeitschr. f. math. Logik und Grundlagen d. Math.* 1, 93–95.

Kleene, Stephen C. 1936. General recursive functions of natural numbers. *Mathematische Annalen* 112(5), 727–742.

————. 1938. On notation for ordinal numbers. *Journal of Symbolic Logic* 3, 150–155.

————. 1954. *Introduction to Metamathematics*. Groningen, Wolters-Noordhoff.

————. 1976. The work of Kurt Gödel. *Journal of Symbolic Logic* 41(4), 761–778.

————. 1981. Origins of recursive function theory. *Annals of the History of Computing* 3, 52–66.

————. 1987a. Reflections on Church's Thesis. *Notre Dame Journal of Formal Logic* 28, 490–498.

————. 1987b. Gödel's impression on students of logic in the 1930s. In P. Weingartner and L. Schmetterer, eds., *Gödel Remembered*. Naples, Bibliopolis, 49–64.

————. 1988. Turing's analysis of computability, and major applications of it. In Herken (1988), 17–54.

Kneser, Adolf. 1925. Leopold Kronecker. *Jahresbericht der Deutschen Mathematiker Vereinigung* 33, 210–228.

Krämer, Sybille. 1988. *Symbolische Maschinen—Die Idee der Formalisierung in geschichtlichem Abriß*. Darmstadt, Wissenschaftliche Buchgesellschaft.

Kreisel, Georg. 1952. On the interpretation of non-finitist proofs II. Interpretation of number theory. Applications. *Journal of Symbolic Logic* 17(1), 43–58.

————. 1968. A survey of proof theory. *Journal of Symbolic Logic* 33(3), 321–388.

Kronecker, Leopold. 1887. Über den Zahlbegriff. *Crelle, Journal für die reine und angewandte Mathematik* 101, 337–355.

Löb, Martin H. 1959. Constructive truth. In A. Heyting, ed., *Constructivity in Mathematics*. Amsterdam, North-Holland, 159–168.

Lucas, J. R. 1961. Minds, machines and Gödel. *Philosophy* 36, 112–127.

Löwenheim, Leopold. 1915. Über Möglichkeiten im Relativkalkül; reprinted in van Heijenoort (1967), 228–251.

Mendelson, Elliott. 1990. Second thoughts about Church's Thesis and mathematical proofs. *The Journal of Philosophy* 87(5), 225–233.

Myhill, John. 1952. Some philosophical implications of mathematical logic. *The Review of Metaphysics* 6(2), 165–198.

Odifreddi, Piergiorgio. 1989. *Classical Recursion Theory: The Theory of Functions and Sets of Natural Numbers*. Amsterdam.

————. 1990. About logics and logicians—A palimpsest of essays by Georg Kreisel, Vol. II: Mathematics. Manuscript.

Parsons, Charles D. 1990. The structuralist view of mathematical objects. *Synthese* 84, 303–346.

————. In press. Quine and Gödel on analyticity. In Paolo Leonardi and Marco Santambrogio, eds., *On Quine*. Cambridge University Press.

Pasch, Moritz. 1918. Die Forderung der Entscheidbarkeit. *Jahresbericht der Deutschen Mathematiker Vereinigung* 27, 228–232.

Post, Emil. 1936. Finite combinatory processes. Formulation I. *Journal of Symbolic Logic* 1, 103–105; reprinted in Davis (1965), 289–291.

————. 1944. Recursively enumerable sets of positive integers and their decision problems. *Bulletin of the American Mathematical Society* 50, 284–316; reprinted in Davis (1965), 305–337.

————. 1965. Absolutely unsolvable problems and relatively undecidable propositions, account of an anticipation. In Davis (1965), 340–433. Originally submitted for publication in 1941.

Rosser, J. Barkley. 1984. Highlights of the history of the Lambda-Calculus. *Annals of the History of Computing* 6(4), 337–349.

Searle, John R. 1990. Is the brain a digital computer? *Proceedings and Addresses of the American Philosophical Association* 64(3), 21–37.

Shanker, Stuart G. 1987. Wittgenstein versus Turing on the nature of Church's Thesis. *Notre Dame Journal of Formal Logic* 28(4), 615–649.

Shapiro, Stewart. 1983. Remarks on the development of computability. *History and Philosophy of Logic* 4, 203–220.

————. In press. Metamathematics and computability. In Ivor Grattan-Guinness, ed., *Companion Encyclopedia of the History and Philosophy of the Mathematical Sciences*. London, Routledge.

Shoenfield, Joseph R. 1967. *Mathematical Logic*. Reading, Mass., Addison-Wesley.

Sieg, Wilfried. 1984. Foundations for analysis and proof theory. *Synthese* 60, 159–200.

————. 1989. Turing's computors and Gandy's machines. Manuscript.

————. 1990a. Relative consistency and accessible domains. *Synthese* 84, 259–297.

————. 1990b. A Review of "S. G. Simpson, Friedman's research on subsystems of second order arithmetic." *Journal of Symbolic Logic* 55, 870–874.

————. 1991. Herbrand analyses. *Archive for Mathematical Logic* 30, 409–441.

Sieg, Wilfried, and Guglielmo Tamburrini. 1991. Does Turing's Thesis matter? (Or: on mechanical and other effective procedures). Manuscript.

Skolem, Thoralf. 1923. Begründung der elementaren Arithmetik durch die rekurrierende Denkweise ohne Anwendung scheinbarer Veränderlichen mit unendlichem Ausdehnungsbereich; Skrifter utgit av Videnskapsselskapet i Kristiana, I. Matematisknaturvidenskabelig klasse, no. 6, 1–38; reprinted in van Heijenoort (1967).

Spruit, Leen, and Guglielmo Tamburrini. 1991. Reasoning and computation in Leibniz. *History and Philosophy of Logic* 12, 1–14.

Tait, William W. 1981. Finitism. *Journal of Philosophy* 78, 524–546.

Tamburrini, Guglielmo. 1988. Reflections on mechanism. Ph.D. diss., Columbia University, New York.

Turing, Alan. 1936. On computable numbers, with an application to the Entscheidungsproblem. *Proceedings of the London Mathematical Society* 42, 230–265; reprinted in Davis (1965), 116–151.

———. 1939. Systems of logic based on ordinals. *Proceedings of the London Mathematical Society* 45, 161–228; reprinted in Davis (1965), 155–222.

———. 1948. Intelligent machinery. In *Machine Intelligence* 5, 3–23. Written in September 1947 and submitted to the National Physical Laboratory in 1948.

———. 1986. Lecture to the London Mathematical Society on 20 February 1947. In B. E. Carpenter and R. W. Doran, eds., *A. M. Turing's ACE Report of 1946 and Other Papers*. Cambridge University Press, 106–124.

van Heijenoort, Jean, ed., 1967. *From Frege to Gödel*. Cambridge, Mass.

———. 1971. Introductory note to Herbrand (1931d). In van Heijenoort (1967), 618–620, and with minor editorial changes in Herbrand (1971), 282–284.

———. 1982. L'oeuvre logique de Jacques Herbrand et son contexte historique. In J. Stern, ed., *Proceedings of the Herbrand Symposium* (Logic Colloquium '81). Amsterdam, 57–85.

———. 1985a. *Selected Essays*. Naples.

———. 1985b. Jacques Herbrand's work in logic and its historical context. In van Heigenoort (1985), 99–122. Translated and expanded version of van Heijenoort (1982).

von Neumann, Johan. 1927. Zur Hilbertschen Beweistheorie. *Mathematische Zeitschrift* 26, 1–46.

Wang, Hao. 1974. *From Mathematics to Philosophy*. London, Routledge & Kegan Paul.

Webb, Judson C. 1980. *Mechanism, Mentalism, and Metamathematics*. Dordrecht, Reidel.

———. 1990. Introduction to Remark 3 of Gödel (1972b) in *Collected Works*, Vol. II, 292–304.

Wiener, H. 1891. Über Grundlagen und Aufbau der Geometrie. *Jahresbericht der DMV* 1, 45–48.

Wittgenstein, Ludwig. 1980. *Remarks on the Philosophy of Religion*, Vol. 1. Oxford, Blackwell.

5

Mathematical Intuition and Objectivity

Daniel Isaacson

1. Mathematics Is Real, and Yet All in Our Minds

Philosophy of mathematics is accountable to mathematical experience. Two features of this experience stand out. First is the inescapable sense that mathematics is constrained by a reality of mathematical facts. Second is the realization that our contact with this reality is entirely through thought.

"I doubt not but it will be easily granted, that the *Knowledge* we may have *of Mathematical Truths*, is not only certain, but *real Knowledge*, and not the bare empty Vision of vain insignificant *Chimeras* of the Brain: And yet, if we will consider, we shall find that it is only of our own *Ideas*." This remark by John Locke (1690, bk. 4, chap. 4, §6) expresses the two features of mathematical experience with which I want to begin this inquiry.

As soon as any particular mathematical notion has been grasped, say addition and multiplication on the natural numbers or that of group and subgroup, we are up against the facts: $3^2 + 4^2 = 5^2$, every natural number is a sum of not more than four squares, the number of elements in a subgroup of a finite group divides the number of elements in the group but not for every group is every divisor of the order of the group the order of a subgroup, and so on. It feels to us that we are in contact with a reality. G. H. Hardy (1929) expressed this feeling as a constraint on the philosophy of mathematics: "It seems to me that no philosophy can possibly be sympathetic to a mathematician which does not admit, in one manner or another, the immutable and unconditional validity of mathematical truth. Mathematical theorems are true or false; their truth or falsity is absolute and independent of our knowledge of them. In *some* sense, mathematical truth is part of objective reality" (p. 4). This sense of reality extends even to the process of defining the notions of mathematics. To formulate a theorem may require first finding a correct definition.

In holding that philosophy of mathematics must respect our sense of the objective reality of mathematics, I am not thereby offering a philosophy of mathematics, nor prejudging a philosophical issue. This demand says nothing in itself as to the nature of any such objective reality. That is for philosophical inquiry to elucidate. The constraint only means that philosophy of mathematics must take account of our impression that mathematical truth is a reflection of fact. Philosophy might still reject this impression as an illusion. The demand that philosophy of mathematics respect our sense of mathematical reality would then be met by providing some explanation of why we feel (mistakenly, as it then would be claimed) mathematics to be an exploration of facts. This constraint of taking into account how it feels when we do mathematics does not rule out skeptical philosophy (though I believe that here, as elsewhere, skepticism is to be rejected), but such rejection is part of philosophy itself, and not given with the pre-philosophical data of the experience we seek to understand.[1]

The perceived reality of mathematics is marked by its classification as a science in the institutional taxonomy by which university faculties are standardly classified. At the same time it is, in its pure form, unique among the sciences in that its notions make no reference to the physical world (this distinction holds even when psychology has been included among the sciences). Thought is the only basis on which the truths of mathematics are obtainable. Of course, to arrive at any truth requires thought. The issue is, what is signified by "basis"? The point about mathematics is that thought is the *only* medium by which the facts which are reflected in its truths impinge upon us.

This observation might be disputed. After all, a fact of arithmetic may be displayed in an array of physical objects. A polynomial equation may be solved by manipulation of symbols handled as concrete marks on paper. A theorem is established by writing down a proof of it. Perspicuous notation is an enormous aid both to creative development of mathematics and to its under-standing by students, and may be essential, so that certain advances, or wide-spread understanding, are impossible without it. Philip Jourdain (1912, 1919) remarks that "It is important to realise that the long and strenuous work of the most gifted minds was necessary to provide us with simple and expressive notation which, in nearly all parts of mathematics, enables even the less gifted of us to reproduce theorems which needed the greatest genius to discover. Each improvement in notation seems, to the uninitiated, but a small thing: and yet, in a calculation, the pen sometimes seems to be more intelligent than the user" (p. 24).

Even so, physical displays and strings of written symbols are not themselves mathematics, but only devices that serve as aids to thought. They no more mean that mathematics consists of physical configurations than notating a symphony or writing down a poem or a novel shows these creations of mind to be distributions of ink on paper. Whitehead and Russell, in the introduction to *Principia Mathematica* (1910, 1927), having outlined the virtues of their "extension of symbolism beyond the familiar regions of number," offer a sensible remark, as it seems to me, on "the limits of useful employment" of symbolism: "In proportion as the imagination works easily in any region of thought, sym-bolism (except for the express purpose of analysis) becomes only necessary as a convenient shorthand writing to register results obtained without its help" (p. 3). David Hilbert appears not to accept this moderate view of the relation of symbolism to thought. In his essay, "On the Infinite" (1926), he states that

> ... as a condition for the use of logical inferences and the performance of logical operations, something must already be given to our faculty of representation [*in der Vorstellung*], certain extralogical concrete objects that are intuitively [*anschaulich*] present as immediate experience prior to all thought. If logical inference is to be reliable, it must be possible to survey these objects completely in all their parts, and the fact that they occur, that they differ from one another, and that they follow each other, or are concatenated, is immediately given intuitively, together with the objects, as something that neither can be reduced to anything else nor requires reduction. This is the basic philosophical position that I consider requisite for mathematics and, in general, for all scientific thinking, understanding, and communication. And in mathematics, in particular, what we consider is the concrete signs themselves, whose shape, according to the conception we have adopted, is immediately clear and recognizable. (p. 376)[2]

It seems to me that Hilbert is either wrong here or means something actually compatible with the view that thought is the only medium by which the facts of mathematics impinge upon us. I will remark on how that is so, both to sustain and to elucidate this view of the nature of mathematics.

In the passage just quoted Hilbert is not explicit as to which concrete objects or signs he takes it must be "intuitively present as immediate experience prior to all thought," but he goes on in the following paragraph to focus on finitary number theory, with numerals in tally notation, and I shall discuss Hilbert's claim as if he had formulated it in terms of these numerals. I begin with the question, how is it that Hilbert considers these numerals to be concrete objects? Isn't any such claim a conflation of the distinction between token and type? It is patently clear that no *particular* set of marks on paper is necessary for the possibility of thought about the natural numbers (indeed also, not least by their finiteness, none is sufficient). Perhaps Hilbert's claim is only that *some* experience with concrete objects of a sort that *could* serve as numerals is requisite to the possibility of thinking about arithmetic (though this reading does not sit very well with his claim that "in mathematics, in particular, what we consider is the concrete signs themselves"). Let us accept that if a being has no experience of concrete objects that have the character of numerals for the natural numbers, then that being could have no thought of natural numbers. It does not follow that our experience of mathematics is *of* those concrete objects, the experience of which made it possible for us to have mathematical thoughts. The supposition is of a nonmathematical experience requisite for transition to mathematical experience. The fact that the one is required for the other does not render them the same.

2. Object Platonism

We have so far identified two basic features of mathematical experience. Our project is to say something as to the nature of mathematics that is compatible with these features and, if possible, explains them. Approaches to the philosophy of mathematics that aim to be compatible with or explanatory of our sense of mathematical reality may be labeled "Platonist." Platonist philosophy of mathematics is by no means restricted to, or even primarily, the philosophy of Plato, and while sharing crucial common features, variants of Platonism can be incompatible with each other. In this essay I shall reject one form of Platonism and argue for the fundamental correctness of another.[3]

Everyday life habituates us to the experience of perceiving objects in the world around us in their varying states and configurations. We consider that how it is with these objects determines the truth or falsity of statements about them. We may find the sensation of being up against the mathematical facts similar. It is not difficult to feel that our experience of mathematics is an experience of objects, those objects which mathematics is about, such as natural numbers, rationals, real and complex numbers, functions, sets, geometrical figures, metric spaces, topologies, differentiable manifolds, and so on. The language in which we express our mathematical thinking has the same grammatical categories of substantival reference as does our talk of the physical world, that is singular terms and the apparatus by which we speak of every*thing* or some*thing* in a given domain. These considerations may lead us to the view that mathematics is about particular mathematical objects in the way that physical discourse is about particular physical objects, and that the objectivity of a mathematical statement is explained by the existence of those mathematical objects that the statement is about. Let us designate such a view "object Platonism."

This rather natural view appears to explain our experience of the reality of mathematics, of its being constrained by the facts. The facts can be understood to be how it is with these particular objects, just as the physical facts are how it is with the physical objects. But there is also a seemingly crucial difference between the two cases. Objects of everyday life can present themselves to us by impingement on our sensory apparatus—depending on what they are and how we are situated in relation to them, we can see, touch, hear, smell or taste them. The objects of mathematics do not seem to be presented to us by any mode of direct perception. We must wonder, then, what corresponds in the mathematical case to our perceptual faculties in the domain of the physical?

Those attracted by this view of mathematics are not necessarily embarrassed by this question. Mathematical intuition is invoked as the human capacity that corresponds in mathematical experience to perceptual capacities in our experience of the physical world. Even so, there is an obvious disanalogy between our sensory capacities and our capacity for mathematical intuition, namely, that there is a passive aspect to our perceptual apparatus and none in our exercise of mathematical intuition. Attention constitutes an active element in sensory perception, separable from the passive reception of a stream of photons impinging upon the retina, sound waves impinging upon the eardrum, and so on. This purely physical substrate to our contact with objects in the physical world may be thought to constitute for us the reality of these objects, which is reflected in their causal impingement upon us. There seems to be no corresponding element in our experience of mathematical facts, and hence no basis in these terms for a Platonist claim for the reality of mathematical objects.[4]

Various considerations may be held to undercut the decisiveness of this point. Physical objects are not all such as can impinge directly upon the perceptual apparatus of human beings. Our understanding of what objects there are in the world around us starts with things that do so impinge ("entification begins at arm's length"[5]), but science tells us of the existence of physical objects far beyond our sensory horizons: microbes, genes, atoms, electrons and elementary particles, quarks, black holes, the background radiation, force fields, the universe, and so on. Physical objects are things we can come to know of when we stumble upon them, as it may be, but very often we can know of them only as the result of a great deal of thought. Even in the case of perception of middle-sized, reasonably compact, near at hand objects—the stone I stub my toe on, the pen I hold in my hand—it may be argued that our capacity to perceive them and our belief in their existence is dependent upon an exercise of conceptual capacities that renders them far more in the nature of theoretical constructs than, on a naive account of the matter, we may have supposed them to be.[6]

Kurt Gödel (1947, 1964) canvases the possibility of a position of the sort I have termed object Platonism: "... the question of the objective existence of the objects of mathematical intuition ... [is] an exact replica of the question of the objective existence of the outer world" (p. 272) (I have removed a pair of parentheses, dropped the words "which, incidentally," and made explicit an implicit "is" of predication). He draws the parallel between mathematical intuition and sense perception, as follows:

> But, despite their remoteness from sense experience, we do have something like a perception also of the objects of set theory, as is seen from the fact that the axioms force themselves upon us as being true. I don't see any reason why we should have less confidence in this kind of perception, i.e., in mathematical intuition, than in sense perception. . . . (p. 271)

Gödel is sympathetic to the claim that appeal to independently existing objects can be explanatory of the mathematics of those objects: "For someone who considers mathematical objects to exist independently of our constructions and of our having an intuition of them individually . . . , there exists, I believe, a satisfactory foundation of Cantor's set theory in its whole original extent and meaning . . ." (p. 262).

For all of its naturalness, such a view immediately faces hostile questions. What is the nature of such objects? Such a question is not only a challenge to this philosophy of mathematics, but may be directed against any appeal to abstract objects—such as virtue, or redness—although how the challenge is met in the case of mathematics might be particular to it. This position is also challenged by the question, What is our access to these objects?

3. Mathematics and Structure

I consider object Platonism to be mistaken, but not because of problems in accounting for our access to the objects which on that view purportedly exist, nor because of difficulties over the nature of such objects. The compelling and immediate reason for rejecting the idea that mathematics is about particular objects is that for any mathematical theory the domain of objects which that theory is taken to be about can always be replaced by a domain consisting of different objects, so long as the second domain has a structure isomorphic to that of the first. What structure must be preserved by the isomorphism depends, of course, on the notions being used in that mathematics, but in all cases mathematics is inherently to do with structure. Isomorphisms between structures in mathematics may be trivial, as in replacing the domain of natural numbers by its proper subset of the even numbers, mapping 0 to 0 and letting the operation of $+2$ in the original domain restricted to this subset correspond to $+1$ in the original structure. Or they may be nontrivial, as in constructing the real numbers by Dedekind cuts of rationals, and as classes of Cauchy sequences of rationals under the equivalence relation of equiconvergence. The particular individuals do not make a difference to the mathematics.[7] What we are concerned with is structure.

Henri Poincaré (1902) insisted on the primacy of structure in mathematics, as against objects: "Mathematicians do not study objects, but the relation between objects. To them it is a matter of indifference if these objects are replaced by others, provided that the relations do not change. Matter does not engage their attention. They are interested by form alone" (p. 20). Paul Benacerraf (1965) establishes this point in reference to competing set-theoretic constructions of the natural numbers. His conclusion is that

> ... numbers are not objects at all, because in giving the properties (that is, necessary and sufficient) of numbers you merely characterize an *abstract structure*— and the distinction lies in the fact that the "elements" of the structure have no properties other than those relating them to other "elements" of the same structure. ... Arithmetic is therefore the science that elaborates the abstract structure that all progressions have in common merely in virtue of being progressions. It is not a science concerned with particular objects—numbers. (p. 70)

It might be claimed that there is one case at least where mathematics does deal with a collection of particular entities, each of which is what it is and not any other thing, namely, pure sets. The empty set is exactly that set which has no elements, the set consisting of the empty set is precisely that set and nothing else, and so on. And foundational work of Dedekind, Frege, Cantor, Russell, and others has shown how all mathematical entities can be made up out of these ontological atoms, as they would then seem to be. However, despite their seeming specificity, sets cannot be held to be particular entities any more than any other elements of mathematics. The two-place relation of set membership can be variously interpreted, and the empty set can be *anything* to which nothing bears that relation. Mirimanoff (1917a, 1917b) observed that sets are isomorphic to trees.[8] Sets exemplify, rather than refute, the general claim that the entities of mathematics are not particular things.

The invariance of mathematical truth with respect to isomorphism shows that mathematics is concerned not with objects but with relations between objects, that is to say, with structure. This structuralism constitutes a definitive characteristic of mathematics, as well as a source of understanding of it. I consider that it must be accepted as a constraint on any philosophy of mathematics, and I shall draw upon it as a means of establishing aspects of the view of mathematics being put forward here.[9]

I have argued that the structural invariance of mathematics renders object Platonism untenable as a view of mathematics. I want now to elucidate this rejection of object Platonism by addressing the question whether the mathematical Platonism espoused by Frege is untenable by these considerations.[10] It would seem so. Frege, in *Die Grundlagen der Arithmetik* (1884), famously held that arithmetic is about particular objects, the identity of which it was a pressing problem, both for philosophy and for mathematics, to discover. He exclaimed, "... surely the number One looks like a definite particular object, with properties that can be specified..." (p. ii), and went on to declare in regard to this number One, "... is it not a scandal that our science should be so unclear about the first and foremost among its objects, and one which is apparently so simple? Small hope, then, that we shall be able to say what number is." Frege considered that "Every individual number is a self-subsistent object" (p. 67). His conception of these objects of mathematics differs from that of Gödel in that for Frege numbers are not objects of intuition.

Frege was motivated in this viewpoint by his antipsychologism, enshrined as one of the three fundamental principles of his inquiry in 1884: "always to separate sharply the psychological from the logical, the subjective from the objective" (p. x). The combination of considering numbers as objects with the view that "we are not able to form of this object which we are calling Four or the Number of Jupiter's moons any sort of idea [footnote: 'Idea in the sense of something like a picture'] at all which would make it something self-subsistent" (p. 69) creates a problem that demands resolution, as Frege clearly saw: "How, then, is a number to be given to us, if we cannot have any ideas or intuitions of it?" (p. 73). Frege sought the solution to this problem in another of his three fundamental principles: "Since it is only in the context of a proposition that words have any meaning, our problem becomes this: To define the sense of a proposition in which a number word occurs" (p. 73). (Frege insists on the context principle at various points in the *Grundlagen*, see pp. x, 71, 72, and 116.) He fixed upon identity statements involving number as the class of proposition whose sense is to be defined: "In doing this, we shall be giving a general criterion for the identity of numbers. When we have thus acquired a means of arriving at a determinate number and of recognizing it again as the same, we can assign it a number word as its proper name" (p. 73), and in thus having determined the meaning of number words, we shall know what numbers are, that is, which things they are.

Is the account Frege provided on this basis an instance of object Platonism, as I previously labeled Gödel's account? The positions of Gödel and Frege on the existence of mathematical objects are in a certain way converses of each other. In the passages quoted from Gödel the existence of mathematical objects is taken to explain the objectivity of mathematics. For Frege, it is rather that the objectivity of mathematics implies the existence of mathematical objects.[11] Frege's enterprise was then to identify objects as the reference of number words in statements of arithmetic. Given the structural nature of mathematics, the question as to whether Frege's account of the nature of the objects of number theory is correct turns on whether Frege considered that he was revealing which unique particular thing each number is. Insofar as he considered this to be what he was doing, the invariance of number theory with respect to isomorphic structures shows him to be mistaken in his philosophical claims arising from his identification of natural numbers with certain extensions of concepts.

But it is not clear whether ultimately Frege considered himself to be revealing what each natural number uniquely is. In leading up to and presenting his account, it sounds as if this is what he takes himself to be doing. But then, in his recapitulation at the end of *Grundlagen*, he states the following:

> In this definition the sense of the expression "extension of a concept" is assumed to be known. This way of getting over the difficulty[12] cannot be expected to meet with universal approval, and many will prefer other methods of removing the doubt in question. I attach no decisive importance even to bringing in the extensions of concepts at all. (§107, p. 117).

For my present discussion, the question whether or not Frege considered that he was revealing which unique thing each natural number is, is not in itself crucial. What is important is just the point that the structural invariance of mathematics tells us that any account of the objects of mathematics that claims to have done so must be mistaken.

4. Concept Platonism

The first constraint on philosophy of mathematics—that it take account of our sense of mathematical reality—favors Platonism in some form. The third constraint, that mathematics is invariant with respect to isomorphism, rules out any philosophy of mathematics based on the unique existence of particular mathematical objects. Because a structure is given by concepts, it favors an account of mathematical reality in terms of the reality of mathematical concepts. A philosophy of mathematics based upon the existence of concepts is also plausible in virtue of the second constraint, that any philosophy of mathematics must take account of the fact that thought is the only medium by which the mathematical facts impinge upon us. The locus of our contact with concepts is the process of thinking about, or with, them. Concepts are the sort of thing with which the mind engages. This can explain how it is that mathematics is achieved entirely by thought. The facts that constrain mathematics are facts about the concepts with which mathematics develops. I shall call such a philosophy of mathematics, based upon the objective reality of mathematical concepts, "concept Platonism." This is the position I advocate in this essay.[13]

The genesis of our mathematical concepts reflects both constitutive features of mind and elements abstracted from experience in the world around us.

Abstracting from experience of the external world means that there is some contingency in the development of mathematical concepts, since differences in experience and interest may give rise to differences in the choice of concepts with which to do mathematics. But insofar as our attention is directed to a particular range of experience, certain concepts will be the ones that apply to mathematical abstraction from that experience, and the kind of mathematics that can be developed out of them will have the determinacy that we experience as being constrained by mathematical facts.

If, for example, our attention is directed to collections of discrete (physical) objects and processes of putting them in an order, abstraction may lead to the mathematical notion of "first element" and "successor of." We may then reach the notion of natural number and arithmetical operations on natural numbers. If, by contrast, our attention is focused on the movement in space of a physical object, we may be led to the notion of a continuum of points, and so to real numbers in mathematics. These are two sorts of experience that present themselves to all human kind (even though it is rare for the individual to reflect upon and abstract from such experiences). Other sorts of experience that, when reflected upon, can give rise to mathematical abstraction may be restricted to limited populations, for example, attempts to determine instantaneous velocity, from which a mathematical concept of derivative of a function has been abstracted.

Many and, as the subject becomes more highly developed, most mathematical concepts arise not from experience in the external world but from mathematical experience itself. Addition and multiplication of natural numbers can be seen as abstractions from physical situations. Exponentiation seems already to be a purely mathematical extension from existing mathematical notions, and clearly so for such notions as p-adic field and Lie group.

What are the constitutive features of mind that enable us to think of mathematical concepts? Thought is the capacity to consider the absent object.[14] Iteration of this capacity brings us to the properties of structure abstracted from the particular, that is, to mathematics. The nature of thought as the capacity to consider the absent object shows itself in the *intentional* nature of thinking.

The situation of an individual thinking of an object is not a two-place relation between the thinking individual and the object being thought of. We may describe a person as thinking of a unicorn, even a particular unicorn (say, the one in *Alice Through the Looking Glass*), without supposing that there is a unicorn which that person is thinking of. Our account of this process of thinking will be in terms of the thinker being possessed of the notion, or concept of a unicorn. Similarly, in the case of someone thinking of a number, or a function, or a metric space, the having of the thought is not a relation of the thinker to an object, but a matter of the thinker being in possession of the requisite concepts.

The cases are similar in being objectless thinkings of objects. But they also differ in a crucial way. Mathematical thought is invariant with respect to change of objects (recall the passage from Poincaré that I quoted earlier). Certain concepts are such that thought in terms of them possesses such invariance. These concepts are, by this characteristic, mathematical. By contrast, thought about a unicorn makes implicit reference to horses and horns of animals (such being the elements, I take it, out of which an account of what we mean by "unicorn" is to be given), and these are particular objects, which if changed, change this concept as given in terms of those objects.

Twentieth-century logic, particularly from the work of Alfred Tarski, formulates precisely a notion of structure on which a structure is a particular set-theoretic object, itself composed of objects (see any current textbook of formal logic or model theory, for example van Dalen 1980, 59). This formulation provides a standard basis for logical and mathematical treatment of structures. Clearly the Tarskian notion of structure is not one that I can, or would wish to, avail myself of in the present context, because the concepts that determine a structure in this sense are given by their extensions, that is, as the collection of objects or ordered n-tuples to which they apply. On the account of mathematics that I am urging, concepts are primary, and concepts in the sense required are not given in extension. Rather, they involve the element of understanding inherently. By a mathematical structure is meant a body of thought whose concepts are mathematical, in the sense that what can be expressed in terms of these concepts is invariant with respect to change of objects. (We see here the sense in which pure mathematics is abstract thought.)

It might be claimed that the account I have just given does not succeed in avoiding the primacy of objects. After all, my condition for a thought to be mathematical was that it be invariant with respect to change of *objects*. In saying this I may appear to have slipped into object Platonism. Such appearance reflects a source of the natural tendency toward object Platonism, namely, that mathematical concepts are concepts of objects.[15] The paradoxical sounding truth of the matter is that mathematics is about objects, but at the same time there are no mathematical objects. The resolution of whatever air of paradox there may be to this formulation resides not in any program of ontological reduction but in reflection upon the nature of mathematical thought. This was the point of my earlier observation about the intentional nature of the state of thinking of objects.

It may also be thought that insofar as there exists a contrast between what I have termed "object Platonism" and "concept Platonism," it corresponds to the difference between finite and infinite. Someone might accept that mathematics is not about *particular* collections of objects in the case of infinite structures, but claim that a finite mathematical structure—for example, a finite permutation group—is a particular object.[16] Consider, for example, the Galois group for the polynomial $x^2 - 2$. This group of automorphisms of $Q(\sqrt{2})$ is isomorphic to the group of permutations on the real numbers $\{\sqrt{2}, -\sqrt{2}\}$. These two finite groups, while isomorphic as groups, are clearly distinct. But the significant point for the present discussion is that neither of these groups is itself a unique particular object. Distinct isomorphic versions of Q and R yield distinct isomorphic structures of $Q(\sqrt{2})$ and $\{\sqrt{2}, -\sqrt{2}\}$, and so distinct automorphisms on $Q(\sqrt{2})$ and distinct permutations on $\{\sqrt{2}, -\sqrt{2}\}$.

It may be replied that these two finite groups each reflect features of infinite structures, namely Q and R, so that the claim that finite mathematical structures are particular objects is not well tested by them. Rather, I should consider the group of permutations on two letters. Here we have a structure that is completely finite (given that letters are themselves finite objects). But the same argument applies in this case just as well as for the isomorphic groups we have just considered. The group of permutations on the letters $\{a, b\}$ is isomorphic to the group of permutations on the letters $\{c, d\}$, giving distinct realizations of the *same* mathematical structure. No single finite object *is* the group of permutations on two letters.

Nor is the point to do with the difference between concrete and abstract. Being abstract is not the same as being mathematical, and the characterization of mathematics in terms of structural invariance distinguishes mathematical from nonmathematical abstract statements. "The whale is a mammal" is a statement about an abstract object, namely, the natural kind consisting of whales. But this abstract object is itself *particular*, by being tied to particular objects, namely, the actual whales that there are (cf. the accounts by Kripke ([1972] 1980) and Putnam (1975) of natural kind terms), and this statement about it is thereby nonmathematical.

I have to say something on how it is that properties of the concepts of mathematics possess reality. I begin by asking how our sense of mathematics being right (or, as the case may be, mistaken) compares with the feeling we can have that solution to a problem in nonmathematical situations can also be seen as right or as mistaken, for example, in writing a novel or designing a building or dealing with a social situation. The solution to a problem in designing a building can elude the designer and then be found, and when found, engender in those who consider the situation the feeling that it is the "right" solution. How is the correctness of such a solution to a design problem to be distinguished from the correctness of a solution to a mathematical problem?[17]

The two features of mathematical experience considered at the outset of this essay—our sense of the reality of mathematics and the fact that our access to this reality is only through thought—do not separate these cases. But the third feature, invariance with respect to isomorphism, does distinguish them. We should note at the same time that recognizing mathematics as concerned with structure is insufficient to distinguish mathematics from the case of designing a building. The design of a new building is a structure, and indeed an abstract structure. The structure in an architectural plan may be subject to propositions that belong to mathematics, for example, that the plan is radially symmetric. The development of an architectural plan may even require use of solutions to problems in geometry or group theory, as in determining how a basic unit of the design can be repeated. But in such a problem situation there will be other constraints than those that belong to pure structure. For residential units, natural light should be maximized while offering occupants as much privacy as possible, and so on. These constraints take the problem outside the domain of mathematics. There is no invariance with respect to isomorphism. The situation is to do with particular things: the earth, sun, human beings, and so on. The sense in which a problem is solved in this situation is that the constraints have been met. Similarly, in the writing of a novel, the sense of getting it right is against the background of human life. Here also there is no invariance with respect to isomorphism. The solution to such a problem may be subject to a constraint of expressing humor, or of being true to certain feelings. These relate to particular things, namely, human beings. The sense in which mathematics is constrained by facts is distinguished from these other cases of constraint by facts by the particularity of their subject matter.

When we embark on mathematics we make a choice. We choose to be concerned only with those features of a given structure that are invariant with respect to that structure. We may do it out of a desire to achieve understanding of a structure that is widely applicable, by abstracting away the particularity of a given situation. Or it may be simply that we find pleasure in this possibility of pure abstract thought that can attain truth. The reality of mathematics is to be understood in terms of the reality of its concepts by which a structure is characterized. That reality is exemplified in the determination of mathematical concepts as correct or not. This is the sense in which the structures of mathematics exist, in which they are real. The reality of a structure lies in the reality of the concepts that characterize it.

More needs to be said by way of elucidation of the key notions of "structure" and "concept" on which the viewpoint I am urging depends. There are $2^{\aleph_0}$ nonisomorphic countable models of the truths of arithmetic (see Kaye 1991, 14). One might consider that each of these nonisomorphic models must be a structure. But if structures are given by concepts, and concepts are the kind of things that are in our minds, there cannot be sufficiently many concepts to characterize these continuum many structures.

I remarked earlier that by structure I cannot mean the extensional notion propounded in set-theoretic terms by Tarski, standard in mathematical logic and implicitly used in this result concerning the number of nonisomorphic models of arithmetic. But what is the difference, then, between the structure of the natural numbers, which I do take to be a structure in the sense I am attempting to develop here, and those structures (which model-theoretically we take them to be) constituting nonstandard models of the truths of arithmetic? If these nonstandard models aren't structures, what are they? And whatever they are, does not the claim that they are not structures contradict the idea that mathematics is always to do with structure?

The mathematics by which we establish the result that there are $2^{\aleph_0}$ nonisomorphic countable models of the truths of arithmetic is model theory. It is this mathematics that requires to be understood in terms of invariance with respect to structure. Nothing in the mathematics of that result is based on our grasp of any particular nonstandard model from the multitude whose multiplicity is there established. In terms of the viewpoint I am urging, these models are not structures. Rather, they are objects within our mathematics—model theory. In making this point, I do not lapse into object Platonism, for, as I already remarked, structures are given by concepts and mathematical concepts are concepts of objects.

It is sometimes claimed that for all we know others may be doing their arithmetic in a nonstandard model, rather than on the standard ω-sequence we consider ourselves to be working with. I take this to be the point of the following argument by Michael Dummett (1967): "Since, for any given formalisation of second-order logic, there will be a non-standard interpretation, we cannot know that other people understand the notion of all properties (of some set of individuals) as we do, and hence have the same model of the natural numbers as we do" (p. 210). Dummett also refers to "... the fact that we can find no method unambiguously to convey what is the standard model we have in mind" (p. 211).

It seems to me that there is no such uncertainty. If the mathematics someone is engaged in is arithmetic, he or she does it with a grasp of the structure of the natural numbers. Articulating that grasp was a subtle and substantial accomplishment (by Dedekind in 1888 and Frege in 1884), but it would be wrong to consider that mathematicians can only have had this grasp after it was articulated, or that formal limitations to that articulation could show that we fail to know what is the structure of the natural numbers. The question whether the structure of natural numbers with which we are working when we do arithmetic is standard or nonstandard is an artifact of overestimating the importance for the practice of mathematics of a formalizable account of our grasp of that structure. When we are concerned with nonstandard structures of the natural numbers we are engaged in a different branch of mathematics from arithmetic. To wonder whether someone engaged in arithmetic is working with a nonstandard model of the natural numbers or the standard one is as plausible as for someone conversant with both finite group theory and functional analysis to be unsure whether the work being presented by a similarly conversant colleague belongs to one of these subjects or the other.

Dummett does seem to allow that it cannot be a puzzle for someone whether he or she does arithmetic with respect to the standard model or a model that is nonstandard, an implication of his remark that "we could not describe a non-standard model without thereby describing it *as* non-standard" (p. 211). Dummett considers this to be a consequence of the fact that "to describe a model for the system, we need to make use of some infinite totality from which to draw its elements, and since the natural numbers are our source for the notion of 'infinitely many', this must be either the natural numbers themselves or something constructed out of them" (pp. 211–212). Acceptance of this fact accords to the (standard) natural numbers a primacy that does not sit well with Dummett's earlier claim (quoted previously) that "we can find no method unambiguously to convey what is the standard model we have in mind." If we cannot describe a nonstandard model without describing it *as* nonstandard, then if someone describes the natural numbers with which he or she is doing arithmetic and does not describe them as nonstandard, we then know that he or she, like us, operates with the standard structure of the natural numbers.

What this observation may show is that for Dummett the problem about nonstandard models is not to know of oneself, or of someone else, that it is the standard natural numbers as opposed to a nonstandard model that one has in mind, but rather to say, even in the situation where nonstandard models have been excluded, *what* the standard model is. But here I want to ask, why is this thought to be such a problem? The structure of the natural numbers consists precisely of elements generated from an element of the structure by iterated application of a successor operation with the property that application of the successor operation to a given element always results in a new element, that is, one that is different from the initial element and from every element generated by application of the successor operation to any element besides the given one.

Such an account, based as it is on the notion of iteration, is circular, as Dedekind pointed out in his letter to Keferstein (1890, 100–101), and the condition that the structure consists of *just* those elements obtained by iteration of the successor operation lacks precision. Dedekind's definition of the chain of a subset with respect to a transformation on a given set (1888, §44) or, equivalently, Frege's definition of the relation "y follows x in the f-sequence" (1879, §26) overcomes this circularity and lack of precision, though this point has been disputed on the basis that these notions depend on use of a second-order quantifier. Whether or not the disputed point is accepted, this initial account of the natural numbers *shows* that the structure of the natural numbers is understood, even if it fails quite to provide foolproof expression of that understanding. Ultimately, Dedekind proved, as a corollary (1888, §132) of his proof of the recursion theorem (1888, §126), that his analysis of the concept of natural number is categorical, demonstrating thereby that it captures the intended structure. This result shows the reality of arithmetic—although, to be sure, number theorists before then did not doubt it, and had no reason to.

It is sometimes supposed that the reality of mathematics turns on bivalence, which reflects an ontology of self-subsistent objects, or an analysis of truth in mathematics by which each statement of our mathematical discourse is determined as true or false. We have seen reasons to reject the possibility that the reality of mathematics can be explained in terms of the self-subsistent existence of the objects that mathematics is about. And Gödel's Incompleteness Theorem shows that for basic arithmetic, and every extension of it, there can be no uniform procedure by which every statement is established or refuted. The reality of mathematics may thereby be thought to be problematic.

The reality of a domain of discourse requires that there be something which that discourse is about. When the discourse is mathematical this something is not particular objects, but a structure.[18] A categoricity result for characterization of a structure (using higher-order quantification) is precisely what is required to show that this situation obtains. I have heard Dedekind's categorical characterization of the structure of the natural numbers dismissed as "a cheap trick."[19] Such a response, it seems to me, is possible only if one is not concerned with the problem of establishing the reality of this region of mathematics, and so cannot see what has been accomplished, namely, a complete characterization of the structure that arithmetic is about. What is not accomplished is a complete characterization of truth in arithmetic.[20]

Dedekind's demonstration of the categoricity of his characterization of the structure of the natural numbers is the sort of thing I have in mind when I speak of the reality of mathematical concepts as the characteristic of concept Platonism. My earlier emphasis on the mind-related nature of concepts may have invited rejection of my label of Platonism and, more seriously, the charge of psychologism, replete with Frege's attendant contempt. In the case of arithmetic, the kinds of concepts that suffice to characterize the required structure are the general one of second-order quantification over a domain and the particular ones of an individual object "zero" and a one-place function "successor of." Such concepts bear more affinity to Frege's objective notion of thoughts than to his psychologistic notion of ideas.

The perception we have of mathematical structures, that is, our basic understanding of them, is what I mean by mathematical intuition. This usage is in accord with "the broadest definition of the term 'intuition'" as "immediate apprehension" (Rorty 1967). Intuition in this sense is the source of our determination of the axioms of a mathematical theory, by which we systematize our immediate apprehension of a given structure. The word "intuition" is used in philosophy with various specific meanings, as shown by its occurrence in the phrases "intuition of" and "intuition that." In keeping with my rejection of self-subsistent mathematical objects, I am not interested here in the notion "intuition of" (and so in particular not interested in the notion of intuition claimed by L. E. J. Brouwer as the basis for his development of so-called intuitionistic mathematics). I am concerned, rather, with the process of mind by which we come to understand what is characteristic of a mathematical structure (where a structure is mathematical when what is true in it is invariant with respect to isomorphism). It might be thought that insofar as this understanding is intuition (immediate apprehension), it is "intuition of," namely, intuition of the given mathematical structure. But I have already stressed that structure in the sense requisite to these considerations is given by concepts (of objects) rather than being itself an object (made up of objects). Our immediate apprehension of a mathematical structure is an intuition *that* certain fundamental facts obtain. In these terms, I endorse Dummett's characterization of intuition as "the womb of articulated understanding" (1967, 214).

The objectivity of mathematics is manifest in the situation that the process of articulating our basic understanding of mathematical structures succeeds or fails (depending upon our perspicuity). It is in this way that mathematical reality is revealed by mathematical intuition. Mathematical intuition is not some low-grade form of mathematical knowledge in which we go by hunches rather than rigorous demonstration. It is rather that experience by which the mathematician first makes contact with reality in mathematics. In these terms, mathematical intuition is the essence of objectivity for mathematics.

5. The Platonist Nature of Intuitionism

Concept Platonism gives a different view of the relationship between intuitionism and Platonist philosophy of mathematics from that usually offered by both proponents and opponents of the intuitionism of L. E. J. Brouwer and of constructivist mathematics generally. I want to say something on this point by way of further elucidating the conception of the reality of mathematics being propounded in this essay.

The image of the intuitionist development of mathematics is of mathematics as the creation of the mathematician. There is no pre-existent reality that the mathematician investigates; rather, the mathematician establishes the domain of mathematical objects by acts of intuition. This conception has been presented as fundamentally in opposition to a Platonist, or realist conception and practice of mathematics, of mathematics as an exploration of facts. Here are two recent examples, one sympathetic to intuitionism, the other to Platonism. Walter van Stigt, in the preface to his book (1990), characterizes the significance of intuitionism in these terms:

> In the broad divide of the historical debate [about the nature of mathematical reality] Intuitionism represents the last great attempt to seek the origin and seat of mathematics in the acting mind of man, challenging the Platonist tradition, which takes mathematics to be an objective, unique and timeless body of truths to be discovered by man. (p. x)

And Penelope Maddy, in the opening paragraph of her paper (1989) remarks that "Intuitionism ... stand[s] in fundamental disagreement with Platonism" (p. 1121). On the contrary, in the terms in which, as it seems to me, Platonism is a viable and indeed the correct view of mathematics, intuitionistic mathematics is just as Platonist as classical mathematics.

The intuitionistic conception and the classical conception constitute two different ways of doing mathematics, both of which exemplify the fundamental nature of mathematics as real. In both cases we are constrained by facts, and are discovering what is true of the notions that we have been led to consider. It is just that the chosen notions differ. Having established certain mathematical concepts by focusing attention on them, in both cases the mathematical facts are determined. In both cases, also, we can be right or wrong in our choice of concepts. Wrong concepts can lead to false mathematics, correct concepts open up ranges of mathematics not otherwise accessible.

Until the first part of the nineteenth century a continuous real-valued function of a real variable was thought of in geometrical terms as a curve traced by a point (as the point of a stylus) moving in the plane. In these terms, it is evident that any continuous function is smooth, that is, has a tangent, at all but an isolated set of points. Bolzano and Cauchy recognized the least upper bound property of the real numbers, which led to an understanding of real numbers that allowed for a correct definition of continuity of a function of a real variable, in terms of which it could be seen that there are continuous functions that are *nowhere* smooth. Nor was it merely optional whether to use this notion of continuous function or the earlier one based on a geometrical notion, since an essential element in our notion of a real variable as a point on the real line is the process of approximating its value to arbitrary precision by rationals. The story of how intuitionistic analysis came to be established, with a domain of objects in process of creation and in which no infinite process is completed, is of an exactly similar character. I have in mind here work from 1907 through the 1970s, by Brouwer, Heyting, Kreisel, Kleene, Troelstra, van Dalen, Kripke and others (comprehending the notion of choice sequence, the difference between choice sequence and lawless sequence, the relation of continuity of operations on real number generators to continuity in the Euclidean metric on the real numbers, the notion of the creating subject, and so on), which, it seems to me, is just as objective and determinate as was the earlier development of classical analysis. Given a particular perspective on the mathematical domain, the concepts that express what one wishes to investigate about that domain need to be discovered, and when they are discovered the correct understanding of the situation that is being investigated can be achieved. The discovery of the concept of free-choice sequence in intuitionistic analysis is comparable to the understanding of the notion of real number achieved by Bolzano in his proof of the intermediate value theorem in the development of classical mathematics, by which it was then possible to achieve truths not otherwise achievable, and indeed such that without that notion "theorems" would have been propounded with, on the later development can be seen to be incorrect.

Those who see Platonism and intuitionism as fundamentally opposed may question whether what I am calling "concept Platonism" falls within what they mean by Platonism. I leave for another occasion consideration of the historical aptness of this label "concept Platonism," except to note that while the position I am here urging as to the relationship between intuitionism and Platonism is not the standard one, I am not the first to have been struck by it. Paul Bernays (1935) expounds a conception of Platonism highly consonant with that of this essay, as when he remarks that "The value of platonistically inspired mathematical conceptions is that they furnish models of abstract imagination. . . . They form representations which extrapolate from certain regions of experience and intuition" (p. 259). On the basis of this conception, Bernays arrives at important insights, as it seems to me, on Brouwer's intuitionism. He begins from the observation that "Intuitionism makes no allowance for the possibility that, for very large numbers, the operations required by the recursive method of constructing numbers can cease to have a concrete meaning" (p. 265). Bernays cites the number $67^{(257^{729})}$, and remarks that "Intuitionism, like ordinary mathematics, claims that this number can be represented by an Arabic numeral," which leads Bernays to the point that "Brouwer appeals to intuition, but one can doubt that the evidence for it really is intuitive. Isn't this rather an application of the general method of analogy, consisting in extending to inaccessible numbers the relations which we can concretely verify for accessible numbers?" (p. 265). Bernays concludes his discussion of intuitionism with the assessment that

> . . . the two tendencies, intuitionist and platonist, are both necessary; they complement each other, and it would be doing oneself violence to renounce one or the other.
>
> But the duality of these two tendencies, like that of arithmetic and geometry, is not a perfect symmetry. . . . we must recognize that the assumptions of platonism have a transcendent character which is not found in intuitionism. (p. 269)

This last remark fits with my viewpoint that describing the reality of mathematics in terms of concept Platonism applies to all mathematics, and thereby to intuitionism as a particular case.

Karl Popper (1968) also discusses Brouwer's intuitionism in terms that are congenial to the viewpoint I am urging here. Popper considers that

> ... it is one of Brouwer's great achievements that he saw that mathematics ... is created by man. This idea is so radically anti-Platonic that it is understandable that Brouwer did not see that it can be combined with a kind of Platonism. I mean the doctrine of the (partial) *autonomy* of mathematics, and of the third world.... (p. 134)

Popper's doctrine of "the third world" is akin to what I mean by concept Platonism, though there are elements of Popper's account that I reject. I will not attempt to indicate here where I disagree with Popper's idea of the third world, except to point out that Popper's third world is much more (and, as it seems to me, too much) a product of human artifact, as when he characterizes it as "the world of *objective contents of thought*, especially of scientific and poetic thoughts and of works of art" (p. 106). This difference in part reflects the fact that Popper's aim in formulating his notion of the third world is to embrace what is objective in all that can be thought, whereas my goal in formulating concept Platonism is to understand specifically the objectivity of mathematics.

Though talk of construction by intuition of the creating subject may make it sound as if the objects of intuitionistic mathematics are particular, it is clear that this cannot be so, since intuitionistic mathematics shares the fundamental characteristic of all pure mathematics of invariance with respect to isomorphism. Intuitionistic mathematics is real and objective in the same way in which all mathematics is.

Notes

Acknowledgments—This essay, based initially on a talk I gave to a philosophy of mathematics seminar in Oxford, is a somewhat revised and expanded version of my contribution to the conference on Mathematics and Mind. I have also read versions of it at the City University of New York Graduate Center, the Mathematical Institute of the Polish Academy of Sciences in Warsaw, and the Mathematical Institute of the Jagiellonian University, Krakow. Some ideas in the present essay go back to much earlier unpublished presentations at a philosophy of mathematics seminar in Oxford, a meeting in Utrecht of the Anglo-Dutch Logic Colloquium, the Cambridge Moral Sciences Club, an Oxford philosophy discussion group, the Oxford Philosophical Society, the St. Andrews Philosophy Club, and the Somerville Philosophical Society. I am grateful for each of these opportunities to expound these ideas and to all those who contributed to the ensuing discussions, both those whom I am able in these notes to acknowledge for specific points and those whose comments had a more general impact on my thinking about these issues. I am also grateful to those who read earlier versions of this essay and gave me comments. My greatest debt in writing this paper is to Alexander George. I am extremely grateful to him for his invitation to speak at his conference on mathematics and mind, for his perceptive commentary on my paper when I presented it there, which provided me with a valuable framework within which to think further about it, and for his tremendously kind encouragement and patience, which made it possible for me finally to publish this material. I am also deeply indebted and grateful to my wife, Kassandra, for her generous patience and encouragement as I worked on this paper.

1. Compare Wittgenstein's remark (1953) that "what a mathematician is inclined to say about the objectivity and reality of mathematical facts is not a philosophy of mathematics, but something for philosophical *treatment*" (§254).

2. Alexander George pointed out the apparent tension between this passage of Hilbert and my claim that our experience of mathematics is purely in thought.

3. This essay does not contain the scholarship requisite to defend the aptness of the label Platonism. It has occurred to me as a possibility and been claimed by some who have heard me present these ideas that the position set out here bears more affinity to Kant than to Plato (I am grateful to Sidney Morgenbesser for arguing this point). The issue is philosophically substantive and one I am interested in pursuing, but I do not have the opportunity to do so here. It might seem preferable to have avoided the need to do so by using a label that does not bear this historical weight, such as "realism" or "objectivism." However, "realism" has been used with a variety of philosophical meanings that would not be mine here, and although "objectivism" is not so much claimed already by established philosophical usage, it seems unsuited to my purposes by its etymological dependence on the word "object."

4. Paul Benacerraf (1973, 671–673) has drawn attention to serious difficulties raised by the issue of causality for any attempt to give an account of mathematical knowledge.

5. This slogan, from the opening page of Quine (1960), occurs in a context where attention is on our predilection for talk of physical things rather than sensations ("things glimpsed, not glimpses"), but Quine's observation is related to the point I am making, as when later in that same paragraph he notes that "Linguistically, and hence conceptually, the things in sharpest focus are the things that are public enough to be talked of publicly, common and conspicuous enough to be talked of often, and near enough to sense to be quickly identified and learned by name; it is to these that words apply first and foremost."

6. Jennifer Whiting put me in mind of this last point by a comment she made in the discussion following a talk I gave on this topic. Consider Berkeley's phenomenalism, in which physical objects are not taken as perceived directly, but rather to be constructs of perceptions. Compare also Russell (1914), which profoundly influenced the Vienna Circle; see particularly Carnap (1928). In more recent times, Quine's doctrines of ontological commitment and relativity have made all objects, including what we consider as physical objects, implicitly theoretical (see Quine 1969).

7. Of course I do not mean that there is no mathematical difference between Dedekind cuts and equivalence classes of Cauchy sequences, which clearly there is. But they have equal claim to be the real numbers.

8. This insight led Mirimanoff to formulate the hitherto unrecognized assumption that the set-membership relation is well-founded. Even with this assumption, sets cannot be taken to be particular things, as Mirimanoff's interpretation of sets as trees showed. Mirimanoff's structural view of sets opened the way to the study of non-well-founded sets, which has recently been seriously developed, most notably by Peter Aczel (1988); see pp. 3–17 for a clear account of tree and graph structures as isomorphic images of sets, and the notion of a picture of a set.

9. Structuralism as a philosophy of mathematics has been significantly developed in recent years. See in particular papers by Resnik (1975, 1981, 1982, 1988), Shapiro (1989), and Parsons (1990).

10. Alexander George raised this point in his commentary on my conference presentation of this essay.

11. This contrast was pointed out by Alexander George in his commentary.

12. The difficulty Frege here refers to is the "Julius Caesar problem," that is, that we cannot "decide by means of our definitions whether any concept has the number JULIUS CAESAR belonging to it, or whether that same familiar conqueror of Gaul is a number or is not" (p. 68), which he formulates in his recapitulation in the following terms: "If we treat the possibility of correlating one to one the objects falling under the concept F with the objects falling under concept G as an identity, by putting for it: 'the Number which belongs to the concept F is identical with Number which belongs to the concept G,' thus introducing the expression 'the Number which belongs to the concept F,' this gives us sense for the identity only if both sides of it are of the form just mentioned. A definition like this is not enough to enable us to decide whether an identity is true or false if only one side of it is of this form."

13. The distinction I am drawing between object Platonism and concept Platonism should be compared with that drawn by Charles Chihara (1973, 61–75) between ontological Platonism and mythological Platonism, and by Mark Steiner (1973) between ontological Platonism and epistemological Platonism.

14. See W. R. Bion (1962, 1967; pp. 111–112) for insight as to the constitutive relation between frustration and the capacity for thought.

15. Robert Tragesser offered this formulation in discussion at a lecture I gave on some of these ideas.

16. Robin Gandy raised this point in discussion.

17. Michael Dummett raised this issue in discussion.

18. Of course, this point applies, in the first instance, to domains of mathematics that have to do with a particular structure, for example, the various number systems, geometries, real and complex function theory, etc. Developments of twentieth-century mathematics such as abstract algebra, the theory of metric spaces, general topology, and so on, in which mathematicians study a class of structures satisfying stipulated axioms—for example, all rings—rather than a particular structure such as the natural numbers do not seem to be covered, and it may be thought that this leaves out of account what is essential to the contemporary development of mathematics (cf. Bourbaki 1948). Two considerations may be offered in response to this challenge. One is that the analysis given here applies to the reality of any particular ring or topological space, etc. The other is that insofar as we are concerned with an entire class of structures and not with any particular one, we will (of necessity) be considering them through use of the mathematical theory that characterizes such structures, for example, ring theory or group theory. This situation corresponds to the case we confronted earlier of the theorem that there are continuum many nonstandard models of the truths of arithmetic.

19. In discussion following my presentation of an earlier version of this essay.

20. For some discussion of the relation between these two aspects of mathematical reality, see Isaacson (1987) and (1992).

References

Page references are to the most recent reprint shown, unless otherwise noted. Quotations from works not originally in English are from the indicated English translation.

Aczel, Peter. 1988. *Non-Well-Founded Sets.* Stanford, CA, Center for the Study of Language and Information.

Benacerraf, Paul. 1965. What numbers could not be. *The Philosophical Review* 74, 47–63.
———. 1973. Mathematical truth. *The Journal of Philosophy* 70, 661–679.
Benacerraf, Paul, and Hilary Putnam, eds. 1983. *Philosophy of Mathematics: Selected Readings*, 2nd ed. Cambridge University Press.
Bernays, Paul. 1935. Sur le platonisme dans les mathématiques. *L'Enseignement Mathématiques* 34, 52–69, English translation by C. D. Parsons, On platonism in mathematics. In Benacerraf and Putnam (1983), 258–271.
Bion, W. R. [1962] 1967. A theory of thinking. *The International Journal of Psycho-Analysis* 43. Reprinted with Commentary by the author, in Bion, W. R. (1967), *Second Thoughts: Selected Papers on Psycho-Analysis*, New York, Jason Aronson, 110–119.
Bourbaki, Nicholas. 1948. L'architecture des mathématiques, F. Le Lionnais, Cahiers du Sud; English translation by Arnold Dresden, The architecture of mathematics. *The American Mathematical Monthly* 57 (1950), 221–232.
Carnap, Rudolf. 1928. *Der Logische Aufbau der Welt*. Berlin-Schlachtensee, Weltkreis-Verlag.
Chihara, Charles S. 1973. *Ontology and the Vicious-Circle Principle*. Ithaca and London, Cornell University Press.
Dedekind, Richard. 1888. *Was sind und was sollen die Zahlen?* Braunschweig, Vieweg; English translation by Wooster Woodruff Beman, The nature and meaning of numbers. In Dedekind (1901), *Essays on the Theory of Numbers*. LaSalle, Ill., Open Court Publishing Company, 29–115; reprinted by Dover, New York, 1963.
———. 1890. Letter to Keferstein, 27 February 1890, Niedersächsische Staats- und Universitätsbibliothek Göttingen, classmark UB, Cod. Ms. Nachlass Dedekind, 13. English translation by Stefan Bauer-Mengelberg, in van Heijenoort (1967), 98–103.
Dummett, Michael. 1967. Platonism. Invited address to the Third International Congress for Logic, Methodology and Philosophy of Science, Amsterdam, 1967. In Dummett (1978), *Truth and Other Enigmas*. London, Duckworth, 202–214.
Frege, Gottlob. 1879. *Begriffsschrift, eine der arithmetischen nachgebildete Formelsprache des reinen Denkens*, Halle, L. Nebert; English translation by Stefan Bauer-Mengelberg, *Begriffsschrift*, a formula language, modeled upon that of arithmetic, for pure thought. In van Heijenoort (1967), 1–82.
———. 1884. *Die Grundlagen der Arithmetik:Eine logisch mathematische Untersuchung über den Begriff der Zahl*. Breslau, Verlag von Wilhelm Koebner; English translation by John Austin (1959), *The Foundations of Arithmetic: A Logico-Mathematical Enquiry into the Concept of Number*. Oxford, Basil Blackwell.
Gödel, Kurt. [1947] 1964. What is Cantor's continuum problem? *The American Mathematical Monthly* 54, 515–525; revised, expanded version in Paul Benacerraf and Hilary Putnam, eds. (1964), *Philosophy of Mathematics: Selected Readings*. Englewood Cliffs, N.J., Prentice-Hall, 258–273. Also reprinted in Benacerraf and Putnam (1983), 470–485. Both versions reprinted, with display of original pagination, in Solomon Feferman *et al.*, eds., *Kurt Gödel, Collected Works*, vol. II: Publications 1938–1974. Solomon Feferman *et al.*, eds. New York, Oxford University Press, 1990, 176–187, 254–270. [Page citations in text are from Benacerraf and Putnam (1964).]
Hardy, G. H. 1929. Mathematical proof. *Mind* 38, 1–25.
Hilbert, David. 1926. Über das Unendliche. *Mathematische Annalen* 95, 161–190; English translation by Stefan Bauer-Mengelberg, On the infinite. In van Heijenoort (1967), 367–392.
Isaacson, Daniel. 1987. Arithmetical truth and hidden higher-order concepts. In The Paris Logic Group, eds., *Logic Colloquium '85*. Amsterdam, North-Holland.

————. 1992. Some considerations on arithmetical truth and the ω-rule. In Michael Detlefsen, ed., *Proof, Logic and Formalization*. London and New York, Routledge, 94–138.

Jourdain, Philip E. B. [1912] 1919. *The Nature of Mathematics*. London, T. C. & E. C. Jack, and Edinburgh, T. Nelson & Sons, revised edition, 1919.

Kaye, Richard. 1991. *Models of Peano Arithmetic*. Oxford University Press.

Kripke, Saul [1972] 1980. Naming and necessity. In Donald Davidson and Gilbert Harman, eds., *Semantics of Natural Language*. Dordrecht, Holland, D. Reidel, 253–355; revised and enlarged edition, Oxford, Basil Blackwell, 1980.

Locke, John. 1690. *An Essay Concerning Human Understanding*. London.

Maddy, Penelope. 1989. The roots of contemporary Platonism. *The Journal of Symbolic Logic* 54, 1121–1144.

Mirimanoff, Dmitry. 1917a. Les antinomies de Russell et de Burali-Forte et le problème fondamental de la théorie des ensembles. *L'Enseignement Mathématiques* 19, 37–52.

————. 1917b. Remarques sur la théorie des ensembles et les antinomies cantoriennes. *L'Enseignement Mathématiques* 19, 209–217.

Parson, Charles. 1990. The structuralist view of mathematical objects. *Synthese* 84, 303–346.

Poincaré, Henri. 1902. La grandeur mathématique et l'experience. In *La Science et l'Hypothèse*. Paris, Bibliotèque de Philosophie Scientifique, Ernest Flammarion; English translation by W.J.G., Mathematical magnitude and experiment. In *Science and Hypothesis*, 17–34. Walter Scott Publishing Company. Reprinted by Dover Publications, New York, 1952.

Popper, Karl R. 1968. Epistemology without a knowing subject. In B. van Rootselaar and J. F. Staal, eds., *Proceedings of the Third International Congress for Logic, Methodology and Philosophy of Science, Amsterdam 1967*. Amsterdam, North-Holland, 333–373; reprinted in Popper (1972), *Objective Knowledge: An Evolutionary Approach*, Oxford University Press.

Putnam, Hilary. 1975. The meaning of "meaning". In Keith Gunderson, ed., *Language, Mind and Knowledge*. Minneapolis, University of Minnesota Press, 131–193.

Quine, W. V. 1960. *Word and Object*. Cambridge, Mass., MIT Press.

————. 1969. Ontological relativity. In *Ontological Relativity and Other Essays*. Columbia University Press, 26–68.

Resnik, Michael D. 1975. Mathematical knowledge and pattern cognition. *Canadian Journal of Philosophy* 5, 25–39.

————. 1981. Mathematics as a science of patterns: Ontology and reference. *Noûs* 15, 529–550.

————. 1982. Mathematics as a science of patterns: Epistemology. *Noûs* 16, 95–107.

————. 1988. Mathematics from the structural point of view. *Revue Internationale de Philosophie* 42, 400–424.

Rorty, Richard. 1967. Intuition. In Paul Edwards, ed., *The Encyclopedia of Philosophy*, Vol. 4, 204–212. New York, Macmillan.

Russell, Bertrand. 1914. *Our knowledge of the external world as a field for scientific method in philosophy*. Chicago and London, Open Court Publishing Company. Rev. ed. W. W. Norton, 1929.

Shapiro, Stewart. 1989. Structure and ontology. *Philosophical Topics* 17, 145–171.

Steiner, Mark. 1973. Platonism and the causal theory of knowledge. *The Journal of Philosophy* 70, 57–66. In Steiner, *Mathematical Knowledge* (1975). Ithaca and London, Cornell University Press, 109–121.

van Dalen, Dirk. 1980. *Logic and Structure*. Heidelberg, Springer-Verlag.

van Heijenoort, Jean, ed. 1967. *From Frege to Gödel: A Source Book in Mathematical Logic, 1879–1931*. Cambridge, Harvard University Press.

van Stigt, Walter P. 1990. *Brouwer's Intuitionism*. Amsterdam, North-Holland/Elsevier.

Whitehead, Alfred North, and Bertrand Russell. [1910] 1927. *Principia Mathematica*, 2nd ed., Vol. 1.

Wittgenstein, Ludwig. 1953. *Philosophische Untersuchungen*; English translation by G. E. M. Anscombe, *Philosophical Investigations*, 2nd ed. Oxford, Basil Blackwell.

6

Intuition and Number

Charles Parsons

How are natural numbers given to us? How do we know that there are such objects? Two responses to these questions have had some currency recently—the first, that they are not given to us (however indirectly) and we don't know that there are numbers because we have no need of that hypothesis (e.g., Field 1980, 1989), and second, that these are not sensible questions at all (e.g., Tait 1986). I am not satisfied with either of these responses, because the first one involves denying what seems obvious to me, that mathematicians and the rest of us make statements involving reference to numbers that are *true*. It is harder to say why I am not persuaded by the second response; a first approximation might be to say that it would have to be justified by some theory about either numbers as objects or number-expressions as merely apparently referring to objects, and then the question arises whether it is really different from other responses, such as the first. It is not my purpose to defend my rejection of these negative responses, however, but rather to explore one more positive approach.

I

The approach I want to consider will seem rather crude at first sight. It holds, roughly, that natural numbers are given in intuition. That would then be its answer to our first question. Relative to that, the answer to the second question seems trivial. If at least one natural number is given in intuition, then we know "by intuition," together with a trivial logical step, that there are natural numbers.

This idea would raise many questions, of which I will now mention only one: In one respect the step from the givenness of numbers to knowledge of their existence is not quite so trivial as it appears. The first is a matter of intuition of objects. The interpretation I want to press, although it is not the only possible one, is that there are instances of intuition the objects of which are natural numbers. Natural numbers would be objects of intuition, just as macroscopic terrestrial bodies are objects of perception. Let us suppose that in an actual case someone A intuits the number 7. (If this sounds silly, bear with me.)

Then this intuition has to have the character that, at least in typical cases, it follows that A knows that 7 exists. Roughly, intuition of an object involves intuitive knowledge of that object. It seems that our idea involves us both in the notion of intuition of objects and in the notion of intuitive knowledge.

As I have stressed in earlier writing on intuition (Parsons 1980; see also 1986), concerning this concept, one has to keep in mind an elementary distinction between intuition of objects and intuition of (apparent) truths. In the former use, the verb "intuit" would take an ordinary direct object, but it is not excluded that it might be intentional (and thus that intuition would be what is called a "referential attitude"). In the latter case, intuition is a propositional attitude. This, at least in contemporary usage, is the more common use. Although the verb "intuit" is not normally used with that-clauses, the noun "intuition" is. When linguists talk of the intuitions of a native speaker, or when philosophers appeal to their own intuitions about a certain matter, the content is propositional, for example, in the former kind of case that a certain sentence is or is not grammatical. I have called intuition in these two "grammars" *intuition of* and *intuition that*. Both occur in the history of philosophy. Kant's *Anschauung* is, in the first instance, intuition of. The *intuitio* of Descartes' *Regulae* is intuition that.

In my usage, what makes such an idea a conception of intuition is that it should be significantly analogous to perception. This holds to a lesser degree in the case of a native speaker's intuitions than in these historical examples. In many cases of philosophers' intuitions, the analogy is still weaker, because of their very fallible and theory-laden character. (I do not mean to say that ordinary perception or other clear cases of intuition are neither, only that they should be so to a lesser degree.) A clearer case of intuition in the sense that interests me is expressed in remarks by Kurt Gödel. He speaks unambiguously of mathematical intuition as "something like a perception of the objects of set theory" (1964, 268). This would be intuition of, and Gödel is as clear a case as one easily finds of a philosopher committed to intuition of mathematical objects. Nonetheless, I would maintain, and have indicated elsewhere (Parsons, in press), that the more basic notion of intuition in Gödel is intuition that. Even "perception of the objects of set theory" is closer to propositional knowledge than appears at first sight, because for Gödel these objects include *concepts*.

In Parsons (1980), where I explored general issues about the concept, I set forth and defended one conception of intuition that in its most plausible form would be intuition of mathematical objects. It was intended to conform to a Kantian idea of expressing a form that is instantiated in sense perception. But the historical model to which it is closest is to be found in the explanations by David Hilbert and Paul Bernays of the intuitive basis of Hilbert's metamathematics (and of finitist mathematics in general). In this case, the objects of intuition are expressions of a formal language. My idea was that the same analysis should apply to expressions of natural languages, although precisely because of their "natural" character it might be better to speak in this case of perception.[1] Other cases of a somewhat similar nature are sense qualities and geometric figures.

All of these cases differ from that of natural numbers in a crucial respect. The objects involved are what I call quasi-concrete; what they are is determined by some instantiation or "representation" in the concrete. Natural numbers, like other important mathematical objects such as pure sets, are not only not quasi-concrete. They have been called *pure* abstract objects (Dummett 1973, 503; Parsons 1983, 19).[2] Pure abstract objects have no intrinsic concrete representation, and they are characterized not by conditions relating them to concrete objects of a specified kind, but by conditions of a highly abstract character, involving objects in general. They thus relate to objects quite generally. There is no limitation on what objects can be "numbered" (either by ordinals or cardinals), unless such a limitation is to be found in the very concept of object itself. Other examples of pure abstract objects are numbers of other number systems and pure sets. Note that any objects (or almost any objects[3]) can be elements of some set, or can have sets of higher rank built up from them.

The fact that natural numbers are pure abstract objects is thus bound up with their generality of application, a fact about them that was emphasized in Gottlob Frege's polemical arguments and thus is familiar at least from that source. There is, however, a subtle difference between the claim that numbers are pure abstract objects and the claim that numbers apply with perfect generality (in the sense that *any* objects can be numbered). It is not obvious that the latter fact puts any constraint on what the numbers are, other than that they instantiate the structure of an ω-sequence. The generality of application of natural numbers amounts roughly to the fact that for any number n and any predicate 'F', it makes sense to say that there are n Fs, or to say of a particular F that it is the nth in some order. But for well-known reasons, for statements of these forms to be meaningful and well behaved it is sufficient that the natural numbers form an ω-sequence; beyond that, they might even be quasi-concrete or even concrete objects.

I propose to argue that these two closely related ideas about numbers, that they apply to objects in general and that they are pure abstract objects, are incompatible with the existence of intuition of natural numbers in the generally Kantian sense I alluded to previously. The discussion will barely touch on the question whether there is some essentially different conception of intuition that would give a different answer. Since the idea of intuition of natural numbers will find few defenders,[4] you may ask why this is a worthwhile exercise. One reason is that it offers an argument against intuition of natural numbers (that is likely to generalize to most other pure abstract mathematical objects) which is independent of a general rejection of mathematical intuition. A second is that it makes clear a limitation of the conception of intuition I have defended in earlier writings. The view of knowledge of numbers that actually fits this conception has elements both of traditional intuitionism and structuralism.

But an objective more or less independent of issues about intuition that I hope the discussion will serve is to clarify the relation of the character of numbers as pure abstract objects and their formal generality of application. I want to argue that it is not just not the case that natural numbers are objects of intuition. A philosophical intuition about the natural numbers that has been widely held is that the natural numbers are quite elementary and transparent; enough of their properties to constitute a beginning of mathematics can be made as clear and obvious as anything abstract can be. This has been explicated by the idea that at least some of elementary arithmetic, typically the finitist part, can be made *intuitively evident*. One way in which arithmetic certainly falls short of intuitive evidence is that the general principle of mathematical induction does not have this character, because of its higher-order nature. Moreover, the actual development of arithmetic goes beyond intuitive evidence, probably as soon as one develops arguments that cannot be formalized in primitive recursive arithmetic (PRA). These considerations, however, do not show that the natural numbers are not *objects* that are intuitively given. How early essentially nonintuitive objects come into mathematics may be a matter of dispute. But if we acknowledge that at some point they do, then of course even small numbers will be applied in statements of cardinality and ordinality involving these objects. Clearly such statements will not be intuitively evident.[5] If natural numbers are objects of intuition of what relevance is this to their application in such contexts, and thus to their generality of application?

II

Hilbert and Bernays' description of intuitive arithmetic makes it *about* a certain sequence of expressions

$$1, 11, 111, 1111, \ldots[6]$$

If one grants that these are objects of intuition, then an interpretation of arithmetic (at least, finitist arithmetic) will have been given that makes the numbers objects of intuition.

The description of the above strings (or of the numbers) as "objects of intuition" glosses over a serious question, which I will mention but not discuss. To say that objects of a certain domain are objects of intuition could be taken to mean that any such object *can* be intuited. But as a practical matter, sufficiently long strings can't be individually grasped; it would not be difficult to describe one that would take centuries to write out, and such that no individual could in a lifetime run through its terms one by one. It could be replied that "can" here is meant in a more abstract way; the string can, in principle, be intuited. But a better reply might be that it is not necessary that every string can be intuited; when we say that physical bodies are objects of perception, we need not be committed to the view that every such body can be perceived. What I have in mind by the idea that numbers are objects of intuition is that in the most favorable cases it should be possible to intuit numbers and that there should be a nontrivial body of intuitive knowledge of numbers.[7]

There is a very well-known problem faced by any philosophical or logical explanation of what the natural numbers are: Any such explanation seems arbitrary. It is not clear that a given account should be preferred in general to another that gives an isomorphic structure.[8] The notorious example is the different representations of the numbers by sets, where the stock examples are those offered by Zermelo and von Neumann:

$$\varnothing, \{\varnothing\}, \{\{\varnothing\}\}, \{\{\{\varnothing\}\}\}, \ldots$$
$$\varnothing, \{\varnothing\}, \{\varnothing, \{\varnothing\}\}, \{\varnothing, \{\varnothing\}, \{\varnothing, \{\varnothing\}\}\}, \ldots$$

The same consideration could be offered if one tried to maintain that the particular sequence of expressions that Hilbert and Bernays use is *the* natural numbers, or that natural numbers *are* strings of the previously mentioned sequence. There is no better case for them than for what is used in the set-theoretic or logicist construction.[9]

A natural remedy that has been often suggested is the "structuralist" view. Numbers are, in Quine's phrase, "known only by their laws, the laws of arithmetic" (1969, 44).[10] It is a little more accurate to say that numbers are *determined* only by their laws. All that is true about the natural numbers is what is contained in, or follows from, a description of them as a structure: there is an initial element and successor operation satisfying the elementary Peano axioms and the induction principle (however the latter is formulated).[11]

The formulation of the structuralist view presents some problems, and it can be developed in different ways, some of which undertake to eliminate reference to numbers (see Parsons 1990). But no matter how it is worked out, this view does not have numbers as objects of intuition in the sense that concerns us, for the obvious reason that the structural condition can be satisfied by a domain not consisting of objects of intuition, provided that there are such objects. On the structuralist view it is natural to regard it as a presupposition of talk about natural numbers that what we are talking about is in some way a possible structure. This could give intuition a fundamental role on this view, because an intuitive model would exhibit an instance of the structure (cf. Parsons 1980, 163, and Parsons 1990, 336). But the intuition in question need not be intuition of *numbers*, and in typical versions of this view it is not. What is asserted to be possible is a structure that is physical, or mental, or intuitive-geometrical, in a way in which, on this structuralist view, numbers are not.

It should be clear that it is not the mere existence of models of arithmetic consisting of objects that are not objects of intuition that leads to the conclusion that numbers are not objects of intuition. It is this existence combined with the structuralist view. If one starts with any domain of objects with some structure, provided it is determined exactly enough so that it makes sense to talk of structures isomorphic to it, then the assumption (obvious for the Hilbertian conception of intuition) that sets of sufficiently high rank are not objects of intuition implies the existence of nonintuitive models of this structure. For surely there is a one-to-one map from those objects whose range consists of sets of high rank, which induces an isomorphism, onto a structure whose domain of objects is the range of this map. No one would conclude that this fact is by itself enough to show that the original objects are not objects of intuition.[12]

I have so far assumed that there are domains of objects that are not objects of intuition in the relevant sense. In the case of the Hilbertian conception of intuition and other possible Kantian conceptions, I take that to be obvious, because some kinds of objects (in particular, sets) lead us to structures that are too rich to be instantiated in space and time. Other examples of non-intuitable objects suggest themselves: other kinds of pure abstract objects, transcendent objects such as God and other objects considered in theology, and theoretical objects in science. Although they are suggestive, I do not want to appeal to any of these: the pure abstract objects because their not being objects of intuition should be the conclusion of an argument, perhaps close to that concerning the natural numbers, transcendent objects because it will not be agreed that they exist, and theoretical objects because, given that they are spatio-temporal, it is at least not obvious that they should not be treated as objects of intuition, although it is not practically possible to perceive them.

It is plausible that the consideration applies rather generally, and not just to the specific conception of intuition I am concerned with. But I am not insisting on that, in the absence of clear statements of other conceptions of intuition. Moreover, it depends on there being domains of objects that are not objects of intuition, and it is not clear that this condition will be satisfied for other conceptions. For example, it is not clear that it holds for Gödel's conception. It isn't clear that on the structuralist view numbers are not objects of intuition on a conception for which the condition fails, because then their being objects of intuition is trivially preserved by any isomorphism from one copy of the structure to another.

A further question is whether, on a structuralist view, any propositions properly about numbers are intuitively evident. This could depend on further details about how the structuralist view is formulated. The answer seems certainly negative on an eliminative version that makes use of second-order logic, which seems to me the most promising form of eliminative structuralism.[13] But I will consider the question again at the end of this chapter.

III

I now want to ask whether we obtain a different result—either with regard to the question of whether numbers are objects of intuition or with regard to the truth of some version of the structuralist view—if we approach the concept of number in a more phenomenological way, beginning with the elements of its application.

The most elementary cardinal and ordinal applications of numerical language do not obviously require numbers as objects at all. I will take as a canonical form for a statement of cardinal number "there are (exactly) $\bar{n}$ Fs," where 'F' replaces a predicate or general term, and $\bar{n}$ is a numeral. I do not think this needs be taken as making a commitment one way or the other as to whether $\bar{n}$ is a singular term. I do choose this in preference to a form making reference to a set. I do not think that the most basic statements of cardinality have to be interpreted as making reference to sets.[14]

In determining by counting that there are n Fs, one sets up a one-to-one correspondence between the Fs and a sequence of n "counters." Something like a canonical way of verifying that there are n Fs is achieved if we have the Fs successively before our minds, by naming or perceiving them, while marking them with the successive counters. This gives to the mth counter the approximate sense "the mth," that is, in the context, the mth F. Of course, we must insure that no object is counted twice, that is, that at each stage the object marked was not marked before, and we must continue the process until every F has been marked. But these two conditions amount to the condition that the marking should be a one-to-one correspondence of the counters used onto the Fs.

The "counters" will typically be numerals of some standard system, perhaps either the number-words of a natural language, or Arabic numerals. I will suppose the system fixed for the present. Now consider what is required for it to be verified by perception that there are n Fs. It is not sufficient that we be able to perceive each individual F; we must be able to survey all the Fs, one by one, and identify them as Fs and as constituting all of them. But this obtains in many everyday situations, where what is counted are objects that either are before one's eyes all at once or can be brought so successively. Consider such cases as counting the plates, glasses, and pieces of cutlery to be put on the table for dinner, or counting the coins in one's pocket.

I have not been very precise about the meaning of the statement "there are $\bar{n}$ Fs," but it should be observed that the claim that in such simple cases it can be verified by perception would run into difficulties on certain conceptions of what it means. Let us take one construal:

(1) There is a one-to-one correspondence between the Fs and the numerals from 1 to $\bar{n}$

On the face of it, this is a second-order statement, and it involves reference to numerals, which for constancy of meaning in different occasions of use will have to be taken as types. Assumptions about the intuitability of finite sets would plausibly imply that, in the kind of favorable case we are considering, (1) might be intuitively known, but even on that assumption it will involve mathematical intuition.

The issues about intuition of sets that these assumptions would raise are of interest in their own right, but their discussion will have to be reserved for another occasion.[15] But I do not think that in order to understand the most elementary applications of the notion of cardinality we need to give a statement of number so much ontological baggage.[16] Consider the following equivalences, which underlie the standard paraphrase of statements of number into first-order logic with identity:

(2a) $(\exists_0 x)Fx \leftrightarrow \neg(\exists x)Fx$

(2b) $(\exists_{\overline{n+1}} x)Fx \leftrightarrow (\exists y)[Fy \wedge (\exists_{\bar{n}} x)(Fx \wedge x \neq y)]$

One way of looking at counting is to suppose that each numeral $\bar{m}$ used in the count has the force of a demonstrative, designating in the context the object with which it is correlated, so that it has the force of "the $\bar{m}$th." To avoid confusion, I will write it in that way. I have been imagining a very favorable case, where at each point the object can be observed to be F and to be distinct from those counted previously, so that we would have

(3a) $F(\text{the } \bar{m}\text{th})$

(3b) the $\bar{k}$th $\neq$ the $\bar{m}$th (for each k, $0 < k < m$)

Moreover, at the nth stage the subject can observe that there are no further Fs. That is, he is also able to observe

(3c) $(\forall x)(Fx \rightarrow x = \text{the 1st } \vee \cdots \vee x = \text{the } \bar{n}\text{th})$

From (3a–c), all that is needed to infer '$(\exists_{\bar{n}}x)Fx$' is the equivalences (2a–b).

That the subject knows (2a–b), or principles from which they follow, is a reasonable enough assumption. But how shall this knowledge be viewed? First of all, for the present we should regard them as rules in which not only 'F' but also '$\bar{n}$' is schematic, in the latter case, of course, for a numeral. This might suggest that "there are $\bar{n}$ Fs" as simply an abbreviation for its expansion according to (2a–b), so that it is simply a first-order consequence of (3a–c). Another view, perhaps representing the next step in the development of the concept of cardinality, represents '$(\exists_{\bar{n}}x)$' as a kind of generalized quantifier, with some of the basic inferences involving it still treated like logical inference. The first-order expansion becomes very unperspicuous, even before n becomes very large. But it should also be possible to see that there are n Fs in a more step-by-step way than that just described. One such way would be to verify at each stage "there are $\bar{m}$ Fs that are G," where 'G' is some predicate coextensive with "counted so far." What 'G' would be would depend on the circumstances, but presumably it would contain an indexical whose reference changes with m. In the case of a set of objects before one's eyes, one might demonstrate a place, so that 'G' would mean "in this place."[17] In any case, a step-by-step procedure would consist of verifying '$(\exists_{\bar{m}}x)(Fx \wedge G_m x)$' at the mth stage (where 'G_m' fixes the previously mentioned indexical in the appropriate way). To pass to the $(m + 1)$st stage, one would observe that for any x

(4) $Fx \rightarrow [G_{m+1}x \leftrightarrow (G_m x \vee x = \text{the } \overline{(m + 1)}\text{st})]$

and then applying (2b).

One clearly will come pretty quickly to the point of using numerical quantifiers with variable n, and also in ways that are no longer reducible to first-order logic. This should remind us that it is only by confining ourselves to a very simple kind of case that we avoid even the appearance of introducing numbers as objects. The obvious way in which reference to numbers comes, from our starting point, to seem forced on us is that we allow the numeral place in the quantifier to be generalized. We would also quickly enlarge the language so that different expressions come to be used to "refer to the same number." Here we might distinguish three kinds of cases:

(i) Terms arising from the introduction of computable operations, beginning with the most elementary ones such as addition. In these cases there will be procedures for reducing terms composed from numerals with these operators to numerals. This reduction must be understood as applicable in contexts such as "there are n Fs"; otherwise, for example, it would not follow that "there are 4 Fs" is equivalent to "there are $2 + 2$ Fs."

(ii) Expressions such as "the number of Fs" and other definite descriptions designating numbers. These presuppose some form of generalization of numeral places.

(iii) Alternative systems of numerals. One might see these as giving rise to questions of translation (or paraphrase, if they are in our own language). However, there is a constraint on a correct translation or paraphrase that is independent of the idea that the numerals refer to numbers. If we consider two systems, call them the N- and the M-numerals, then we will render the (perhaps foreign) M-numeral $\bar{n}^*$ by (our own) N-numeral $\bar{n}$, just in case there are n M-numerals up to $\bar{n}^*$.[18] Another way of looking at the matter, which gives the same result, and which may be more appropriate if the M-numerals belong to our own language, is to regard them as terms introduced by recursion.

My remarks about (i) and (iii) suggest that, at least before we have constructions comparable to variables and quantifiers for numbers, we have a conception of what it is for expressions to "designate the same number" that does not presuppose an antecedent conception of the numbers as objects. And by an expression that "designates a number," at present we need to mean no more than simply a numeral of our initial system or an expression that, according to the conception just mentioned, "designates the same number" as such a numeral. This encourages us to think of the introduction of variables and quantifiers "ranging over numbers," as in the first instance, substitutional. And in fact, substitutional interpretations of arithmetic have been constructed and defended on philosophical grounds (see especially Gottlieb 1980).

Such an interpretation might be viewed either as an explanation of reference to numbers or as an elimination of it.[19] As we shall see, the latter view suffers fatal objections if it is to be more than an explication of a certain stage in the development of the concept of number. But, in any event, it does not make numbers objects of intuition, because it amounts to a denial that numbers are objects at all.

Let us consider the relevance of the former view to the question whether numbers are objects of intuition. On this view, numbers would be constituted by the use of language, and in particular by the expressions that refer to them. It is the understanding and use of certain language that counts as consciousness of numbers. This does involve ordinary perception—for example, of the objects counted—and intuition of linguistic expressions, in particular, numerals.

Could we still describe the understanding of a numeral as intuition of the number? If so, how would this be related to perception? Not in the same way as in the conception of intuition that has concerned us. Unlike an expression type, the number is not a *form* instantiated by the numeral; we do not explain what the number is by saying that its nature is to be instantiated in just that way. The numeral is here playing the role of a linguistic expression; one thing that shows this is that the number would be just as "present" if it were represented by a corresponding numeral in a different system, perhaps totally different perceptually.[20] Thus, if we were to describe this situation as intuition of a number, the analogy with perception would be less close.

The understanding of reference to numbers that we are considering is a special case of a general conception of object that has been applied in the foundations of constructive mathematics, where an object is given by a canonical expression for it—in the case at hand, a numeral—that in general shows its construction from the basic constructions for that domain of object. Other rules would give rise to noncanonical expressions, which should reduce computationally to canonical expressions. Such rules arise naturally from the constructions manifested in the canonical expressions; for example, if canonical numerals are constructed from 0 by means of successor, the predecessor function δ (introduced by the trivial recursion $\delta(0) = 0$, $\delta(Sn) = n$) simply undoes the last step of the construction of a non-initial number.[21]

The conception of mathematical objects as given by canonical expressions for them does not model the conception of intuition with which I have been concerned, but, rather, models in certain respects that of Edmund Husserl. In general, terms for mathematical objects would express intentions that are fulfilled by their reduction to canonical expressions, and having a canonical expression is then analogous to the presence of the "object itself." In the constructive setting in which this conception arose, one can understand a mathematical proposition as an intention that is fulfilled by the construction that proves it.[22]

It is easy to see, however, that a purely substitutional theory of arithmetic along the lines we have intimated cannot be adequate. There is no difficulty in giving a substitutional interpretation of first-order arithmetic as a stand-alone theory (see Parsons 1971b, note 1),[23] and this can be extended to a ramified second-order theory, at least within the limits of predicativity. Moreover, it can be further developed, along the lines just sketched, to include a treatment of numbers as cardinals (see Gottlieb 1980, Parsons 1982). This treatment supposes, however, that the objects numbered come from an antecedent domain. Of course, in mathematical practice we apply the notion of cardinality to *numbers* and to mathematical objects of other kinds that might depend on natural numbers. Moreover, we do not restrict it to the finite.

This rather commonplace observation could be offered as an argument in favor of the view that this explanation of quantification over numbers really is an explanation of domain of objects. The "cash value" of this view in this context, however, is the same as that of what, on another view, would be the further conceptual leap of regarding the substitutional quantification as objectual. The point is that in mathematical practice, and to some extent in ordinary life, numbers are treated as on a par with other objects, so that they themselves not only can be numbered (which implies that number variables mark an argument place of a *predicate*[24]) but further can be elements of sets and sequences and arguments and values of functions.

But now in what would this further conceptual leap consist? It would consist of steps taken after we have substitutional quantification of numerals, perhaps segregated from other quantification. Perhaps after noting the formal analogy between the behavior of these substitutional quantifiers and that of object quantifiers, and the fact that the former could be generalized to numerical quantifiers in the same way that the latter were, we might then come to treat the number quantifiers as just restricted quantifiers with an underlying predicate "is a number." In addition, the equality predicate that underlies both computable operations and the use of numerical definite descriptions would have to be treated as identity. Talking of sets of and functions on natural numbers would involve still further steps. Evidently it is only at a rather late point in this development that the questions to which the structuralist view responds can even arise. Without allowing numbers into a common domain of quantification with other objects, the question whether any identities hold between numbers and objects given in some other way can of course not be formulated, and the numbers can also not be identified as a structure and a general description of that structure given.

I might at this point make some comments about the famous Fregean criterion of identity of numbers, which in the *Grundlagen* played such a central role in Frege's argument for the thesis that numbers are objects and thus in his explanation of what reference to numbers is. The suggestion made previously is that in an account of the origin of reference to numbers, this criterion introduces more ontology than it is plausible to attribute to a beginning stage in the development of such reference. In application to the natural numbers in a fully developed stage of mathematics, one might still object to it on structuralist grounds, because it treats natural numbers first of all as *cardinals*. But, of course, as a criterion of cardinal equivalence, and therefore as a criterion that cardinal numbers as objects have to satisfy, it is undoubtedly extensionally correct. Moreover, there seems to be no escape from taking this criterion as the most basic one in generalizing the notion of cardinal number to the infinite case. This fits with the fact that the historical situation in which the criterion came to be seen as the basic one was the creation by Cantor of the theory of transfinite numbers. In that context, it is the unique one that yields a coherent theory with anything that can reasonably be called an arithmetic of infinite cardinals. But in standard set theory it does not play the role it played for Frege: as a criterion of identity that was part of an explanation of reference to a certain kind of object.

IV

Now let us return to the question of the relation of the generality of application of numbers to their intuitive or transparent character. To begin with, we might observe that it is not evident that the picture we suggested of the beginnings of reference to numbers makes them pure abstract objects, although they are undoubtedly abstract and not quasi-concrete. But we imagined that in their cardinal role their application had not been generalized beyond a previously given domain of objects, and we did not yet have the setting in which to consider them abstractly as a structure.

When we do understand numbers in a general enough setting so as to realize the idea of them as pure abstract objects, is the intuitive evidence of elementary statements about them preserved? Let us suppose, with Hilbert and Bernays, that certain such statements are intuitively evident when understood in relation to an intuitive model. Do they remain so when interpreted as being properly about *numbers*? Consider a very old chestnut, '$7 + 5 = 12$'. This statement certainly implies the validity of the schema

$$(5) \quad [(\exists_7 x)Fx \wedge (\exists_5 x)Gx \wedge (\forall x)\neg(Fx \wedge Gx)] \rightarrow (\exists_{12} x)(Fx \vee Gx).$$

It should be clear that there will be instances of this schema that are not intuitively evident, once the domain over which the quantifiers range no longer consists of objects of intuition. Does this imply that, in drawing such a consequence, we have come to understand '$7 + 5 = 12$' so that it is no longer intuitively evident? We have an argument for this conclusion only if I assume that even in this setting *logic* preserves intuitive evidence. But precisely because it is being applied where the domain of quantification has a nonintuitive character, we can question this assumption. Thus, the conclusion that the lack of intuitive evidence of such an instance of (5) reflects back, so that '$7 + 5 = 12$' is itself not intuitively evident, is not forced on us.

That the matter is not quite as simple as that can be seen by reflecting on the structuralist view of numbers. I have remarked that the most promising eliminative version of this view paraphrases arithmetical statements, '$7 + 5 = 12$' included, as statements of second-order logic, generalizations about arbitrary ω-sequences. An alternative would take talk of numbers to result from a kind of abstraction, once one is given an ω-sequence.[25] Either one makes reference to numbers derivative either from the general notion of ω-sequence or from the identification of a specific instance, and therefore from some formulation or other of induction as a general principle.

The ideas sketched in this chapter about the genesis of reference to numbers differ from both of the just mentioned versions of structuralism, in that according to them, some form of reference to numbers is present before the questions giving rise to the abstraction or generalization can even arise. The eventual integration of arithmetic with set theory (and possible highly abstract empirical scientific theories) does bring the numbers into a sort of holistic connection with highly nonintuitive modes of reference and knowledge. It is not clear, however, that statements that were intuitively evident before this expansion of our conceptual resources need to lose that evidence. What is clear from examples like that of '7 + 5 = 12,' given above is that their *applications* outside the intuitive sphere in general will not have the same intuitive character. If we model the "transparency" of the numbers by our concepts of intuition and intuitive evidence, then we are committed to the view that the generality of their application—thus, one aspect of what is involved in their status as pure abstract objects—is something added to what is transparent about them. Although some will no doubt disagree, I do not find this an unwelcome result.

Notes

Acknowledgments—Earlier versions of this essay were presented at Brandeis University and Manhattanville College. I wish to thank Palle Yourgrau and Billy Joe Lucas both for their hospitality and their comments, from which the version presented at Amherst benefited. My greatest debt is to my commentator at Amherst, Thomas Tymoczko, whose comments prompted nearly all the revisions made in preparing the paper for publication.

1. There are, however, two dimensions of the relation of intuition and perception that should be distinguished. If I hear what someone else has said, I am aware of (say) a sentence, thus of something abstract (the sentence as type). (I leave out of consideration the question whether I might also be aware of something further, such as a proposition. Obviously that would raise additional issues.) But I also, typically, perceive the physical sound and come to know that the speaker has uttered the sentence in question. Thus, one reason for speaking of perception would be that the whole episode contains cognition of an actual event and not just of abstract objects and their relations. Intuition of the same sentence founded on imagination would not have this character, and would presumably be miscalled perception.

2. Dummett's explanation of the meaning he gives to this term relies on ideas of Frege, and his intended meaning appears to differ from mine. But I think we have much the same objects in view, and I think the same holds for uses of the phrase "pure abstract object" by other writers.

3. Of course, a question arises about proper classes, which, however, might be held not to be objects.

4. Among major philosophers of the past hundred years, the only one known to me who clearly defends it is Edmund Husserl. Moreover, Husserl's articulate defense is in the early work *Philosophie der Arithmetik* (1891), so that the question naturally arises how much of it is compatible with his later philosophy. Although I will say a little more about Husserl in what follows, I do not think it would be rewarding to examine his discussion in detail. Gödel's views on mathematical intuition in general might commit him to intuition of numbers, but he is in fact silent on the matter.

In the preface to Butterfield (1986), the editor attributes to my paper in that volume the view that "constructivism requires that numbers can be intuited" (p. xi). That is a misinterpretation. However, the construction of section 3 of Parsons (1971a) *was* intended to justify the claim that, in a sense at least, numbers can be intuited. It should be clear from the following discussion why I no longer think such a construction could accomplish that end; see, in particular, note 20.

Intuition of numbers is defended in Tieszen (1989). Because the primary model for his conception of intuition is Husserl's, it is not clear how directly his view is affected by the argument of the present essay.

5. In fact, on this view of intuitive evidence, truths that are not intuitively evident can be formulated without reference to such objects. Assuming for the sake of argument that PRA is the limit of intuitively evident arithmetic, then a relatively trivial such example would be "there are 0 proofs of contradictions in PRA."

6. Hilbert and Bernays say explicitly that from their finitary point of view (1934, 21) these symbol-strings (*Ziffern*) are the *objects* of number theory. Cf. also Hilbert (1926, 171, trans. 376–377).

7. Cf. Parsons (1986, 222–227). One might raise the objection that the conception of intuition with which I am concerned here rests on a grossly oversimplified conception of the relation of token and type in actual symbolisms. Such an objection is made in Tymoczko's comments, and a similar objection was made to me in conversation by Linda Wetzel (cf. Wetzel 1989). This is a serious issue for the viability and interest of this conception, and I hope to address it elsewhere. Since the present essay makes a negative claim about intuition so conceived, I do not think the truth of its claims would be affected by such an objection. But I do not answer the objection that what my discussion shows is that numbers are not objects of an intuition that does not exist anyway.

8. The qualification "in general" is of some importance because in particular contexts one might have very good reasons to prefer one. In fact, the von Neumann representation has the great advantage that it is part of a very elegant and natural representation of *ordinals*; in standard set theory that is a pretty decisive reason in its favor. But other representations, or keeping the numbers as primitive, will be used in other contexts.

9. Indeed, Hilbert and Bernays (1934, 20–21) make the following remark: "In number theory we have an initial object and a process of continuation. Both must be fixed intuitively in a definite way. The particular manner of fixing is nonessential, but the choice once made must be held to for the whole theory. We choose the numeral 1 as initial thing, and appending a 1 as process of continuation" (my translation).

One might read this as saying that the sequence of strings of 1's is an intuitive *model* of arithmetic, clearly one among many possible such. The question would then arise of what meaning the notion of model has in the conceptual framework of their metamathematics.

10. In the same place Quine expresses an analogous view of expressions and sets.

11. This statement is not entirely accurate because among the truths that can reasonably be said to be about natural numbers are those involving relations to objects of other kinds, such as that 9 is the number of planets. Such statements, however, do not require more of the numbers than that they form an ω-sequence. See Parsons (1983, 189–190, or 1990, 309).

12. However, there is a large issue here that I do not claim to be addressing. The thesis of the inscrutability of reference is defended on grounds similar to those offered for the structuralist view of mathematical objects; does it amount to a structuralist view of objects in general? If so, could not my argument be used to show that the inscrutability thesis implies that there are no objects of perception (since intuition, as I understand it, includes ordinary perception)? I think not. Suppose that a proxy function that witnesses the inscrutability of reference maps certain objects that are, intuitively, objects of perception, onto objects that are not. One has inscrutability, it seems to me, only because predicates like "x perceives y" are also caught up in the reinterpretation, so that, if ϕ is the proxy function, "x perceives y" is reinterpreted as "$\phi(x)$ perceives $\phi(y)$."

But relations involving perception are not part of the structures at issue in the structuralist view of mathematical objects.

About the relation of inscrutability and the structuralist view, more needs to be said. I am indebted to William Bracken for making me aware of this.

13. Cf. Parsons 1990. A version of the view that is not directly subject to the criticism in that paper is presented in Hellman (1989). He is not concerned with questions of intuitive evidence, and the remark in the text does apply to his construction.

14. But, of course, the form given in the text does subsume one obvious one involving sets, because 'F' might be "is an element of a" where 'a' designates some set.

15. The strongest such assumption would be that any finite set of intuitable objects is intuitable. If we think of the correspondence as a set of ordered pairs, then it follows that the correspondence is intuitable if we either understand the ordered pairs by the Wiener-Kuratowski definition or assume (independently and, in my opinion, with as much plausibility) that ordered pairs of intuitable objects are intuitable. These assumptions could, however, be questioned on a number of grounds.

16. I might remark that the second-order aspect of (1) would not have caused any concern to Frege, because he would have taken it to be a logical consequence of a statement of the form "H is a one-to-one correspondence of the Fs and the numerals from 1 to $\bar{n}$," for a specific predicate 'H.'

Of course Frege would not have interpreted statements of number by way of reference to numerals. On the reading of the *Grundlagen* the statement "the number of Fs in $\bar{n}$" would be a second-order consequence of the usual translation of "there are $\bar{n}$ Fs" into first-order logic and instances of the Fregean criterion of identity for numbers:

the number of Fs = the number of Gs iff there is a one-to-one correspondence of the Fs and the Gs,

(which in turn is, as is well known, provable with the help of Frege's axiom V from his definition of "the number of Fs" using extensions). In the kind of maximally favorable case we are considering, by Frege's lights "the number of Fs is $\bar{n}$" would thus be a logical consequence of facts verifiable by perception.

17. Of course, one could say that what is demonstrated is the *set* of so-far-counted Fs, so that 'G' means "in this set." This is clearly of more general application and thus represents one entry point for the set concept.

This might seem to give comfort to Penelope Maddy, who maintains that in verifying by perception some such thing as that there are three eggs in a carton, one perceives a set of three eggs (1990, 58). Maddy seems to infer "Steve sees a set of eggs that has three elements" from "Steve sees that there are three eggs in the carton." This has considerable plausibility if one assumes that the statement "there are three eggs in the carton" involves reference to a set. But I do not see that such reference needs to be assumed to analyze elementary perceptual evidences of the sort that Maddy is concerned with.

Maddy's conclusion that there is perception of sets might, however, be justified by the claim that in slightly more complicated cases than the one she describes (say, if there are seven eggs in the carton), at each stage of counting one must demonstrate the set of eggs counted so far. Given that demonstration of a place would also serve the purpose, I do not see this. But one might be able to make the case with examples of another kind.

18. If the initial element is taken to be 0, "up to n^*" is replaced by "less than n^*"; if it is taken to be 1, "up to n^*" is taken to mean "up to and including n^*." Note that these relations are decidable by a computational procedure, in some cases a trivial one.

19. Gottlieb defends the latter view. The former view would be suggested by the

general view in Parsons (1971b). With more specific attention to arithmetic, I examine the question further in my review article (1982).

20. However, this does suggest a way of viewing numbers as objects of intuition, by taking them as "generalized types": numeral-tokens even in *different* systems are of the same type if they "represent the same number" in the sense explained in the text. (See Parsons 1980, 163–164; also Parsons 1971a, 43–47, where, however, this conception is given a modal nominalist interpretation.) This conception seems to me to lose much of its motivation once one sees the relation of alternative numeral systems to our own as a matter of translation. In any event, supposing it be developed so that the case is made that numbers so understood are objects of intuition, one can then raise the structuralist objection that it is just one more *construal* of the natural numbers. What is there about the concept of natural number that makes it true that numbers are these objects rather than some other ω-sequence?

21. The conception of mathematical objects as given by canonical expressions for them underlies Per Martin-Löf's intuitionistic theory of types, a powerful constructive theory that is susceptible of still further extensions. See especially Martin-Löf (1984). I discuss this ontological conception (mostly with reference to quite simple cases) in 1986. The rather obvious considerations given in the following text to show the inadequacy of the straightforward substitutional interpretation do not apply to a theory like Martin-Löf's. In fact, the treatment of higher types in his theory rules out taking the conception as an elimination of ontology.

22. Cf. Tieszen (1989, esp. chap. 4, §5). It is probable that Husserl exercised at least an indirect influence on the origins of intuitionistic logic in the early work of Arend Heyting.

23. For a fuller treatment, see Kripke (1976, §§8–9).

24. Assuming the form of the basic statement of number I have assumed. But taking number to attach to sets would have the same implication (cf. note 16).

25. This is modeled by W. W. Tait's notion of "Dedekind abstraction"; see Tait (1986, 369 n. 12). Cf. Parsons (1990, 308, 336).

References

Butterfield, Jeremy, ed. 1986. *Language, Mind, and Logic.* Cambridge University Press.

Dummett, Michael. 1973. *Frege: Philosophy of Language.* London, Duckworth.

Field, Hartry. 1980. *Science without Numbers.* Princeton University Press.

———. 1989. *Realism, Mathematics, and Modality.* Oxford, Blackwell.

Gödel, Kurt. 1964. What is Cantor's continuum problem? (revised and expanded version). In Solomon Feferman, John W. Dawson, Jr., Stephen C. Kleene, Gregory H. Moore, Robert M. Solovay, and Jean van Heijenoort, eds., *Collected Works, Vol. II: Publications 1938–1974*, Oxford University Press, 1990, 254–270.

Gottlieb, Dale. 1980. *Ontological Economy: Substitutional Quantification and Mathematics.* Oxford, Clarendon Press.

Hellman, Geoffrey. 1989. *Mathematics without Numbers.* Oxford, Clarendon Press.

Hilbert, David. 1926. Ueber das Unendliche. *Mathematische Annalen* 95, 161–190; reprinted in Jean van Heijenoort, ed., *From Frege to Gödel: A Source Book in Mathematical Logic, 1879–1931.* Cambridge, Mass., Harvard University Press, 1967, 369–392.

Hilbert, David, and Paul Bernays. 1934. *Grundlagen der Mathematik I.* Berlin, Springer.

Husserl, Edmund. 1891. *Philosophie der Arithmetik*. Halle, Pfeffer.

Kripke, Saul. 1976. Is there a problem about substitutional quantification? In Gareth Evans and John McDowell, eds., *Truth and Meaning*. Oxford, Clarendon Press, 325–419.

Maddy, Penelope. 1990. *Realism in Mathematics*. Oxford, Clarendon Press.

Martin-Löf, Per. 1984. *Intuitionistic Type Theory*. Naples, Bibliopilis.

Parsons, Charles. 1971a. Ontology and Mathematics. In Parsons (1983).

———. 1971b. A plea for substitutional quantification. In Parsons (1983).

———. 1980. Mathematical intuition. *Proceedings of the Aristotelian Society* N.S. 80, 145–168.

———. 1982. Substitutional quantification and mathematics. (Review of Gottlieb 1980.) *British Journal for the Philosophy of Science* 33, 409–421.

———. 1983. *Mathematics in Philosophy: Selected Essays*. Ithaca and London, Cornell University Press.

———. 1986. Intuition in constructive mathematics. In Butterfield (1986), 211–229.

———. 1990. The structuralist view of mathematical objects. *Synthese* 84, 303–346.

———. In press. Quine and Gödel on analyticity. In Paolo Leonardi and Marco Santombrogio, eds., *On Quine*. Cambridge University Press.

Quine, W. V. 1969. *Ontological Relativity and Other Essays*. New York, Columbia University Press.

Tait, W. W. 1986. Truth and proof. *Synthese* 69, 341–370.

Tieszen, Richard L. 1989. *Mathematical Intuition: Phenomenology and Mathematical Knowledge*. Dordrecht, Kluwer.

Wetzel, Linda. 1989. Expressions vs. numbers. *Philosophical Topics* 17, 173–196.

7

Hilbert's Axiomatic Method and the Laws of Thought

Michael Hallett

The nature of thought was frequently appealed to in discussions of the foundations of mathematics and natural science towards the end of the nineteenth century, as were its capacities and, indeed, its laws. This very term was used, of course, by Boole as the title of the work that Russell called, with wicked humor, the first book ever written on pure mathematics (1901). Something like it also appears in the title of another well-known work, Frege's *Begriffsschrift* of 1879, for recall that this is only an abbreviation for *Begriffsschrift, eine der arithmetischen nachgebildete Formelsprache des reinen Denkens,* (*Concept writing, a formal language for pure thinking modelled on arithmetic*). At the time, this seems to have been no empty reference, for in the *Vorwort* to this work, in explaining how he approached the question as to the nature of arithmetical judgments, Frege says that he first sought to investigate "how far one could proceed by inferences alone," thus basing oneself only on "the laws of thinking, which transcend all particulars" (1879, pp. III–IV; English trans., 5). Dedekind, too, states in the *Vorwort* to his 1888:

> In saying that arithmetic (algebra, analysis) is only a part of logic I wish to state that I hold that the number concept is completely independent of ideas or intuitions of space and time, and that I hold it to be an immediate consequence of the laws of pure thought.[37] (p. III; English trans., 31)

Moreover, in isolating the notion of one-to-one correspondence (or "imaging": *Abbildung*) in the concept of counting, and thus in the claim that this is one of the main components behind the concept of number, or ω-sequence, Dedekind says that we are confronted here with

> ... the capacity of the human intellect to relate things to things, to let one thing correspond to another, or to image a thing with a thing, and that this capacity is such that without it no thinking at all is possible. (ibid., pp. III–IV; English trans., 32)

There is no doubt that a serious examination of the appeal to thought and its laws as it appears in the later nineteenth century would be an extremely complicated one, not least because of the relation of this both to what we now treat as logic, to the desire, common in the nineteenth century, to want to describe the workings of the mind along naturalistic lines, and also to what Frege attacked as "psychologism." (Indeed, after his *Die Grundlagen der Arithmetik*, Frege avoided the suggestion that logic is concerned with the laws of thought and preferred instead to speak of the general laws governing truth or being true.) Thus, it is extremely unlikely that the notions of thought and of the laws of thought are meant by the various authors who appeal to them in the same sense whenever or wherever they occur. Indeed, even when one restricts the considerations somewhat, it might be salutary to reflect on the fact that such divergent schemes as those of Cantor and Brouwer represent two striking examples of insistence on "inner" mathematics and were taken by their authors to rest in some way on an analysis of the nature of mind and the "necessary" structure of its products. One of the specific purposes of this essay is to expose and draw out a somewhat less dramatic opposition in the way the laws of thought might be approached, namely between that of Frege (modulo his later avoidance of this term) and Hilbert. I hope also that the detail will serve to show that there is a good deal more to Hilbert's approaches to the foundations of mathematics than is often assumed.

1. The Background

One thing that is common in all the appeals to the notions of thought and its laws in the nineteenth century, in first approximation, is the insistence on the view that mathematics, or even physical theories involving mathematics, are products of the mind and as such responsible to the mind in some sense. This phenomenon goes back at least to Gauss, certainly in some form to Kant, and probably at least as far back as Descartes. Gauss, for example, calls number, as distinct from objects of geometry (considered here as the theory of physical space), "a product of our intellect [*Geistes*]," and *therefore* something for which *we* can prescribe laws in an *a priori* way.[1] It is hinted at, too, in the remark of Poncelet from 1822 meant partly, one supposes, to be pejorative, that imaginary elements in geometry are "creatures of reason [*êtres de raison*]" (1865, 12),[2] and also in Hertz's later recognition that a physical theory is built upon what he calls "inner *Scheinbilder* or *Symbole* of outer objects which we make for ourselves" (1894, 1), thus on products of the intellect.

This insistence is found in a sharpened form in the demands of Bolzano, Cantor, and Dedekind, expressed most clearly perhaps by Frege (1884), to make (most of) mathematics autonomous, to rid it, as Frege put it, of "foreign elements" (§103), or in the frequent clear statements of all of these mathematicians (and others) that mathematics, or at least arithmetic and analysis, should be developed so as to be free of intuition. It is perhaps difficult to say precisely what a "foreign element" is, but it is plausible, at least in Frege's case, to understand the term intuition in the somewhat more precise, Kantian sense, thus as referring to spatial and temporal cognition or its preconditions, for

Frege's (1884) is meant in part to constitute a reply to Kant's view that mathematics rests on truths secured only through such intuition. Space and time are repeatedly regarded as "foreign elements" (e.g., by Bolzano, Cantor, and Dedekind, as well as Frege), and were almost certainly seen as the main intruders, for on them depends any suggestion of movement or change, thus of kinematics or dynamics. Hence, excluding appeals to space and time (thus, intuition in the sense just made clear) will then perhaps be enough to exclude the foreign. In a somewhat more restricted sense, it was a commonplace demand, although not universal, that proof itself (i.e., deductive procedure) must be freed from "intuition," whatever more liberal position might be taken towards the content or the source of the premises. For instance, Frege insists that it should not be necessary to call on intuition in the midst of a proof (1879, *Vorwort*, 1884, §§90–91). Hertz (1894, 4) demands that a system of "principles" of mechanics has to satisfy the condition that it be possible to ". . . develop the whole of mechanics from [these] purely deductively, without calling on experience."[5] And in his treatise on geometry Pasch (1882, 98) insists on clearly formulated axioms and the carrying through of its construction in a neutral way based only on these. He says:

> In fact, if geometry is to be genuinely deductive, then the process of inferring must always be independent of the *sense* [*Sinn*] of geometrical concepts, just as it must be independent of diagrams. Only the *relations* between the geometrical concepts must be taken into account in the propositions, respectively definitions, treated. In the course of the deduction, it is certainly legitimate and useful, though *in no way necessary*, to think of the reference [*Bedeutung*] of the concepts concerned. Indeed, if it is necessary to do so, then the inadequacy of the deduction is revealed, and even the insufficiency of the proof method, if the gaps cannot be removed through a modification of the reasoning.[6]

The claim that *logic* can be appealed to in proofs but intuition cannot is, if not entirely empty, then at best programmatic. At any rate, it came before Frege set about erecting a positive system in which it is clear exactly which principles can be used in a proof. Nevertheless, one tradition, as Pasch says, is that proofs should proceed, once constructed, without any reflection on the content or even the denotation of the terms involved, even if this content is secured, as it were, from "without," as Pasch (and indeed Frege) think is the case in geometry, and as Hertz thinks is the case in mechanics, for some terms at least. And this corresponds to Frege's insistence, quoted earlier, that the logic used in derivations should be independent of "all particulars," and his insistence later that there is indeed a certain "thinking in symbols" or "mechanical operation" with a properly constructed logical calculus.[7]

It is not difficult to fit Hilbert into that part of the nineteenth century tradition concerned with rigorization. Hilbert often used the phrase "pure thought" (*reines Denken*), as one can see by looking at the first few pages of his essay on mathematical problems (1900b). For instance, he points out there that mathematical problems, and hence mathematical disciplines that grow out of their treatment, have often had their origins in empirical questions. But he stresses that:

> . . . in the further development of a mathematical discipline, the human intellect becomes conscious of its self-sufficiency, encouraged by the achievement of solutions in the past. Out of itself, and often without recognizable stimulation from without, intellect creates new and fruitful problems, through purely logical combination, through generalization, through specialization, through separating and collecting concepts in the cleverest way, and thus steps forward itself as the real questioner. (1900b, 257; reprint, 213)

It must be emphasised that Hilbert *never* plays down the importance of influence from the external world. Far from it, for even here, just after this passage, he goes on to say that there is a powerful and insistent interplay between thinking and experience, and (recalling Hertz somewhat) an apparent "pre-established harmony" between the "means of inquiry, the methods and the concepts of different domains of science."[8] However, it is also clear that one of Hilbert's constant aims was to make mathematical theories self-sufficient, the most striking example being geometry, traditionally taken to be the mathematical discipline closest to the study of nature. The whole of Hilbert's geometrical work is colored by this, although perhaps the most graphic example from within geometry of Hilbert's striving for independence in this sense is provided by his work on the notion of congruence, and the desire, in which he was successful, to make this independent of the concept of the movement of rigid bodies, with its dependence in turn on the concepts of space and time.[9]

Nevertheless, there are subtle and significant differences between Hilbert's approach and Frege's that go beyond the concern with precision, rigor, the removal off foreign elements, and gapless deduction, and that go to the heart of Hilbert's distinctive approach to the foundations of mathematics. Any attempt to understand this has to rest on a recognition of the importance Hilbert places on what he calls the axiomatic method, and on an understanding of what the point of axiomatization is for Hilbert. He first talks about the axiomatic method explicitly in his paper on the number concept (1900a), but the application of it stems from his work on the foundations of geometry, which culminated in his treatise on geometry (*Grundlagen der Geometrie*, 1899b). To some extent, stress on this reinforces some similarities with Frege. But nonetheless, a closer examination of the *purpose* of axiomatization for Hilbert reveals and underlines the differences, and such an examination is thus essential in trying to understand Hilbert's approach to the laws of thought. Certainly, Hilbert himself sees the axiomatic method as closely tied to the nature of thought. For one thing, he sees the ability to axiomatize as fundamental for the formulation of a precise mathematical claim, and sometimes even goes further, asserting that this is basic to *any* scientific [*wissenschaftliche*] work whatsoever. As he said later (1922, 161): "The axiomatic method is and remains the indispensable tool, appropriate to our minds, for all exact research in any field whatsoever. . . ."[17] On the same page, he implies that what distinguishes this "modern" insistence on the use of axioms from earlier approaches in science is the insistence on articulation of assumptions that previously were part of background belief. Consequently, "To proceed axiomatically means in this sense nothing other than to think with consciousness: ..." And in some lectures of 1905, he is reported as saying that "The general idea of this method [the axiomatic method] always lies behind any theoretical and practical thinking" (*1905c, 7).[10] These passages indicate quite clearly that Hilbert regarded the axiomatic method not only as foundational, but as connected *in some way* either to the preconditions (the "form") or to the operation of thought. It should become clearer in the course of this essay why Hilbert held this view.

2. The Axiomatic Method

The first thing to be clear about is that for Hilbert the concern with the axiomatic method is not just a concern with independence, precision, and deductive rigor, although all of these things were important.

If rigor were Hilbert's sole concern, then the remarks cited previously, say those taken from Pasch and Frege, should be enough to indicate that the stress on the axiomatic method as a means of pursing deductive precision was not unique to Hilbert, and does not differentiate clearly his own approach from Frege's. Even if Hilbert was not at this time aware of Frege's work, he was certainly aware of Pasch's, one of his important and immediate predecessors in the analysis of the foundations of geometry. That rigor in something like the sense of Pasch or Frege was *part* of Hilbert's concern is obvious, not just from the passages previously quoted, but also from statements Hilbert made relatively early on, statements like this one concerning the role of figures in proofs taken from some lectures on geometry given in 1894:

> A system of points, lines, planes is called a diagram or figure [*Figur*]. The proof [of the theorem he is discussing] can indeed be given by calling on a suitable figure, but this appeal is not at all necessary. [It merely] makes the inter-pretation easier [*erleichtert die Auffassung*], and it [the appeal to diagrams] is a fruitful means of discovering new propositions. Nevertheless, care, since it [the use of figures] can easily be misleading. A theorem is only proved when the proof is completely independent of the diagram. The proof must call step by step on the preceding axioms. The making of figures is [equivalent to] the experimentation of the physicist, and experimental geometry is already over with the [laying down of the] axioms. (*1894, 11)[11]

This is very close to what Pasch says in the passage quoted previously where he insists that deduction in geometry must be independent of diagrams. And in his essay on mathematical problems (1900b), addressing the question of what general demands are to be put on the satisfactory solution of a mathematical problem, Hilbert says:

> ... above all, I stress that a solution is to be achieved by giving the answer through a finite number of inferences, and indeed based on a finite number of

assumptions, assumptions which are involved in the very posing of the problems, and which can be precisely formulated. This demand of logical deducibility through a finite number of inferences is nothing other than the demand for rigour in the carrying out of proofs. In fact, the demand for rigour, which in mathematics, as is well known, has become proverbial, corresponds to a general philosophical requirement of reason [*Verstandes*]. Indeed, only through its satisfaction are the conceptual [*gedankliche*] content and the fruitfulness of the problem fully clear. (1900b, 257; reprint, 293)

But precise articulation of assumptions and deductive rigor as such were *not* Hilbert's sole concern. That there was a considerable distance between Hilbert and Frege on the use of axiom systems, despite the obvious similarities, is clear, if from nothing else then from the Frege-Hilbert correspondence. What does the difference amount to?

One central difference, putting it in modern terms, is that Hilbert's work on the axiomatics of geometry lays considerable stress on the notion of what became the modern notion of *non-logical constant*, something that is neither so free in its interpretability as a variable, nor so fixed as is a *logical* constant. In other words, the stress is on the idea that once an interpretation is given, then the reference of the non-logical terms is fixed, whereas that of the variables is still not, and on a view which allows for variation in reference *across* interpretations, thus the very possibility of essentially different interpretations. The notions involved are not taken to be meaningless,[12] thus, we might say that they have sense, a sense which is given to them in some way by the axiom system in which they play a role. But the varying reference *does* mean a rejection of the Frege doctrine that sense determines reference.[13] In the light of this, the difference might be expressed suggestively by saying that although both Frege and Hilbert would agree that logic should operate in a way that is independent of concern with reference (Frege's "particulars"), what Frege rejected and what Hilbert affirmed is that this doctrine of "reference independence" should apply to the truth of axioms as well. For want of a term, we might call Hilbert's view a "reference-free" view.

The root of this difference between Frege and Hilbert is one of philosophical aim, and it is connected to their differing attitudes to the laws of thought. Frege's philosophical aim is fairly easily identifiable from the first paragraphs of the *Vorwort* to his *Begriffsschrift* (1879), and then from §3 of *Die Grundlagen der Arithmetik* (1884). He states quite clearly that his central purpose is the *foundational* investigation of arithmetic, not in the sense of wanting to show *how* we can know arithmetical truths, but rather in the sense of wanting to show *why* they are truths, that is, what the *basis* of their truth is.[14] Frege takes this basis to be an all-embracing logic, and he presents us with the body of knowledge that he thinks constitutes this, both in the 1879 work and then more fully in the two volumes of the *Grundgesetze der Arithmetik* (1893, 1903a). Hence, Frege's aim from the beginning is what we might call a reductionist one, this meant in the limited sense of aiming to show that one body of truths can be derived from another. (This, together with other assumptions, puts various formal demands on the theory, as I will show.) On the other hand, since Hilbert has no such clear, philosophical aim (rather a complex mixture of mathematical and philosophical aims), and in particular no all-embracing view of logic, there is consequently no such impulse towards reductionism and the formal demands that this makes. This, in one sense at least, makes Hilbert's project much less ambitious than Frege's. Of course, as mentioned, it *is* Hilbert's aim to show that geometry, for instance, can be specified and developed independently of both mechanics and analysis, and thus independently of "foreign" elements, and for the purposes of the derivations this does involve a call on logic, although Hilbert fails to specify a logic, at least publicly, until the 1920s, whereas presumably it has to be part of Frege's project from the beginning to do just that.[15] And again with respect to the issue of "foreign" elements. Hilbert's procedure is negative in the sense that it is clearly enough for him to demonstrate that geometry can be developed *without* having to call on mechanics or analysis, that is, that it can be framed in a neutral way, without having to show in addition that it requires only concepts from a certain prescribed domain. Again, it is part of Frege's project to show that *only* notions from the prescribed domain of logic are used, and this is what determines Frege's insistence on so-called constructive definitions, for this constitutes in the end the key to the demonstration. The need for such definitions represents the principal technical difference between the approaches of Hilbert and Frege.

What underlies Frege's attitude to arithmetic here is a universal attitude towards logic in the sense that Frege views this as an umbrella theory which deals with the general aspects of operation with *any* concepts and which governs the structure of *all* scientific (i.e., *wissenschaftlich*, or declarative) discourse—in one way of putting it, the framing of any judgments whatsoever (see van Heijenoort 1967a, Ricketts 1986). This is reflected in the fact that in his works 1891, 1892a, and 1892b, Frege attempts to give a general view of the structure of sentences, ultimately based on the use of function and argument and the difference between concepts and objects, a view derived from the requirements of his analysis of mathematics, but a view that he nevertheless wants to transform into a general one. This is understandable, given the philosophical need to establish a quite general sentential analysis decisively different from (and more adequate than) that of the received division of sentences into subject and predicate. Thus, since for Frege every scientific discipline requires the framework of the general laws that logic expresses governing the operation of concepts, it is of course natural to ask the kind of question that Frege asks of arithmetic, namely, does arithmetic require recourse to a source of knowledge other than this general logic? Or, more generally, what is the relationship of arithmetic and geometry to the general logic within which all scientific discourse (any systematic stating of truths) takes place? Frege proposes a negative answer to the first question, thus asserting that arithmetic is derivable from logic alone. If we add to this the extra step which Frege takes that number theory also has to concern objects, that is, that numbers themselves must be objects—then Frege's project leads us to the conclusion that logic must treat of objects produced by logic, "logical objects" as Frege called them later (1903, §147), and that numbers are just some amongst these. This latter, of course, has to be shown explicitly, that is, demonstrated by explicit, constructive definitions.

Let us try to be as clear as possible about how this connects to considerations of the laws of thought. For Frege, thinking (or better: the framing of judgments) consists of establishing connections between concepts. Hence, in giving the laws of thought, we should try to specify general principles that apply to all concepts, no matter how constituted. Given the assumption that thought has to operate with the extensions of concepts as well as with concepts themselves (and there is the growing realization that for mathematics the important things *are* the extensions), then it is natural to think that the correct general laws governing extensions will be "laws of thinking," or logical laws. Arithmetic fits into this picture in the following way. Number, or numbering, must apply to every*thing* there is, or, more strictly, to every sortal concept that there is. It it thus natural to think that arithmetic must belong to, or rather follow from, the general principles governing any concepts whatever, that is to say, from the laws of thought.[16] Frege's later way of putting it, avoiding reference to the laws of thought, would be similar in the relevant respects, namely: What are true (or what denotes the True) are Thoughts, and Thoughts are expressed by sentences. Sentences, in their turn, are formed from concept expressions and object expressions, with the help of quantifiers and so on. Again, given the assumption that extensions of concepts are of necessity linked to the concepts themselves, then once the correct laws have been given for the expression of this linkage, these ought to suffice for the derivation of the laws of arithmetic for the reasons recently given. Thus, this latter follows from laws of truth transmission, or the laws of being true or whatever. Given this view of logic, then the reason for maintaining the thesis of fixity of reference, certainly for arithmetic, becomes plausible, as mentioned earlier, for there is the need to show that the arithmetical objects, the numbers, are just certain of the logical objects, certain definite extensions. The reduction to these is then indispensable for Frege's philosophical purpose.

This issue of the fixity of reference is really central to what divides Hilbert's conception of the axiomatic method from what, in modern terms, appears as Frege's use of an axiomatic presentation of logic, and thus, arithmetic. Hilbert's declarations to Frege in the correspondence makes it clear that his reference-free view is not a new one for him, but rather the fruit of long reflection on developments within mathematics. This is supported by the fact that the correspondence was in large part provoked by the publication of Hilbert's *Grundlagen der Geometrie* (1899b), and this itself was the culmination of nearly a decade of detailed examination of this material, a fact that can be seen clearly in the notes for the various series of lectures on geometry that Hilbert gave throughout the 1890s.[17] Moreover, it is to be expected that any attempt to understand Hilbert on the axiomatic method must be based primarily on an attempt to understand his attitude towards geometry, just as any attempt to understand Frege's work must be based on an examination of his approach to arithmetic.

At the beginning of the sequence of lectures from the 1890s, Hilbert seems inclined to the view that geometry is really the study of (perhaps idealized) physical space, and that the solid core of this is furnished by some mixture of experience and what he calls intuition. But he moves quickly towards the view that axioms are not truths in the straightforward sense that their truth was guaranteed by the way that the outer, spatial world is. He takes it that spatial intuition might very well furnish us with a body of "facts" (*Tatsachen*), as he calls them, which geometry has to take seriously, but that, nevertheless, geometry, as a developed science, is independent of these. For example, it can be related to the real world by taking particles as points, or stretched threads as straight lines. However, Hilbert is clear about two things: (1) There can always in principle be interpretations other than the one given. We might, for instance, take stars as points and light rays as straight lines, and in the correspondence with Frege he lays particular weight on the fact that there may be manifold interpretations.[18] But some five years before this he was already saying quite clearly:

> In general we must state: Our theory furnishes only the schema of concepts connected [*verknüpft*] to each other through the unalterable laws of logic. It is left to human reason how it wants to apply this schema to appearance, how it wants to fill it with material [*Stoff*]. This can happen in manifold ways. But whenever the axioms are satisfied, then the theorems must apply too. The easier the application and the more kinds of application there are, the better* the theory.
>
> * Any system of units and axioms which gives a complete description of the appearances is as justified as any other. Show nevertheless that the axiom system specified here is, in a certain respect, the only possible one.[19]

(2) These interpretations are, in any case, *approximate*. Among other things, this means that not enough precision can be given by an interpretation to make it clear whether something like the parallel postulate is true or not. Hilbert is clear that this will not be decided even by interpretation plus clever experimental checking, which is as precise as one can get and already in 1894 he recognizes it as a positive advantage that mathematics has worked out geometries other than Euclid's, not least because they might be used to give a description of the physical world.[20] The kind of indeterminacy towards the physical world that Hilbert sees in geometry is strengthened by the fact that he recognizes in addition that: (*a*) there can be different choices of basic concept—say the circle and sphere instead of point, line, and plane, that is, that the world and intuition of it does not fix basic terms for us; and (*b*) even given a choice of basic concepts, there will still be immense freedom as to what to take as axioms and what to allow to stand the test of proof.[21]

In sum, then, the view is clear in Hilbert that geometry must relinquish finally any claim to offer in a straightforward way a description of the shape and/or the behavior of bodies in space. Hilbert gives a direct comparison between his axioms and Hertz's *Bilder* (1894, 10): "The axioms are, as Her[t]z would say, *Bilde[r]* or symbols in our intellect,..." and he insists (as we have seen) that "experimenting finishes with the setting up of the axioms." As Hilbert says somewhat later in his notebooks, "The points, lines, planes of my geometry are nothing other than things of thought [*Gedankendinge*], and as such have nothing whatsoever to do with real points, lines and planes."[22] Thus, geometry comes to be recognized as a product of the mind, a product largely independent of the outer world, an independence reflected, to repeat, in the example of Hilbert's work on the notion of congruence.

But it is not sufficient to let any account of Hilbert's work on geometry rest there. For another crucial part of it was the attempt to show that geometry can be constructed independently of arithmetic and analysis as well. This proceeded mainly in two directions. First, there is the clear attempt to show that many key results can be achieved without full continuity assumptions, and that, even so, continuity principles can be formulated independently of analytic or arithmetic assumptions. In showing this, Hilbert developed a *segment calculus*, which mirrors the behavior of the rational numbers purely geometrically, thus a modern form of the theory of proportions, which can then be appealed to in the formulation of the Archimedean Axiom, one of the pillars of Hilbert's continuity axioms. Part of this, then, consists of showing that at no point in the development of geometry are we forced to assume that geometry must be concerned at root with a number manifold, a common assumption in the nineteenth century (see Freundenthal 1960, 1962). It is important to note, however, that this runs parallel to Hilbert's use of arithmetic and algebraic interpretations to show that various principles he employs in the geometrical constructions are independent of one another.

Thus, part of what we see here is the importance of the geometric axiom system itself, independently of its source and the reason for its original creation. In short, Hilbert's geometry is a concrete demonstration of the thesis that it is not just logic which operates "independently of particulars," to use Frege's expression again, but mathematics in its full extent, for what we have is precisely the illustration of the thesis of variable reference. Atoms or stars or real numbers or certain complex sets are not *the* referents of the geometrical term "point," but rather all the things mentioned are *possible* referents; geometry can (or, better, should) proceed quite happily without the need for specifying such references. This kind of independence goes further than dispensing with "foreign elements"; it is in fact full independence of subject matter. In his 1922–1923 lectures, Hilbert says that: "To have stressed a separation into the things of thought [*die gedanklichen Dinge*] of the [axiomatic] framework and the real things of the actual world, and then to have carried this through, that is the service of axiomatics"[11] (*1922–1923b, 122; limited ed., 87). We might go further: the axiomatic method, in Hilbert's conception, strives for this separation even when only other mathematical theories are involved. In his 1921–1922 lectures, Hilbert speaks of the "mapping" (*Abbildung*) of a "domain of knowledge" (*Wissensgebiet*) onto a framework of concepts in an axiomatic theory. Then he says:

> Through this mapping, the investigation becomes completely detached from concrete reality. The theory has nothing more to do with real objects [*realen*

Objekten] or with the intuitive content of knowledge. It is a pure thought construction, of which one can no longer say that it is true or false. Nevertheless, this framework has a meaning for knowledge of reality, in the sense that it presents a possible form of actual connections. The task of mathematics is then to develop this framework of concepts in a logical way, regardless of whether one was led to it by experience or by systematic speculation. (*1921–1922, 3)[23]

The brief discussion here might give the impression that, for Hilbert, geometry, and thus (if we take geometry as the model of an axiomatic theory) *any* axiom system, is *fully* independent, thus cut off not only from the outer world, but also from other mathematical theories. But this would be to lose sight of why Hilbert must adopt the kind of view which we have been considering. It is not the case that Hilbert sought to destroy connections; in fact, isolation of theories seems to be just the opposite of what he intends, for recall Hilbert's remark to Frege that the *more* interpretations a theory has, the better. It is rather that he wants to weaken any connection to a unique, fixed subject matter or range of referents, and in doing so open up the possibility of many connections.

Hilbert was always at pains to stress the unified nature of mathematics. That he is not an isolationist is perfectly clear from his later work (1918), his sustained hymn to the axiomatic method, entitled, incidentally, "Axiomatic *thinking*." It begins thus:

Just as in the life of nations, the individual nation can only thrive when all its neighbours are in good health; and just as the interest of states demands, not only that order prevail within every individual state, but also that the relationships of the states among themselves be in good order, so it is in the life of the sciences. In due recognition of this fact the most important mathematical thinkers have always exhibited great interest in the laws and the structure of the neighbouring sciences. They have always cultivated the relations to the neighbouring sciences, especially the great empires of physics and epistemology, above all for the benefit of mathematics itself. I believe that the essence of these relations, and the reason for their fruitfulness, will appear most clearly if I describe for you the general method of research which seems to be coming more and more into its own in modern mathematics: I mean the *axiomatic method*. (1918, p. 405; reprint, 146)

In this respect, there is also an interesting passage in Hilbert (1900b, 257; reprint, 293–294):

A new problem, even when it originates in the world of outer phenomena, is like a young rice plant, which can only thrive and bear fruit when it is carefully grafted onto an old stem according to the rules of art of the gardener, the stem here being the secure treasury of mathematical knowledge.

But perhaps the most forcible expression of this sentiment is in the following passage:

... in my view, mathematics is an indivisible whole, an organism whose ability to live is governed by the connection between its parts. No matter how various is the stuff of mathematical knowledge in its details, we recognise very clearly the sameness of the logical tools, the close relations between idea formation across the whole of mathematics, and the innumerable analogies between its distinct domains. Thus, we notice that the further a mathematical theory is developed, all the more harmoniously and uniformly does its construction unfold, and unexpected relations are discovered between hitherto separate branches of this science. The extension of mathematics, therefore, does not threaten its uniform character, but on the contrary brings it out all the more clearly.

The unified character of mathematics is embedded in its inner nature, for it is the foundation of all exact natural scientific knowledge. (1900b, p. 297; reprint, 329)

The way in which Hilbert thought theories must be integrated and related is central to any understanding of his quite distinctive attitude to the laws of thought.

3. The Unity of Mathematics

There are two aspects to the unity that Hilbert saw which must be distinguished, although they are indirectly and importantly related. Both are hinted at in Hilbert's own conditions on the adequacy of axiom systems and will be dealt with in this section and the next respectively. The first is based on the inter-connectedness made possible by the "reference-free" view recently considered; the second is connected to Hilbert's later "program."

It is well known that, at an early stage, Hilbert lays down certain explicit conditions on the acceptability of an axiomatic theory, both in (1899b) and elsewhere, conditions that are needed if, in the construction of axiom systems, the various indeterminacies which we have noted are not to collapse into arbitrariness. Briefly, these conditions are the insistence that the axiom system be *complete, consistent,* consist of only a *finite number* of axioms (although sometimes the less precise but potentially more flexible epithet "simple" is used), and also that the axioms be *independent* of one another.[24] Hilbert's criteria are not new. To take one example, Toepell (1986, 59) points out that the demand for independent axioms was clear in much work on geometry in the twenty years before Hilbert began his own work. To take another, the demand for consistency in setting up new theories had been suggested, with varying degrees of clarity, by both Dedekind and Cantor, and then later by Hertz, who also insisted on independence and a kind of completeness for the chosen principles of physics (1894, 4). Having said this, though, it should be added that Hilbert was probably the first to state these conditions together and explicitly tied to an axiomatic method. On the face of it, these conditions do not seem to be related to the interconnectedness of mathematical (and physical) theories, particularly not if one considers the requirement of completeness, surely a demand for self-sufficiency of a kind. This seems even clearer when one recalls that Hilbert means consistency in more or less a syntactic sense, even in respect of relative consistency proofs, that is, a relative consistency proof is taken to show that a contradiction provable in the domain being checked can be translated into a contradiction in the domain being taken as a base. (The emphasis on the syntactic sense of consistency is clear from Hilbert 1900b and from the 1905 lectures.)

Nevertheless, the fact that both Dedekind and Cantor were natural predecessors in this concern is important. At first sight, the question which interests them is somewhat different from that which concerns Hilbert, namely, how to integrate a new theory into an existing body of theory, there being, of course, no talk of axiom systems. Cantor, for instance, was concerned essentially with producing arguments for the acceptability of a theory of transfinite numbers, and then in particular with the integration of these numbers into existing systems of number. Dedekind too (1854, in particular) focuses on what we might call "canonical extensions" of theories, thus is concerned with how a new theory is to be introduced with respect to existing theories.

However, some of the discussion in section 2 of this essay should have indicated that a large part of Hilbert's concern was also with conceptual compatibility, however much stress comes to be placed on consistency. If this is not already obvious from the passages cited, it *is* obvious from other statements Hilbert makes. In the following passage, for example, he stresses the relations between theories and "neighboring" theories. The context concerns physical theories, although there is no reason to suppose that the same demand will not arise for relations between mathematical theories: "But particularly in physics it is not sufficient that the propositions of a theory be in harmony with each other; there remains the requirement that they not contradict the propositions of a neighbouring field of knowledge" (1918, 410; reprint, 151). This is an explicit recognition that mere consistency—internal consistency—is not enough. Hilbert then goes on to illustrate this with various examples, drawn from the kinetic theory of gases and thermodynamics, from mechanics and electromagnetism, from radiation theory, and so on.[25] In these contexts, Hilbert sometimes uses the term *verträglich*, "compatible," and it is important to see that this need not just emphasize the relative consistency of the theories in question, although it certainly can be taken in this way. However, the term can also be taken to stand for something more like the conceptual compatibility or integrability of the theories involved; that this is closer to Hilbert's meaning here follows from his own example of the reconciliation of electromagnetism and mechanics through the special theory of relativity. This is not just a case of the relative consistency of two theories or even of their simple amalgamation, but a striking example of what Hilbert calls the *Tieferlegung der Fundamente*, the importance of which was stressed by in Hilbert (1918). Thus, the message seems to be: if it is not clear how two theories S and T are related, then look for a new, "deeper" theory U, possibly with quite a different conceptual base, for which, however, it is clear how each of S and T is related to U and thus indirectly to each other. As Hilbert puts it: "Similarly, *electrodynamic inertia* and *Einsteinian gravitation* are compatible [*verträglich*] with the corresponding concepts of the classical theories, since the classical concepts can be conceived as limiting cases of the more general concepts in the new theories" (1918, 410; reprint, 151).

But even suppose we do think officially more in terms of relative consistency than compatibility directly; in practice this too involves showing the kind of compatibility we have mentioned rather than simply showing that a contradiction derived from one theory will be matched by one in another. For although on the surface it looks as though this involves merely a translation of the terms and concepts of one language into those of another, in practice this is only a formal reflection of a prior appreciation of the sense(s) in which the structures are similar, that is, can be seen to be conceptually compatible. The construction of such a translation need not be a simple matter at all, and it may be deeply revealing, as it is, say, in Gödel's relative consistency proof for the Axiom of Choice and the Generalized Continuum Hypothesis. Hilbert's further insistence on the demonstration of any suspected independence makes the emphasis on the demonstration of structural similarity even more apparent, for again this demands (generally) the creating of interesting substructures from existing structures, or perhaps the embedding of a known structure in a hitherto unknown one composed, nevertheless, of known materials. Thus, *Verträglichkeit* in its strongest sense is deeply involved in the Hilbert enterprise; it is intended, in short, to guarantee the interconnectedness of mathematics, the integrability of new theories. Minkowski's work on the "geometry of numbers" shows exactly the fruitfulness of investigations of the kind that Hilbert has in mind, of the interrelations between apparently disparate domains, of the way that various propositions of one theory fit together, either with each other or with propositions of the other domain, and which axioms are essential for the proving of a given theorem and which not.[26] This partly explains Hilbert's emphasis on impossibility proofs with which he ends his *Grundlagen der Geometrie* (1899b), as well as what Hilbert there calls "the basic tenet of elaborating a matter in such a way that we check simultaneously whether its resolution is possible or not in a prescribed way with restricted means," and that this is "closely connected to the demand for the 'purity' of proof method which many mathematicians in recent times have stressed."[27]

This shows two things clearly.

Firstly, it shows that any shift to consideration of mere consistency, in the sense of the underivability of contradictory statements, whether this be taken in the relative sense or even more in the absolute sense, will involve the loss of much of this part of the spirit of the Hilbert enterprise. Hence, even though Hilbert naturally did become involved in the problem of absolute consistency proofs after 1900, this concern is to be seen as an addition to his foundational concerns hitherto, and no substitute for them. This observation is of great importance for the way in which Hilbert's consistency program is to be viewed in the light of Gödel's work.

Secondly, it emphasizes that the non-fixity of reference is intrinsic to Hilbert's project, in this respect thus quite counter to Frege's project, for this is precisely what facilitates comparison of structure involved in both the kind of independence investigation demonstrated by Hilbert (1899b) and the comparison of structure in wider investigations of mathematical unity.

The differences between Hilbert and Frege in this respect are underlined if we look at their approaches to definitions.

It is often said, with some justice, that Hilbert supported a view of what is called "implicit definition." Certainly this is right when we compare Hilbert's account to what is often called *constructive* or *explicit* definition. Very loosely, what is meant by an implicit definition is that rules or principles (axioms) are laid down as conditions and it is then said, "By a point (or whatever) is meant whatever satisfies these conditions."[28] In a definition by construction, on the other hand, one employs the designated term as a shorthand for a certain entity constructed from a given domain. To take an example, the term "imaginary number" can be taken to stand for pairs of real numbers, with certain operations on pairs of these pairs now designating imaginary multiplication, addition, and so on. Given this, it has to be proved that the "right" algebraic rules for the constructed objects are obeyed; of course, there are now other, apparently irrelevant, things that can be proved about these "new" entities over and above what falls in the purview of complex number theory ordinarily understood, for instance, that the numbers are pairs of a certain kind.

Nevertheless, the primary philosophical advantage of constructive definition is presumably clear. Instead of having to say, for example, that statements involving the term $\sqrt{-1}$ are meaningless because this term denotes nothing, or having to say that indeed it does denote, but that we have no idea as to what it denotes, we can say instead that it denotes a complex made up of things whose existence is quite happily accepted—in this example, real numbers. This procedure has been followed frequently in the development of mathematics: points at infinity in projective geometry were interpreted as "bundles" of parallel lines; in some versions of the Dedekind theory, real numbers are seen as Dedekind cuts in the rational numbers, thus, in effect, as certain sets of rationals; the Frege theory treats natural numbers as extensions of certain complex concepts; and in some versions of nonstandard analysis, infinitesimals are given by complex algebraic constructions over nonstandard models of Zermelo set theory. What these procedures show is that there is no need for any extra existential worry over and above that involved in the acceptance of the base theory, although one obvious problem is that of accepting the propriety of the means used to effect the constructions, thus of constructing pairs of reals, equivalence classes of points or concepts, arbitrary subsets of rational numbers, nonstandard models, or whatever. And this is no empty worry, for often it has turned out that what was thought to be straightforward at the time the construction was first introduced turns out not to be straightforward, as the examples of Dedekind and Frege both show, the latter leading to an inconsistency frustratingly complex in its ramifications, and the former to serious debates about the nature of the set-theoretic principles involved. These experiences no doubt strengthened the desire to use a neutral (and hopefully safe) base theory in which the constructions can always be carried out, a theory like Russell's or that of Zermelo-Fraenkel. Nevertheless, whatever problems thereby caused, the discovery of such constructions has frequently represented enormous progress and clarification over the previous stages. And in Frege's case, there is (or so Frege thought) the added philosophical purpose of the reduction to logic.

Several interesting things can be pointed out now with respect to Hilbert. The first is that what he characterized as the "genetic" method, just the method to which Hilbert says his axiomatic method is to be preferred, very often comes to rest on just this method of construction. For example, Hilbert's main example of the genetic method is the way that the concept of number was successively extended by the use of constructions:

> Starting from the concept of the number 1, one usually imagines the further rational positive integers 2, 3, 4 . . . as arising through the process of counting, and one develops their laws of calculation; then, by requiring that subtraction be universally applicable, one attains the negative numbers; next one defines fractions, say as a pair of numbers, so that every linear function possesses a zero; and finally one defines the real number as a cut or a fundamental sequence, thereby achieving the result that every entire rational, indefinite (and indeed every continuous, indefinite) function possesses a zero. We can call this method of introducing the concept of number the *genetic method*, because the most general concept of real number is *generated* by the successive extension of the simple concept of number. (1900a, 180)[29]

The second interesting thing, connected with the progress that seems to have been made with constructions, is that it brings with it the recognition that the objects involved are no longer "simples" or "primitives" but can be considered as "complexes." This has often been of enormous importance, particularly in the attempts to loosen the ties with what was thought to be intuition.[30]

In this sense, then, the view that the use of constructions opposes, whether it be in geometry or arithmetic, is that which thinks of the basic objects of the theory as having no further structure, of being primitive, not just in the sense of lying at the bottom of the theory, but in the sense that if there is to be any further explanation of their nature it must be sought outside the development of the theory itself.[31] On the accounts of Gauss, Frege, Weierstrass, Cantor, and (some versions of) Dedekind, the kinds of number treated turn out not to be simples in this sense, but highly structured complexes, a fact best demonstrated by looking at the structure of the defined objects in something like Russell's type hierarchy.

In this respect, Hilbert's stress on the axiomatic method might be seen as an attempt to go back to the view of these fundamental objects as "structureless," to insist that there be no asking after the "real" nature of the objects concerned, whatever the complexity of the constructions used in the "genetic" (i.e., pre-axiomatic) history. There is thus some ontological point to it, if only negative. But if the main purpose of Frege's use of constructive definitions is philosophical, the main point of Hilbert's eschewal of them, at least in the mature construction of a theory, is mathematical, namely, of being able to select "things" that satisfy the axioms from anywhere within the mathematical (or even physical) realm. And the point is then to put as few requirements as possible on the choice of these things, in particular, to shun the kind of external "explanations" that Euclid provides for his primitives or that Cantor gave for the notion of set.[32] From this point of view, thus from the point of view which underlines interconnectedness and integrability, it is perfectly understandable that Hilbert saw the proliferation of "models" of axiom systems, as we would now say, as a good thing, as is clearly expressed both in his lectures (*1894) and then later in a letter to Frege, as mentioned previously (see p. 166). It is a good thing precisely because it allows for the sort of exercise carried out in the *Grundlagen der Geometrie*; insistence on fixity of reference as a necessary condition of meaning, as is the case with Frege, would thwart this.[33]

The availability of constructions now appears in a different light, for these are to be seen no longer as addressing the ontological question as to the "real" nature of the objects concerned, but rather that of showing how an axiomatic theory might be embedded in already accepted mathematical theories. The central difference is that construction will no longer be *definition* by construction, but rather only "interpretation" by construction, of which the interpretation via what are now known as "inner models" is only a part. Thus, real numbers will not be Dedekind cuts in the rational "line," but, on the other hand, this collection of cuts is shown to exhibit the properties that the axiom system for real numbers demands. In this case, axiomatization really uncovers certain structural relations that in general will be common to various structures, for instance, common to that of equivalence classes of Cauchy sequences of rationals as well as the collection of cuts in the rationals.[34] Indeed, the formulation of axioms then becomes one natural means of attempting to isolate structure, one elementary example being the axiom of compactness in general topology that isolates the general structural property exhibited in the reals by the Heine-Borel Theorem, a property that is then transferred to other domains. This shows that construction in general will still be necessary in so far as it is one creative means of showing that the axiomatized theory can be embedded in the mathematical corpus or that the axioms have models.[35] But, at the same time, by insisting that we are not dealing with definition by construction, we are freed from the necessity of regarding real numbers as, say, cuts in the rationals or equivalence classes of Cauchy sequences or line segments in Euclidean geometry, or, more generally, from regarding a fixed reference for the terms involved as being part of their meaning. (Indeed, according to Hilbert, the ontological question is to be addressed in quite a different way from that envisaged by the giving of constructions. Construction, in short, has a different purpose.) It should be remarked here that Dedekind's insistence that real numbers are not defined by the Dedekind cuts, but rather are primitive things whose structure is mirrored by the system of rational sections, goes a long way towards this aspect of Hilbert's position.

The upshot of this is that Hilbert's axiomatic method is based on what are known as implicit definitions in the sense that there is deliberately no attempt made to say what the basic objects are outside of the fact that they are supposed to satisfy the conditions laid down in the axioms.[36] Constructive "definitions" are, of course, still taken seriously in the sense that the exhibition of construc-tions is one way in which the incorporation of a mathematical theory within the body of mathematics might be demonstrated. But two questions remain to be answered. First, why is Hilbert's approach not formalist, as is, say, Leibniz's approach toward "imaginary quantities"and infinitesimals, both of which he regarded as involving strictly meaningless terms, but ones which nevertheless were useful for purposes of abbreviation?[37] And second, how is the Hilbert approach related to the postulation of entities? The short answer to both of these questions is that Hilbert still took the existence question seriously, a question which is at the root of the philosophical difficulties with both postulation and formalism. The reasons for this are fairly clear. If one postulates the existence of an entity of a certain sort, then, in addition to what-ever mathematical questions one may be forced to tackle, one still has the philosophical question to face of what this entity is. On the other hand, if one adopts not postulation, but implicit definitions taken in a formalist sense, then the charge of meaninglessness seems to rest on the admission that the terms in question do not have a denotation. Thus, Hilbert's method of avoiding both sets of difficulties is to take seriously the question of whether (and in what sense) there can be said to be entities that the terms in question denote. His way of doing this, as is well known, is to tie the existence question to the question of consistency, and the tackling of this is itself seen as an intra-mathematical problem. How successful Hilbert is in this depends on how one regards his approach to consistency. Nevertheless, it is important to see clearly emerging here the central attitude of modern metamathematics, and with it, a shift towards examining the important properties of the theoretical system instead of being concerned with questions of the existence and description of objects or sets of objects that those systems purport to describe.[38] And what has been presented above might be enough to suggest that this should not be assessed merely in terms of the failure of the later consistency programme.

Seen in the light of this difference between Hilbert and Frege, it might be said that their approaches embody two quite distinct ways of achieving generality. For Frege, to repeat, arithmetic is a body of assertions derived from the most general body of knowledge there is, logic, the framework within which all scientific work must take place and which concerns the operation with any kind of concepts whatever. On the other hand, the kind of generality Hilbert's approach embodies is more that of a structural generality derived in part from being quite uncommitted about what objects the theories in question are about. Once this has been said, Hilbert's approach admits, and indeed invites, a range of questions that Frege's does not, in particular, all those questions which have to do with the nature of the axiom system itself, thus, what we would now call meta-questions, which Hilbert always regarded, not only as questions that it makes sense to ask, but questions that it is part of mathematical activity to ask and that must be treated as far as possible by mathematical means. Of course, Frege's approach to arithmetic admits some questions as internal to the theory that for Hilbert are external. Thus, for the Hilbert approach, arithmetic has to be applied, say, to the planets; it will not follow automatically that the number of planets plus the number of the earth's moons is ten (or eleven, if Ceres is to count as a planet), and this will, in general, require separate, extra investigation. For Frege, however, it will follow automatically, given the way arithmetic and the definition of numbers are set up—that if sortal concepts are involved (for example, being a planet, being a moon), then the arithmetic laws will apply to them. On the other hand, there will be other questions that for Hilbert can only have an external sense (again, external to the theory, not external to mathematics), and ought, for Frege, to have no sense at all, for instance, that concerning the syntactic consistency of a system or its completeness or categoricity.[39]

Seen under this first aspect, unity is clearly a loose and fluid notion, deliberately so. But there is another aspect to the stress on unity, one that is closely related to what has been discussed hitherto, to the lack of reliance on constructions, and to the issues of integrability and consistency. It is, however, rather more directly connected to the issue of the laws of thought.

4. Logical Unity

The second aspect of unity is concerned centrally with the operation of theories and their internal structure, and is hinted at as far back as Hilbert's *Zahlbericht* of 1897. In the introduction, Hilbert says:

> Certainly, in terms of the simplicity [*Schlichtheit*] of its assumptions, number theory is *the* branch of mathematics whose truths are most easily grasped. But arithmetical concepts and methods of proof demand for their understanding and full mastery an advanced ability of reason to abstract, and this fact was hitherto held against arithmetic. I am of the opinion that all other branches of mathematical knowledge demand at least as advanced an ability of the reason to abstract—assuming that also in these areas one wishes to investigate the foundations with the necessary rigour and completeness. (p. 175; reprint, 64)[40]

And only a little later, in his essay on mathematical problems, Hilbert writes this about the demand for rigor:

> If I put forward rigour in proofs as the requirement for a complete solution of a problem, then at the same time I would like to counter the opinion that only the concepts of analysis, or even just those of arithmetic, are capable of fully rigorous treatment. Such a view, represented by the foremost authorities, is thoroughly mistaken. (1900b, 258; reprint, 294)

He goes on to say that geometry and natural science, once treated properly by axiomatic means, will produce concepts whose "... sharpness ... and ... applicability in deduction in no way falls short of the old arithmetical concepts[11] (p. 258; reprint, 295). And recall also from the same essay the passage quoted earlier in which Hilbert pointed to the "sameness of the logical tools" in stressing the unified nature of mathematics (see p. 169). In short, in all these remarks there seems to be the suggestion of an underlying structure which all (properly treated) mathematical theories ought to share, a structure which lies in the nature of the axiomatic and deductive arrangement.

The need for some such claim is implicit in what has already been examined. One advantage of the method of definition by construction, certainly when carried through so universally as it is in Russell's theory or in modern set theory, is that the ontological unity rests on a theoretical, conceptual unity. Even if one stops short of an all-embracing scheme like the two mentioned, one aim of definition by construction is surely to cut conceptual diversity to a minimum. On the other hand, if definition by construction is eschewed, then the common properties of theories must be sought at a different level. The insistence that there be a considerable measure of theoretical embedding, of compatibility, among theories in the mathematical corpus presupposes that all theories have something in common, independent of considerations of content, for otherwise it would be hopeless to look for possible, and surprising, embeddings. The conjecture behind Hilbert's reference to "sameness of logical tools" is that the requisite similarity of structure is to be found in similarity of underlying *logical* structure, or more loosely, similarity of logical background.

Given the emphasis on rigor and deduction that one finds throughout Hilbert's foundational work, for Hilbert, logic has to be intrinsic to the way theories are constructed and the way they operate. Hence, logic must be used in developed mathematical thought, and is therefore general in the sense that it is available or built into all theories. One gets the impression, if from nothing else, then from Hilbert's negative reaction when confronted with a challenge to classical logic by Brouwer's and Weyl's work, that Hilbert views this logic as unique, as indeed is suggested by reference to the "sameness of the logical tools." But, although unique and available to all theories, for Hilbert, logic is not the universal framework that it is for Frege, that is, a framework within which all scientific investigation has to take place. Indeed, it cannot be, for logic is part of what constitutes the framework of a mathematical theory, and, as we have said, Hilbert's early conception of the axiomatic method leads naturally to the view that mathematical theories must, of necessity, be legitimate objects of mathematical study. An axiom system is no longer a means used to express truths about a certain domain of objects (e.g., the real numbers) and relations between them, but this axiom system *is* real number theory, and mathematics has to study its properties, its relations to other theories, its consistency, and so on.

What follows in Hilbert's subsequent foundational work, and especially that after 1918, is an attempt to make explicit what is to be meant by logic, how this is involved in the construction of an axiom system, and hence what is to be accepted as an inference—as Hilbert says, an attempt to "subject the concept of specifically mathematical proof itself" to precise investigation (1918, 415; reprint, 155).[41] Part of the incentive for this comes from the recognition that the paradoxes challenge not just set theory, but also what was taken to be logic, thus the notion of inference, and, therefore, indirectly the whole of mathematics.[42] But, even apart from the paradoxes, there is the need to work out a general schematic framework that can be used in the application of the axiomatic method. This is a natural extension of the earlier view, for it is assumed that formalization (in the sense of the explicit and conscious use of a logic) will contribute to precision, and will therefore make the conceptual independence of an axiom system clearer and also facilitate the investigation of the connections both between its own axioms and those of other theories. This is connected to what Hilbert calls the necessity of "rendering the language precise,"

> ... insofar as it concerns the presentation of mathematical facts and their logical connections. This rendering precise occurs through the formalisation of the logical calculus, in which all logical inferences, even those of a transfinite nature, are represented formally. (*1922–1923a, 30)

In this sense, then, a precise treatment of logic is fully in accord with the axiomatic method. As Hilbert goes on to remark,

> In order to be clear about the nature of the formalisation needed here, it will be useful to look at the relation and the analogy in method between the logical calculus and axiomatics.
>
> The logical calculus forms an appropriate completion of the axiomatic way of proceeding. For, when we consider the axiomatic enterprise in its original sense, then the point of it rests in giving a precise account of the *assumptions* of a theory. With the application of the logical calculus one goes a step further, in that one investigates the nature of the *inferences* in detail. (*1922–1923a, 30–31)

Second, and in addition to this, a more formal treatment of logic is a natural consequence of the view that because axiom systems themselves are to be objects of mathematical study, and since logic is admitted to be a key part of an axiomatic system, this, too, should be subject to the axiomatic method, being one basic tool of mathematical investigation. Note that this, too, is indirectly connected to the paradoxes, for some of the point of investigating logic is to obtain a way of defusing the criticism of classical analysis, with its unrestricted use of classical logic, put forward (in particular) by Weyl. In this respect, then, it is important for Hilbert to isolate and make clear the classical aspects of logic and the way they are involved in classical analysis.[43]

This view that axiom systems, and hence logic, are legitimate objects of mathematical study is decisive for Hilbert's later position. It can be interpreted as making two separate claims. The first and weaker claim is simply that mathematicians have, of necessity, to study axiomatic frameworks as part of doing mathematics. But the stronger claim, one that comes to the fore in Hilbert's later work, is that there are common, mathematically describable features to be discovered in the underlying frameworks of all theories, thus, that it is possible to isolate mathematical theories with which the study of locally formulated axiom systems can be conducted. Hence, since Hilbert claims that the use of axiom systems is "basic to thought," it then seems that any attempt to isolate and describe common mathematical features behind the application of axiom systems will at the same time, be an attempt to investigate mathematically the laws of thought. It is at this point that Hilbert asserts that there must be a source of mathematical knowledge *other than* the logical, and where what is called by Hilbert "finite point of view [*finite Einstellung*]" is decisive, imposing strong conditions on the kind of mathematics to be permitted in describing what underlies thought.[44]

Let us try to understand more precisely what gives rise to this position. The first important thing to note is that from the beginning of his concern with the foundations of mathematics Hilbert emphasizes one basic thing which is common to all mathematical theories in their developed form, and thus, in particular, to the application of logic, that is, the use of *signs*, and indeed, the combinatorial operation with those in accordance with what is permitted by the axioms. For instance, comparing arithmetic and geometry in his essay on mathematical problems, no doubt for heightened dramatic effect since these two disciplines were seen traditionally as the two opposing poles of mathematics and of mathematical thought, Hilbert says that "... arithmetical signs are written diagrams, and geometrical diagrams are drawn formulas..."[45] More primitively, what is behind this is the use of symbolic representation, the ability to represent *things* by *signs*. Hilbert is quite clear about this in his unpublished lectures of 1905. In setting out to give a "simpler form" to the logical calculus than had yet been given, Hilbert claims, we need,

> ... an *Axiom of Thought*, or, as one might say, an *Axiom of the Existence of an Intelligence*, which can be formulated approximately as follows: I have the capability to think *things* and to denote them through simple signs (*a, b*; ..., *X, Y*, ...; ...) in such a fully characteristic way that I can always unequivocally recognise them again. My thinking operates with these things in this designation [*Bezeichnung*] in a certain way according to determinate laws, and I am capable of learning these laws through self-observation, and of describing them completely.[46]

Then follow some logical laws, for example, laws governing identity. This seems to be a clear statement of Hilbert's view that the principles for manipulating symbol systems are a priori, thus, that with these considerations, we have reached something basic. Indeed, in a marginal note to this passage he remarks that this assumption is "the *a priori* of the philosophers." Moreover, what is important about it is the claim that the mental ability to think about objects or things is reflected in the ability to represent these (in some cases to replace them) by signs, that is, by something arguably nonabstract, something qualitatively different, say, from a number or a set, and something which is subject to what Hilbert frequently calls "logico-combinatorial intuition." In short, what is taken as basic here is the ability to let a (possibly simple) sign stand for a (possibly complex) object.

This is extremely close to the basic ability presupposed in the use of embeddings or modeling, the translation of one language into another, or in other words, the replacement of one sign (or complex of signs) by another. We might go so far as to say that this ability is revealed by the reference-free view, and then emphasized by the insistence on interconnections and so on, and it is also worth noting that this is closely related to Dedekind's remark that "the capacity of the human intellect to relate things to things" is such that "without it no thinking at all is possible" (see p. 158, this essay). Indeed, this is one reason why the later view can be seen as a development of the earlier one and not simply an addition, for the continuity with the earlier work is direct. Recall that in Hilbert (1922), perhaps the first paper in which he begins to elaborate what is known as Hilbert's program, in saying that he will take the "signs themselves as the objects of number theory," Hilbert wrote: "In this there lies the firm attitude which I regard as necessary for the grounding of pure mathematics, as well as for all scientific thought, understanding and communication: *In the beginning is the sign*" (p. 163; reprint, 163).[47]

The second thing to point out is that Hilbert assumes early on that the ability to operate correctly with symbolic representations is an arithmetical one. The thought behind this seems relatively simple, namely, that the symbol systems which form the basis of a language are ultimately made up of discrete arrangements of signs, given that we have the ability (not explicitly mentioned by Hilbert in the quote from 1905 previously cited, but clearly presupposed) to recognize signs as single, individual objects. Given this, and the fact that the natural numbers are the paradigm of the discrete, it is already clear that the ability to operate with mathematical language systems is close to the ability to operate with a simple system of arithmetic. More precisely, as became clearer in Hilbert's remarks about elementary arithmetic (see below), the claim is that the ability to set out, according to fixed rules, a simple stroke or numeral system based on |, ||, |||, etc, or on 1, $1 + 1$, $1 + 1 + 1$, etc, where "$+$" stands for concatenation (see p. 185 of the present essay), and then to recognize that a sign **a** composed according to these rules is different from sign **b**, is at root the same ability as that required to set up a restricted number of symbols as an alphabet for a language and to compose complex linguistic units out of them, again according to a number of fixed rules, and thus to be able to recognize that a sentence σ is different from a sentence τ. In other words, the conjecture is that the basic linguistic and the basic arithmetic abilities are identical (see note 40). In this sense it is perhaps no accident that Hilbert uses the sign '1' (1905a) to stand for a "thought object" (*Gedankending*), and then considers combinations of this sign (with brackets), for example (11), or (111), or 1(11), as paradigmatic of the structure of more complicated objects generated from 1.

These two features, the recognition of the basicness of the use of signs plus the conjecture about the arithmetic, algebraic nature of the way these are used, are summed up in the following passage from Hilbert's 1922–1923 lectures, *Wissen und mathematisches Denken*:

> Calling on mathematical methods for the investigation of the logical language is not artificial, but fully appropriate and even inevitable. For the role of the language in the expression of the logical connections between thoughts corresponds to the sign language in calculation. In following a logical passage of thought with the help of this logical language, we carry out simultaneously a calculation, in which manifold logically elementary processes are put together according to practised rules. It is even self-evident that, when we exclude the

accidental features [*zufälligen Momente*] in the derivation of words, then a form of mathematical sign language arises. (*1922–1923b, 130; limited ed., 93)[48]

As Hilbert says, the restriction "to the essential" will make it possible "... to frame the rules of the grammar in such a surveyable way that logical inference can be carried through automatically by calculation according to simple, determined rules." (*1921–1922, 76). The further assumption that fundamental syntactic abilities can indeed be described and accounted for in a simple *finitary* arithmetic, thus, where no direct or indirect reference to infinities is made, is something fundamentally tied to the decisive influence (or the building in) of the *finite Einstellung* in the formalization of the logic. Formal proofs will then be nothing more than surveyable, inspectable *finite* sequences of *finite* formulas, "figures," or "diagrams," as Hilbert calls them (1922), and no different in basic, syntactic form from a finite sequence of strokes $\|\|\| \dots \|$.[49] According to Hilbert (*1922–1923a, 30), once the requisite formalization has been done,

> ... the signs and formulas of the logical calculus are thoroughly finite objects, even though they can represent transfinite inferences. Thus, we have the possibility of making these formulas themselves objects of contentual, finite considerations, wholly corresponding to what happens in elementary number theory with number signs.
>
> Naturally, the formalism with which we have to do here is far more involved and complicated than that of the number signs. Nevertheless, it embraces all mathematical relations which are expressible in formulas.[50]

The mathematical problem is then to investigate such "figures," an investigation which will give rise to a form of mathematics alongside formalized mathematics. As Hilbert puts it,

> In addition to proper mathematics formalised in this way, there is a mathematics that is to some extent new, a metamathematics necessary for securing mathematics, and in which—in contrast to the purely formal modes of inference in mathematics proper—one applies contentual [*inhaltlich*] inference, but only to prove the consistency of the axioms. In this metamathematics we operate with the proofs of mathematics proper, and these proofs are themselves the object of the contentual investigation. Thus the development of mathematical science as a whole takes place in two ways that constantly alternate: on the one hand we derive new provable formulas from the axioms by formal inference; on the other, we adjoin new axioms and prove their consistency by contentual inference. (1923, 153; reprint, 179–180)

Now the strengthened claim is seen quite clearly, namely, that the investigation of unity in the looser sense examined in sections 2–3 of this essay is not only intrinsic to what mathematicians do, but that there should be a mathematical theory through which the investigation of unity can be pursued. This is part of what the Hilbert method aimed to achieve, the complete mathematization of the philosophical concerns, for example, the complex of issues connected to the problem of mathematical existence. As Bernays (1922a, 19) put it,

> ... one sees through this also that what one has to carry out here are *mathematical* considerations in the proper sense.

> The great advantage of the Hilbert procedure lies exactly in this. The problems and difficulties which the founding of mathematics offers are taken out of the domain of the epistemological and placed in the domain of the properly mathematical.

In some ways, Bernays makes it clearer than Hilbert that the mathematics used to effect the investigation of formal structures must involve arithmetic, in that he is clear that a weak form of induction is bound to be involved in drawing general conclusions about sign- and proof-structures (1922a, 18–19). But in this respect it is important to recall that the concentration on finitude (and hence, indirectly, on the notion of finite number) goes back to the origins of Hilbert's concerns with foundational questions. Recall that already in 1900 the finitude (or "simplicity") of the collection of axioms is one of Hilbert's conditions on the adequacy of axiom systems, and that he connected the finiteness of proof to a general "requirement of reason." Moreover, in his notebooks, in remarks that are grouped around 1905, Hilbert repeatedly says that it is this finitude, both of the axiom systems and of proof, that forms the basis of an answer to the constructivism of Kronecker, a concern that seems quite independent of any additional concern with the paradoxes. Note also that Hilbert was certainly not the first to recognize the need for a logical language as a means of achieving precision, and even that the use of this in drawing inferences has to be, to a certain extent, automatic and mechanical. To take only a modern example, this is clearly expressed in Frege's letter to Hilbert of October 1, 1895, or in his two papers "Ueber die wissenschaftliche Berechtigung einer Begriffsschrift" and "Ueber den Zweck der Begriffsschrift" from 1882.[51] However, aside from the incorporation of considerations of logic into his view of the axiomatic method, the novelty of Hilbert's approach is the conjecture that the combinatorial element can be investigated by mathematical means based on elementary arithmetic, and which are therefore governed by a weak kind of intuition.

There is a certain parallelism between the earlier use of the axiomatic method and the later use of formalization. In the earlier treatment, singular terms were divorced from the suggestion that they have unique referents; thus, a certain way of construing the sentences as meaningful is blocked. The later formalization suggested after 1918 goes further in that the sentences which result from formalization are temporarily taken as having no meaning at all.[52] Nevertheless, there is an important difference in that the formalizing of mathematics is solely for the restricted purpose of investigating consistency. The limited nature of this purpose, although stressed by both Hilbert and Bernays, is often overlooked. It is not, as is sometimes said, that mathematics is to be replaced completely and finally by a meaningless formalization and that the only contentual, meaningful part of mathematics is the unformalized, elementary number theory, this then being served by the formalized mathematics in an instrumentalist way. Rather, the formalized mathematics is to replace proper mathematics only for the investigations of consistency and independence.

Some of Hilbert's own statements on this are somewhat ambiguous. Take, for instance, the phrase "purely formal modes of inference in mathematics proper" in the last but one passage quoted, or the following:

> For this purpose, the usual contentual considerations of the mathematical theory must be replaced by formulas and rules, and imitated by formalisms. In other words, a strict formalisation of all mathematical theories, inclusive of proofs, must be carried through, so that—following the example of the logical calculus—the mathematical inferences and definitions are drawn into the edifice of mathematics as formal components. The axioms, formulas and proofs that make up this formal edifice are precisely what the number-signs were in the construction of elementary number theory described earlier. And with these, then, just as with the number-signs in number theory, contentual considerations take place, i.e., proper thought is practiced. In this way, the contentual considerations, which of course we can never wholly do without or eliminate, are removed elsewhere, as it were, to a higher plane and with this it becomes possible in mathematics to draw a rigourous and systematic distinction between the formulas and formal proofs on the one hand, and contentual ideas on the other. (1922, 165; reprint, 165)

One could perhaps be forgiven for forming the impression that "proper thought" is that which is concerned with the finitary. But it is important here not to overlook the phrase "usual contentual considerations of the mathematical theory." Similarly, Hilbert (1926) says that in the process of formalization, "signs are detached from their contentual meaning"; but this, of course, implies that they have such a meaning to be detached from (see 177; English trans., 381). Some of Hilbert's unpublished writings are much clearer on this. For example, comparing the "reduction" of mathematics to its formalization and the "reduction" of geometry to arithmetic, Hilbert and Bernays say: "However, the reduction [of geometry] to arithmetic does not show that all geometrical and physical considerations ought to be replaced [*ersetz werden sollen*] by arithmetical considerations; just as little does *Beweistheorie* aim to show that all mathematical proofs ought to consist in schematic formal writing."[53] And it is important to stress that the elementary arithmetic, or the elementary arithmetical considerations of the symbol and proof systems, are not *inhaltlich* in virtue of being finitary; rather they are *inhaltlich* because they are not formalized. Unformalized mathematics, say analysis or set theory, is *inhaltlich* too, for it embraces the "usual contentual considerations." It is simply that the *inhaltliche Mathematik* involved in elementary number theory or the investigation of axiom systems does not need investigating for its consistency because it happens to be finitary, that is, accessible to a certain kind of intuition. Indeed, it is supposed to be in the nature of the finitary, and hence, fundamental, for the enterprise, that this is so. In other words, elementary number theory is contentual *and* finitary, whereas the bulk of unformalized mathematics, say analysis or set theory, is just *inhaltlich*, that is to say, not accessible to finitary intuition. (Indeed, sometimes Hilbert uses the phrase "*inhaltlich-anschauliche Überlegungen*" when *both* features are to be stressed. See, e.g., 1928, 71, English transl., 469.) This way of looking at the matter fits well with the relative way

Hilbert interpreted his own theory of ideal elements.[54] As for instrumentalism meant in the sense that it will always be possible to reduce statements of higher mathematics to statements about the theory of numbers, a view prevalent in Hilbert's youth,[55] Hilbert quite clearly repudiates it, and felt able to do so through his recognition that formal proofs must be finite figures. He says:

> We see ourselves occasioned by this to deviate from the fundamental principle that held sway earlier, according to which every proportion of pure mathematics was in the last analysis only a statement about the whole numbers. This principle, in which was seen a basic truth, and one which was to shape the way mathematics proceeds, must not be given up as a prejudice. (*1921–1922, 4a; i.e., 100 + 4)

Thus, far from this kind of instrumentalism being embraced by Hilbert's program, rightly or wrongly, Hilbert saw this program as a means by which this view can be finally and comfortably rejected.

It is important to say something briefly about Hilbert's repeated assertion (e.g., in 1922 and 1926) that he is taking the number signs themselves as the numbers, saying explicitly that these signs are to have no meaning/reference (*Bedeutung*), and that these are "the objects of our consideration [*Betrachtung*]."[56] In many ways, understanding this is the key to understanding Hilbert's entire later position.

First, it can be argued that this approach (just as with the formalization of mathematics) does not represent Hilbert's final view of arithmetic, but is adopted only for a specific purpose. It is also rather clear as to what the specific purpose is. For one thing, the relevant assertions come directly after Hilbert's claim that there must be something "extra-logical" in mathematics, something prior to "all scientific thinking, understanding and communication" (1922, 163; reprint, 163), something in virtue of which one can make true assertions, the ground for whose truth is not derivation from axioms, but which rather arises from the fact that the assertions are about objects that are discretely arranged, finite, and concretely presented, and thus whose truth stems from "immediate intuition."[57] As Hilbert (*1921–1922, 51) said, "... in elementary domains of arithmetic, in particular in that of elementary number theory, there is that complete certainty in our considerations. Here we get by without axioms, and the inferences have the character of the tangibly certain [*handgreiflich-Sichern*]." The "formal" theory of number is what Hilbert put forward in support of this, thus as an argument that the primitive intuition being appealed to can in fact yield some significant truths: "We wish to develop the theory of numbers as an intuitive [*anschauliche*] theory of certain simple figures, which we wish to call *number-signs*. (The connection between these number-signs and the cardinal numbers will emerge afterwards in a natural way.)" (*1921–1922, 52).

It is also clear what underlies this, namely, that the important role of numerals in counting can be exploited to yield a simple sign, counting theory of number. The first thing to notice about this is that what Hilbert put forward here is not a formalist account of number in the sense that none of the terms and statements of ordinary, full number theory are to have meaning or reference. On the contrary, Hilbert allows the sign 1 to stand for itself, and then the sign '+' to stand for the concatenation of signs. Given this, "the objects of consideration" in the theory are '1,' '1 + 1,' '1 + 1 + 1,' etc.; hence, the usual term '2' (or the successor operation applied to 1) will have as reference '1 + 1,' the term '3' (or the successor operation applied to 2) will have as reference '1 + 1 + 1,' etc., whereas the usual sign for addition '+' will stand for the concatenation of two objects. Thus, '2 + 3 = 4' interpreted in this way will then be the false proposition that 1 + 1 concatenated with 1 + 1 + 1 will yield the string 1 + 1 + 1 + 1. It is important to see that there is a strong connection between this and the reference-free view of mathematics explained in section 2. This latter view to a certain extent enables the adoption of the approach taken towards number theory just described without prejudice to the overall significance of mathematics or number theory. According to the reference-free view, mathematics, and thus number theory in particular, can and should proceed perfectly well with no fixed referents for its terms. But, given that Hilbert's position seems to encourage the multiplicity of possible referents rather than their complete absence, it follows that it should not really matter if some specific subject matter is chosen as the domain of reference, provided it can be shown that the domain chosen possesses the right theoretical properties. Thus, the term '1' can be assigned the formal object | or ● or itself, the term '+' can be assigned the (intuitive) operation of concatenation; '2' can be assigned the object ‖ or ● ● or 1 + 1, and so on, whereas the terms '∀' and '∃' are assigned nothing, that is (on this system of assignments), *are* strictly meaningless [*Bedeutungslos*].[58] There are two remarkable things about this. The first is that there is now accessibility to the primitive intuition. The second, is that, despite inessential properties, the sign domain does manage to preserve enough of the essential aspects of the mathematical structure. But this does not mean that these signs are the numbers. Bernays sums this up in an important footnote (1931). Concerning the representation of numbers through these number signs, he writes:

> The philosopher is inclined to speak of this representation as a relation of meaning [*Bedeutungszusammenhang*]. However, one should note that, in contrast to the usual relation between word and meaning, there is here the essential difference that the object doing the representing contains the essential properties of the object to be represented. Thus, the relations which are to be investigated between the objects represented are to be found in the objects doing the representing, and thus can be established through consideration of these. (1931, 32, n. 4)[59]

It is this that makes it possible to exploit fully the freedom given by the reference-free view.

The original proviso, of course, is crucial, namely, showing that the domain of the "representing" objects really does possess the right properties, in other words, can yield number theoretic theorems, or is a "model" of the ordinary, elementary arithmetic. In this case, it is not clear that any such conclusive argument can be given, for it is not clear exactly what theory the sign model is supposed to be matching. (See Parsons 1980 and Tait 1981 for related discussions.) Nevertheless, Hilbert is clearly sensitive to the need for some such argument, and he gives indications in two ways. First, he shows that the sign-arithmetic can indeed demonstrate some nontrivial theorems, for example, Euclid's theorem that for any given prime number there is a larger one. And, if it is accepted that the results are obtained on the basis of the primitive intuition, thus yielding the "tangibly certain," then it will be clear that the intuition involved is not merely trivial. Second, Hilbert argues that the sign-arithmetic is related in the right way to counting with ordinary whole numbers, and thus to the ordinary, basic number concepts, in that the cardinal number arrived at via this sign system (the appropriate array of '1's and '+'s) is independent of the order of counting of the objects to be counted (*1921–1922, 51–65).[60] In short, number theory is not trivialized or devalued: it has not become "merely formal."

This way of looking at the matter suggests that the detour through the sign-arithmetic is made, not to show the "true nature" of, or the certainty attached to, a fragment of mathematics, but rather to demonstrate that one way of acquiring knowledge that is as primitive and basic as any we have can also yield elementary (and significant) mathematical, indeed arithmetical, knowledge. Thus, in so far as knowledge gained in this way does not need further support, and in so far as it is accepted that knowledge of the properties of the proof figures is based on the same kind of "tangible," intuitive considerations, then neither does this require further support. It is clear from the beginning, of course, that what can be proved directly on the basis of this primitive intuition is quite limited. Hilbert himself is absolutely clear on this; and indeed, it is part of the point that the intuition be limited, for it is only supposed to concern what is assumed to be in the domain of the finitary, thus, what eschews the transfinite. Instead, the important thing for Hilbert at this stage is to show that *some* significant truths can be established in this way, and crucially to be able to argue that the reasoning involved need not be subjected to axiomatization for the purposes of investigating its consistency, something that would lead to a regress. If anything, then, something is being shown about a certain primitive form of outer intuition rather than about elementary number theory, an intuition that lies behind our ability to use and arrange signs, and is thus a precondition for "all scientific thinking, understanding and communication" (1922, 163; reprint, 163). In particular, what is being illustrated is the potential force of applying this intuition to proof figures arising from *any* formalized system. As Hilbert and Bernays (1934, 2) later put it, this intuition constitutes "that primitive method of obtaining knowledge [*diejenige primitive Erkenntnisweise*], which is a precondition for every kind of exact, theoretical research," and must be behind all use of axiomatics.[61] In this context, Gödel's and others' subsequent work surprisingly reveals the nonelementary nature of the main metamathematical goal, a proof of consistency.

5. Conclusion: The Laws of Thought

Let us come back to the laws of thought. What shapes Hilbert's treatment of formal logic, and hence *Beweistheorie*, is the *finite Einstellung* and the realization that, in their concrete manifestation, sentences are finite and discrete arrangements of individual signs. The understanding of propositions, their formulation, and the performance of operations with them (in deductions, etc.), and, indeed, the very possibility of communication, must be based, Hilbert thinks, on a certain primitive form of outer intuition, an intuition activated by the syntactic presentation via the signs, and thus the combination and resolution of these into finite, discretely arranged figures. This intuition then appears as a precondition for exact and communicable thought, and, in particular, for the use of logic. The focus on signs as basic goes right back to the essay on mathematical problems from 1900, the early period of Hilbert's concern with foundations, and is indeed closely bound up with the reference-free view adopted in this period. Moreover, recall that in 1900 Hilbert says that the basic requirement of rigor, that there be only a finite number of inferences involved in the carrying out of a proof, "corresponds to a general philosophical requirement of reason" (quoted previously, p. 163). And later (1923, 160; reprint, 187) he says quite explicitly that: "Our thinking is finite [*finit*]; when we think, a finite process occurs." This claim is made even more explicit in Hilbert (1928, 79–80; English trans., 475):

> The formula game that Brouwer so deprecates has, besides its mathematical value, an important general philosophical importance [*Deutung*]. For this formula game takes place according to certain definite rules, in which the *technique of our thinking* [*Technik unseres Denkens*] is expressed. These rules form a closed system that can be discovered and definitively specified. The fundamental idea of my proof theory is nothing other than to describe the activity of our understanding, to take down a protocol of the rules according to which our thinking actually proceeds. Thinking takes place parallel to speaking and writing through the formation and concatenation [*Aneinanderreihung*] of sentences [*Sätze*]. If any totality of observations and phenomena deserves to be made the object of serious and thorough research, it is this one . . .[62]

In short, what the *finite Einstellung* expresses is a principle, albeit weak, about the actual workings of the mind, namely, that a (deductive) thought process can be resolved formally into finitely many atomic units. When associated with the assumption that reasoning can be formalized, the essential precondition for understanding (and for thoughts being transferable from one mind to another) is transformed into the claim that the mind is able to make the step from one atomic unit to the next in a "mechanical" way, without the need to reflect on the content of what is being asserted. This corresponds to some aspects of the Fregean ideal as expressed through and around the *Begriffsschrift*, although note that without further argument this is only supposed to apply formalized thought.[63]

Neither the *finite Einstellung* nor the elementary arithmetic that can be treated by means of it are made sufficiently precise by Hilbert or by Bernays. Nevertheless, it is clear that any attempt to identify and describe the specifically Hilbertian (i.e., finitary) metamathematics to be based on this simple insight will at the same time be a description of Hilbert's laws of thought. The working out and analysis of recursive and primitive recursive arithmetic resulting from Gödel's and others' subsequent work (particularly Turing's) makes precise the conjectures both about the mathematical describability of metamathematics, its arithmetical nature, and the weakness and mechanical nature of the arithmetical theories involved. If this is taken to be the mathematical clarification of Hilbert's laws of thought, then it is clear that these laws are not strong enough to prove the consistency of interesting mathematical theories. Nevertheless, the framework is strong enough for the formulation of basic metamathematical questions, itself a remarkable confirmation of Hilbert's approach. And, interestingly, if primitive recursive arithmetic is taken as a plausible reconstruction of the minimal arithmetic that Hilbert's attitude towards the laws of thought suggests, and if we regard the search for *relative* consistency proofs as the natural model-theoretic correlate of Hilbert's insistence on the widespread use of theoretical integration, then it is remarkable to note that all the known relative consistency proofs can be carried out solely within primitive recursive arithmetic.

The contrast with Frege's view of the laws of thought is now striking. This is a *maximal* view of these laws, a view that involves the claim that mathematical objects are to be regarded as constructions within the framework given by the laws.[64] This maximal view was not Hilbert's. Rather, his was a *minimal* view, according to which the laws of thought form a regulative system of minimal restraint with which mathematical theories must not clash, but where we do not demand that mathematics be developed *within* that system. This view, or something like it, is perhaps hinted at in Hertz (1894), for one of Hertz's conditions on the adequacy of a system of *Bilder* was the condition of "permissibility": "As impermissible, we will denote such *Bilder* which already contain in themselves a contradiction with the laws of our thinking [*Widerspruch gegen die Gesetze unseres Denkens*], and we thus demand first that all our *Bilder* are logically permissible, or for brevity permissible[65] (p. 2). The concern with the preconditions for the operation with symbols, and the later attempt to develop a minimal arithmetic furnishing absolute consistency proofs which this inspires, might be seen as a far-reaching development of this. Note that Hilbert's minimal system is arrived at by forming conjectures about the basic operations of actual thought, thus, of human capacities to use language; perhaps this, too, is foreign to Frege's project.[65]

Notes

Acknowledgments—I would like to acknowledge the generous and kind support of Günther Patzig, the Alexander von Humboldt Stiftung, the Akademie der Wissenschaften zu Göttingen, the Social Sciences and Humanities Research Council of Canada, as well as McGill University for the granting of a sabbatical year in 1990–1991, during which this paper was prepared. I also wish to thank both the Niedersächsische Staats- und Universitätsbibliothek Göttingen and the Mathematisches Institut of the Georg-August Universität, Göttingen for permission to quote from various unpublished manuscripts of Hilbert in their possession. I am grateful to those who attended the conference, and also to seminar audiences at the Universities of Göttingen and Heidelberg for useful discussion. In particular, I wish to thank Emily Carson, Lorraine Daston, Lorenz Krüger, Ulrich Majer, and Erhard Scheibe for their questions and comments, and also Moshe Machover, Mihaly Makkai, John Mayberry, Stephen Menn, and William Demopoulos for very helpful remarks on this and closely related work, most of which I have unfortunately not been able to do justice to in this essay. The translations are always my own, although I have tried wherever possible to give references to published English translations as well.

1. See, for example, Gauss, letter to Bessel of April 9, 1830, reproduced in Gauss (1880, 497).

2. For excellent discussions of geometry in the nineteenth century, see Nagel (1939), the three papers by Freudenthal (1957, 1960, 1962), and Daston (1986). See also Enriques (1907).

3. The phrase "ideas foreign to it [arithmetic] (*ihr [Arithmetik] fremden Vorstellungen*)" is also used by Dedekind (1872, §1); in addition, in §3 he says that it is wrong to try to base the number concept on the "foreign considerations" of geometry.

4. For clear statements of this aim, see both Frege (1879) and (1884, *passim*), Cantor (1883, esp. 191–192), and Dedekind (1872, *Vorwort* and §§1–3).

5. This recalls Hilbert's (1928) statement about derivations in physics.

6. A similar passage, with only minor alterations, can be found in Pasch (1926, 91). See also Nagel (1939), especially pp. 193–198, and Freudenthal (1957, 1960, 1962). One notable exception to the insistence that proofs be free of intuition was Klein. See (1890, 381), where he expressly says that his statement of this position is directed against Pasch.

6. See Frege, letter to Hilbert, October 1, 1895, in Frege (1976 or 1980), Frege (1882, and 1882–1883).

8. Ibid. Hilbert's third notebook to be found in the Hilbert Nachlass in the Niedersächsische Staats- und Universitätsbibliothek in Göttingen (under Cod. Ms Hilbert, 600, 3) makes frequent reference to "pre-established harmony" between mathematics and the world of physical phenomena, all of these references falling within a short temporal span, probably a little later than 1900. There are also similar references in Hilbert's later lectures (*1922–1923b, 135; 98 of the new typescript), and (1926, 176; p. 381, English transl.).

9. See the abstract treatment of congruence in Hilbert (1899b, §6).

10. This *Mitschrift* stems from Max Born. The other extant *Mitschrift* of these lectures, stemming from Ernst Hellinger, is Hilbert (*1905b). Much the same point is made in Hilbert (*1922–1923b, 122; new typescript, 87).

11. Also quoted in Toepell (1986, 64). Note the rather abstract characterization of diagram or figure.

12. Hodges (1985–1986) compares them to indexicals like "today" in ordinary language. See pp. 148–149.

13. I am indebted to Demopoulos (1994) for this way of putting it in terms of nonlogical constants, as well as to Hodges (1985–1986).

14. It has been stressed frequently that the point of this is not that of rendering arithmetical truth certain, but rather of showing something clearly about the structure of the body of truths of arithmetic.

15. I should note that Hilbert did start to develop a distinctive attitude to logic from around 1905 on. However, in keeping with the spirit of his letter to Frege of October 4, 1895, he did not begin to develop a logic until he was clear concerning exactly what function it would fulfill.

16. In this case, the general structure of the argument is somewhat the same as with Dedekind, namely, that once we are in possession of the basic equipment, we are also in possession of arithmetic.

17. These are (among others) Hilbert (*1891, *1894, *1894–1895, *1898–1899, *1899a, as well as 1895). The issues are also reflected in many other works. The lecture notes mentioned here are particularly valuable because they were written down either by Hilbert himself or dictated to, or copied by, his wife, and are not lecture notes prepared by others, as was mostly the case later. A thorough account of their contents can be found in Toepell (1986).

18. Letter of December 29, 1899, reproduced in Frege (1976, 66–69). Unfortunately, not all of the relevant remark of Hilbert's is rendered in the English translation in Frege (1980).

19. Hilbert (*1894, 60 and footnote, quoted from Toepell 1986, 85). I assume that the comment in the footnote alludes to the problem of demonstrating what we would now call *categoricity*.

20. There is an interesting passage in Hilbert's 1894 lectures on geometry concerning the "prejudice" expressed by the philosopher Lotze that non-Euclidean geometry is to be rejected out of hand as a possibility for providing a description of physical space. Hilbert says:

> To come back to Lotze's prejudice, naturally no experiment can force us to accept hyperbolic geometry. Rather, in case an experimental result did show the angle sum $< \pi$ [Hilbert is referring to the fact that in Euclidean geometry the angle sum in a triangle $= \pi$, in hyperbolic geometry it is $< \pi$, and in elliptic geometry it is $> \pi$], then it is still always possible to get by with ordinary Euclidean space. In this case, we would have to assume that there is a sphere, in whose interior we find ourselves, whose surface is never reached by translating a [measuring] rod, no matter how often we execute this. Each rod turned in itself, i.e., each axis, forms a circle, so likewise does every light ray, every tightly drawn thread, and indeed these form circles which are orthogonal to the surface of the sphere. However, it is much more perspicuous and simpler, and it requires fewer axioms, if under these circumstances we postulate the hyperbolic nature of space. And this [presumably this simplicity] is the only determing factor for us when we adopt an hypothesis and recognise it as the truth. Nobody could force us to accept the Copernican world system; rather we can still hold to the Ptolemaic if we patch it up [*ausflicken*] properly. And how much more of a transformation, how much more spoke against the view of the earth as the resting central point than now speak against the assumption of hyperbolic geometry. Lotze is far stupider than the opponents of Copernicus at that time, and far worse, since he energetically rejects [this] in advance, for there are still no observations which contradict Euclidean space. (*1894, 88–89. Also quoted in Toepell 1986, 92–93.)

Among other things, this is an interesting anticipation of the situation that Henri Poincaré and later Hans Reichenbach start from. It also gives an early indication that truth for Hilbert is to depend on properties of the system, here simplicity, later consistency.

21. Klein, geometrical empiricist though he was in a certain sense, recognizes that there is bound to be some imprecision that mathematics has to abstract from, even if we claim that intuition fixes the basic terms. Klein says:

> The element of spatial intuition . . . is not the point but the three-dimensional body. We may conceive of the body as diminished in size, but we never obtain in this way the

intuition of a single point. Similarly, it is impossible to represent a curve exactly; what we can see is always only a body of which two dimensions fall into the background with respect to the third. (1873; reprint, 214)

22. Hilbert, Notebook 3, Cod. Ms. 600, 3, p. 101. The use of the term *Gedankending* here suggests Hilbert's paper (1905a), thus a data of around 1904–1905. A passage a little later on the same page mentions Zermelo's "principle of choice", suggesting that the date is at least as late as 1904.

23. For similar remarks, see also Bernays (1922a, 11 and 15, and 1922b, 95–96).

24. See, for example, Hilbert (1899b), (1900a, 181), and (1900b, 264, 299–300 of the reprint). Hilbert (1899b) says that a complete [*vollständiges*] geometrical system should prove all the "most important" geometrical theorems. Hilbert (1900a, 181) has changed this to *all* theorems. In his lectures of 1905, Hilbert (*1905b, 12) says that a system is complete [*vollständig*] when it has all the facts [*Tatsachen*] that one is presented with as logical consequences. Hilbert (*1905c, 8) has all the "remaining" facts. However, in the same lectures (and in notes from around this time) Hilbert lays weight on what we would now call (following Veblen 1904, p. 346) the *categoricalness* of the axiom system he gives for the real numbers. (See, e.g., *1905b, 21; *1905c, 16–17.) Moreover, it is difficult not to think of Hilbert's *Vollständigkeitsaxiome* for the systems of real numbers and Euclidean geometry (1900a, 183, and 1903, 16) as demanding a form of categoricity; indeed Veblen interprets it in just this way. This would, of course, imply completeness in a strong sense, since if the system is categorical, then for every proposition σ in the language either σ or $\neg\sigma$ is provable. However, categoricalness is never, to my knowledge, put forward by Hilbert as a condition on axiom systems generally. For interesting discussion of this, which reflects the increasing complexity of the issues, see Fraenkel (1923, 227–228), and (347–354). (There is no discussion of these matters in the first edition, Fraenkel 1919.)

25. A glance at the list of *Mitschriften* for lecture courses held by Hilbert indicates that he had gone into all of these subjects rather carefully. Certainly Hilbert's own work on, for example, radiation theory, shows intense interest in compatibility between physical and mathematical theories, and the "ergodic problem" reflected in the debate between Zermelo and Boltzmann, mentioned by Hilbert (1918), can also be seen as a problem of compatibility of this kind. Hilbert's work on geometry, as has been explained, can be seen partly as grappling with this question for relations between mathematical theories.

26. At the core of Minkowski's investigations is a new geometry, obtained by replacing one of the standard Euclidean axioms dealing with the congruence of triangles (for example, Hilbert's Axiom IV 6, 1899b, 12–13—the axiom is differently numbered in subsequent editions, e.g., III 6 in 1903) with an essentially weaker Euclidean *theorem*, the proposition that any two sides of a triangle are together greater than the third. (This theorem is proved as Proposition 20 in Book I of Euclid's *Elements*.) Minkowski then applies this system to quite a different domain, namely, number theory. For Hilbert's comments on Minkowski, see Hilbert (1909; reprint, 345). For Euclid, see Heath (1925, Vol. 1, 155, 224–225, 286–287).

27. See pp. 89–90. It is not clear which mathematicians Hilbert has in mind, but no doubt they include Cantor and Dedekind, and probably Bolzano and, to some extent, Frege. Bolzano is mentioned in Hilbert (1900b, 262). Hilbert, of course, had been in personal contact with Frege since 1895, and no doubt knew something of Frege's work from Frege himself, even if he had not studied it.

28. However, for a general discussion of the extent to which Hilbert's definitions

are implicit, see note 36. For an excellent and very thorough discussion of Frege's use of definitions, see Dummett (1987).

29. Hilbert mostly sees the application of the axiomatic method as depending on a body of *Grundtatsachen* which it is the job of the axiom system to treat, although not to respect religiously. Intuition, although taken in a looser sense than the Kantian, can usually be thought of as playing a significant role in the setting up of the *Grundtatsachen*, and the "genetic method" often plays a large part in the development here.

Two things seem to be characteristic of the genetic method: the fact that it is not always clear that definite or clearly articulated principles are being appealed to, and (connected to this) the fact that very often unclear notions of generation are involved, thus raising the danger of dependence on something temporal.

30. For an account of the history of geometry in this respect, see Nagel (1939, esp. 178).

31. According to Pasch, this is in fact what Euclid's notorious "explanations" of points, lines, etc., amount to, explanations which actually play no part whatsoever in the construction or development of the axiom system. See Pasch (1882, 16–17). Note that Hilbert is careful to give no such "extra" explanations, and also to make it clear that none is needed. See Hilbert's letter to Frege, December 29, 1899, (Frege 1976, 66). (Also given in Frege 1980.) It is interesting that Russell's work on the foundations of geometry from the 1890s is based on taking certain things as "primitives" or "simples," and that the main foundational philosophical task of the logicist (1903) is taken to be that of finding the right logical "simples" from which the whole of mathematics is to be built up.

32. There is some stress on this in Hilbert's letter to Frege of December 29, 1899: see Frege (1976 or 1980). For Euclid's "explanations," see Heath (1925, Vol. 1, 153–154). According to Emmy Noether, Cantor once described a set as being "like an abyss [*Abgrund*]." See Becker (1964, 316).

33. Frege recognizes that it is part of the point of proofs to illuminate "the dependence of truths on one another" (1884, §2). It could be said that part of Hilbert's foundational project is a radical extension of this, that for Hilbert this is largely what mathematics is about, whereas for Frege, the demonstration of (some) connections is primarily of philosophical interest.

34. Connected to this is another general problem with genetic definition, which John Mayberry pointed out to me, namely, that genetic procedures may not be canonical. Suppose, as happens with the Cantor and Dedekind accounts of real number, that there are different ways of extending some given domain. Do we not now have to investigate whether these are essentially similar or not? This will involve an investigation of whether they satisfy the same principles, which, of course, is close to investigating whether they satisfy the same axioms or whether their consequence classes are the same.

35. It should be stressed that the Hilbert view seems to underline the creative side of the provision of models. Indeed, the remarkable creativity involved is illustrated by such diverse (and randomly chosen) examples as the illustration of non-Euclidean behavior in Euclidean objects by Beltrami, and the subsequent building of "inner models" out of this, the construction of Gödel's inner model of constructible sets in the cumulative hierarchy, and then Cohen's construction of forcing models. It must be stressed that the term "embedded" used here should be taken only in a weak sense, and not as meaning that a model of the whole theory somehow has to be provided with the help of already existing materials. Modeling of the whole theory will only be possible some of the time.

36. Of course, Hilbert did not give implicit definitions in the sense that the axioms,

either individually, or as a whole, fixed the concept of point (to take an example) completely and unequivocally. Indeed, the mathematical force of Hilbert's work depends precisely on this *not* being the case, on it being possible to choose points, lines, and planes from anywhere. Hilbert, by the way, seems quite clear in his letter to Frege of December 29, 1899 (in Frege 1976 and 1980), that is not the individual axioms that define anything, but the axiom system as a whole. On the other hand, as Hodges points out (1985–1986, 141), Hilbert's later assertion that the axioms would "contain a precise and complete description of the relations involved [*eine genaue und vollständige Beschreibung derjenigen Beziehungen enthalten*]" (1900b, 264; reprint, 299) seems to contradict the flexibility required in the above presentation. If the "relations involved" are dependent on the elements that fall under them, this will certainly not be the case. It would perhaps be more accurate to say, as Hodges points out (ibid.), that what the (geometrical) axiom system fixes is the concept of a (Euclidean) system of points, lines, and planes, that is, something of higher order. Despite the later remark, this does seems to emerge from the Hilbert letter to Frege mentioned above. Bernays is particularly clear on the situation (1942).

37. This attitude is best seen in Leibniz's letter to Varignon, February 2, 1702, in Leibniz (1859, 92–93).

38. A graphic illustration of the shift in concern from individually defined objects towards systems is Hilbert's attitude towards the real numbers. This is fairly clearly presented in his 1900a, 1900b, and 1922. In his 1921–1922 lectures, Hilbert says that the essential thing with the axiomatic method is the "investigation of logical connections," and that this is separated off from the question as to the "material truth" of the statements involved. See *1921–1922, 3; also 7a–8a, i.e., $100 + 7-100 + 8$. Another reason for guarding against the formalist connotations associated with implicit definitions here is that the strong suggestion of instrumentalism is quite counter to Hilbert's attitude to the so-called "ideal elements." I cannot go into this here, but for some preliminary discussion, see Hallett (1990). See also p. 183.

39. The completeness question is explicitly mentioned by van Heijenoort (1967a). Of course, the situation changes once it is shown that the various meta-theoretic questions are capable of being tackled by a form of arithmetical investigation.

40. Twice in his third notebook Hilbert says that number theory plays the role in mathematics of a kind of "grammar," thus perhaps anticipating and elucidating the later primacy of arithmetic in the foundational study of axiomatic structures. See Hilbert, Cod. Ms. 600, 3, pp. 22 and 133–132. (Hilbert paginates in reverse here!) The remarks are difficult to date, but a guess based on some surrounding material would put them between 1905 and 1910.

This view of number theory as the "grammar of mathematics" is common to all of Hilbert's post–1900 considerations of the foundations of mathematics. It appears later as the assumption that it is possible for there to be a single mathematical theory within which to do metamathematics. This even figures as late as Hilbert and Bernays (1934); see, for example, p. 2.

41. To some extent, this view is already present in Hilbert (1905a).

42. This is made clear by Hilbert in his 1905 lectures. See (*1905b, 217), or (*1905c, 141–142).

43. It is not just the availability of the Law of Excluded Middle that has to be taken into account by Hilbert; classical logic also has to be appropriately adapted to the use of what Hilbert calls "ideal elements." This is undoubtedly one of the motivations behind the introduction of the ε-calculus and its predecessor, the τ-calculus. There also is the need to develop a logic that is amenable to the reference-free view stressed in the

earlier parts of this essay, of great importance in the evolution of the notion of a nonlogical constant.

44. This English translation of *finite Einstellung* stems from Bernays.

45. Hilbert (1900b, 259; reprint, 295). See also p. 260 (p. 296). Hilbert later recognizes a difference between certain arithmetical signs and geometrical ones, for in his 1921–1922 lectures, he suggests that geometrical figures are different in so far as they are taken to have properties that cannot be described in purely discrete (and thus not in finitary) terms. They are not therefore amenable to the primitive intuitions of the *finite Einstellung*, unlike elementary arithmetical and proof "figures." See (*1921–1922, 5a, i.e., 100 + 5).

46. Hilbert (*1905b, 219). Virtually the same passage is to be found in the other *Ausarbeitung* of these lectures stemming from Max Born (*1905c, 143). In Hilbert (1905a) Hilbert hints at much the same thing, for there he begins his presentation of his logical theory: "Let an object of our thought be called a *thought-object* [*Gedankending*] or, briefly, an object [*Ding*] and let it be denoted by a sign." (176; English trans., 131). Although I cannot go into it here, it is clear that the importance of this idea was recognized by Frege too, as well as by Helmholtz and Hertz.

47. Note that the term "program" to describe the project of investigating the mathematical means of proof itself is used already in 1918 (415; reprint, 155), although this paper contains very few details of Hilbert's program. It does, however, set out some of the broad aims and problems that use of what is now known as mathematical logic faces. (See *op. cit.*, pp. 412–413; reprint, p. 153.)

48. See also pp. 128–130 (resp. pp. 92–94). Bernays gives arguments (1922a, 18–19, and 1931, 30–31) as to why number theory must be involved in the study of a logical calculus, for instance, in considering the number of argument places in a predicate, the number of certain logical operations or the number of appearances of a certain symbol in an inference.

49. See Hilbert (1922, 169; also 169 of the reprint). Hilbert also makes this point in his 1923 work 152; reprint, 179) and in the 1926 paper (177; English trans., 381).

50. The designation of this as "far more involved and complicated" was, of course, prescient. Note that both Brouwer and Zermelo, for quite different reasons, of course, thought that it will not be possible to represent mathematical thoughts and proofs in a circumscribed and finite language. See the interesting discussion in Sieg (1990, 272–273).

51. The letter appears in Frege (1976, or 1980).

52. It should not be assumed that the achievement of formalizations is automatic. For instance, because of the initial vagueness of the separation axiom, rendering Zermelo's axiom system for set theory formalizable is by no means an automatic task.

53. An undated manuscript from the Hilbert Nachlass in the Niedersächsische Staats- und Universitätsbibliothek, Göttingen, Cod. Ms. 601, Blatt 17. The manuscript (four pages long), is mostly in Bernays's hand, but there are remarks and alterations added in Hilbert's hand, including one long paragraph glued on. See also Hilbert (*1921–1922, 7a, i.e., 100 + 7). That formalized axiomatic theories cannot dispense with their contentual counterparts is also stressed in Hilbert and Bernays (1934, 2).

54. For a preliminary discussion, see Hallett (1990, 234–239).

55. See, for example, Dedekind (1888, p. VI, English trans. 35) or Cantor (1883, 172–173 of the reprint). This goal was pursued in quite different senses by Kronecker and Dedekind; see Sieg (1990), 262–265.

56. See (1922, 163; reprint 163) and (1926, 171; English trans., 377).

57. Ibid.

58. As Bernays (1923, 160) points out, it is to some extent irrelevant what are taken

as the concrete objects here, so long as they possess the right discreteness properties. See also Bernays (1931, 32), where he seems to stress this freedom. One of Bernays's ways of stressing what here I call the "reference-free view" is to point out the "abstractness" of mathematics.

59. As John Mayberry has pointed out to me in hindsight one might see precisely this correlation between the natural number structure and the representing symbols as foreshadowing the difficulties thrown up by the Gödel theorems. The transfinite cannot be bypassed as simply as Hilbert thought.

60. This connection, of course, is no accident, given the origins of number theory in a simple counting stroke arithmetic.

61. As for this intuition being "outer intuition," at one point in his 1921–1922 lectures, Hilbert calls his elementary sign arithmetic "number geometry," thus recalling the Kantian outer intuition that is supposed to govern geometry. See op. cit., 5a (i.e., 100 + 5). See also Gödel's note b to his own 1972 revision of an English translation of his 1958 work, where he says: "What Hilbert means by 'Anschauung' is substantially Kant's space-time intuition confined, however, to configurations of a finite number of discrete objects" (272).

62. The reference to "formula game" here is to Hilbert's description of Brouwer's dismissal of classical existence assertions: "Brouwer declares existence statements, one and all, to be meaningless in themselves, in so far as they do not contain constructions for the forms they assert to exist. For him they are worthless scraps of paper, and their use causes mathematics to degenerate into a game" (1928, 77; English trans., 474).

63. As has been illustrated, and as is made clear by Bernays (1931), in this respect, elementary number theory presented as a theory of signs is an exception in that some of the content of the theory can be deduced from the form of the numerals. See op. cit., 30–32.

64. Gödel also seems to have had a "maximal" view, since he thought that the general concept of set, described, say, by the iterative conception, is a concept through which we "think" mathematically, or better, which is necessarily employed in the formulation of mathematical assertions. See Gödel (1964).

65. The previous two sections are to be regarded as giving only a very brief sketch of the situation. For further discussion on many closely related subjects, see Sieg (1988, 1990), as well as the numerous papers by Bernays, only some of which are specified in the references.

References

Works with an asterisk before the date are unpublished.

Becker, Oskar. 1964. *Grundlagen der Mathematik in geschichtlicher Entwicklung*, 2nd extended ed. Freiburg and München, Karl Alber Verlag; reprinted as Vol. 115 in the Suhrkamp Taschenbuch Wissenschaft series. Frankfurt, Suhrkamp, 1975.

Bernays, Paul. 1922a. Über Hilberts Gedanken zur Grundlegung der Arithmetik, *Jahresbericht der deutschen Mathematiker-Vereinigung* 31, 10–19.

———. 1922b. Die Bedeutung Hilberts für die Philosophie der Mathematik, *Die Naturwissenschaften* 10, 93–99.

———. 1923. Erwiderung auf die Note von Herrn Aloys Müller: "Über Zahlen als Zeichen," *Mathematische Annalen* 90, 159–163.

———. 1931. Die Philosophie der Mathematik und die Hilbertsche Beweistheorie, *Blätter für deutsche Philosophie*, 4, 326–27; reprinted in Bernays (1976), 17–61, Page numbers in the text refer to this reprinting.

————. 1935. Hilberts Untersuchungen über die Grundlagen der Arithmetik. In Hilbert (1935), 196–216.

————. 1942. Review of Max Steck: "Ein unbekannter Brief von Gottlob Frege über Hilberts erste Vorlesung über die Grundlagen der Geometrie," *Sitzungsberichte der Heidelberger Akademie der Wissenschaften, mathematisch-naturwissenschaftliche Klasse* (1940), no. 6, in *Journal of Symbolic Logic* 7, 92–93.

————. 1976. *Abhandlungen zur Philosophie der Mathematik*. Darmstadt, Wissenschaftliche Buchgesellschaft.

Cantor, Georg. 1883. Über unendliche lineare Punctmannigfaltigkeiten, 5, *Mathematische Annalen* 21, 545–585; reprinted in Cantor (1932), 165–209; English translation in Ewald (1994).

————. 1932. *Gesammelte Abhandlungen mathematischen und philosophischen Inhalts*. Herausgegeben von Ernst Zermelo. Berlin, Julius Springer.

Daston, Lorraine. 1986. The physicalist tradition in early nineteenth century French geometry. *Studies in the History and Philosophy of Science* 17, 269–295.

Dedekind, Richard. 1854. Über die Einführung neuer Funktionen in der Mathematik: Habilitationsvortrag, gehalten im Hause des Prof. Hoeck, in Gegenwart von Hoeck, Gauss, Weber, Waitz, 30 Juni 1854. In Dedekind 1932, item LX, 428–438.

————. 1872. *Stetigkeit und irrationale Zahlen*. Braunschweig; reprinted in Dedekind (1932); English translation in Dedekind (1901).

————. 1888. *Was sind und was sollen die Zahlen?* Braunschweig; reprinted in Dedekind (1932); English translation in Dedekind (1901).

————. 1901. *Essays on the Theory of Numbers*; English translations by W. W. Beman of Dedekind (1872) and (1888). LaSalle, Illinois, Open Court Publishing; reprinted by Dover Publications, New York, 1963.

————. 1932. *Gesammelte mathematische Werke, Band 3*. Herausgegeben von Robert Fricke, Emmy Noether and Öystein Ore. Braunschweig, Friedrich Vieweg und Sohn; reprinted by Chelsea Publishing Co., New York, 1969 (with some omissions from the third volume).

Demopoulos, William. 1994. Frege, Hilbert and the conceptual structure of model theory, *History and Philosophy of Logic* 15.

Michael. 1987. Frege and the paradox of analysis. In Michael Dummett, *Frege and Other Philosophers*. Oxford, Clarendon Press, 1991.

Enriques, Frederico. 1907. Prinzipien der Geometrie. In *Encyklopädie der mathematischen Wissenschaften*, III, *Erster Teil, Erster Hälfte*, 1–129.

Ewald, William (*ed.*) 1994. *Readings in the Philosophy of Mathematics*, Vols. 1 and 2. Oxford, Clarendon Press.

Fraenkel, Adolf. 1919. *Einleitung in die Mengenlehre*. Berlin, Verlag von Julius Springer.

————. 1923. *Einleitung in die Mengenlehre. Zweite erweiterte Auflage*. Berlin, Verlag von Julius Springer.

————. 1928. *Einleitung in die Mengenlehre: Dritte umgearbeitete und stark erweiterte Auflage*. Berlin, Verlag von Julius Springer.

Frege, Gottlob. 1879. *Begriffsschrift, eine der arithmetischen nachgebildete Formelsprache des reinen Denkens*. Halle an die Saale, Verlag von Louis Nebert; reprinted in Frege (1964); English translation in van Heijenoort (1967b), 1–82.

————. 1882, Ueber die wissenschafliche Berechtigung einer Begriffsschrift. *Zeitschrift für Philosophie und philosophische Kritik* 81, 48–56; reprinted in Frege (1964), 106–114.

————. 1882–83. Ueber den Zweck der Begriffsschrift. *Jenaische Zeitschrift für Naturwissenschaft* (9) 16, 1–10; reprinted in Frege (1964), 97–106.

————. 1884. *Die Grundlagen der Arithmetik*. Breslau, W. Koebner; English translation by J. L. Austin (1953) *The Foundations of Arithmetic*, 2nd ed. Oxford, Basil Blackwell.

————. 1891. *Über Funktion und Begriff*. Jena, Hermann Pohle; reprinted in Patzig (1986), 18–39; English translation by Max Black in Frege (1984), 136–156.

————. 1892a. Über Sinn und Bedeutung. *Zeitschrift für Philosophie und philosophische Kritik* 100, 25–50; reprinted in Patzig (1986), 40–65; English translation by Max Black in Frege (1984), 157–177.

————. 1892b. Über Begriff und Gegenstand. *Vierteljahrschrift für wissenschaftliche Philosophie* 16, 192–205; reprinted in Patzig (1986), 66–90; English translation by Max Black in Frege (1984), 182–194.

————. 1893. *Grundgesetze der Arithmetik, Band 1*. Jena, Hermann Pohle; reprinted in Frege (1966).

————. 1903. *Grundgesetze der Arithmetik, Band 2*. Jena, Hermann Pohle; reprinted in Frege (1966).

————. 1964. *Begriffsschrift und andere Aufsätze, Zweite Auflage, Mit E. Husserls und H. Scholz' Anmerkungen herausgegeben von Ignacio Angelelli*. Darmstadt, Wissenschaftliche Buchgesellschaft.

————. 1966. *Grundgesetze der Arithmetik, Bände 1 und 2*. Hildesheim, Georg Olms.

————. 1976. *Wissenschaftlicher Briefwechsel*, edited by G. Gabriel, H. Hermes, F. Kambartel and G. Thiel. Hamburg, Felix Meiner.

————. 1980. *Philosophical and Mathematical Correspondence*. Oxford, Basil Blackwell; partial English translation by Hans Kaal of Frege (1976).

————. 1984. *Collected Papers on Mathematics, Logic and Philosophy*, edited by Brian McGuiness. Oxford, Basil Blackwell.

Freudenthal, Hans. 1957. Zur Geschichte der Grundlagen der Geometrie: zugleich eine Besprechung der 8. Auflage von Hilberts Grundlagen der Geometrie. *Nieuw archief voor wiskunde* 5, 105–142.

————. 1960. Die Grundlagen der Geometrie um die Wende des 19. Jahrhunderts. *Mathematisch-physikalische Semesterberichte zur Pflege des Zusammenhangs von Schule und Universität* 7, 2–25.

————. 1962. The main trends in the foundations of geometry in the nineteenth century. In Ernest Nagel, Patrick Suppes and Alfred Tarski (eds.). *Logic. Methodology and the Philosophy of Science*. Stanford, Calif., Stanford University Press, 613–621.

Gauss, Carl Friedrich. 1880. *Werke. Ergänzungsreihe, Band II: Carl Friedrich Gauss— Wilhelm Bessel, Briefwechsel*. Leipzig, Wilhelm Engelmann Verlag; reprinted by Georg Olms, Hildesheim, 1975.

Gödel, Kurt. 1958. Über eine bisher noch nicht benützte Erweiterung des finiten Standpunktes, *Dialectica*, 12, 280–287. Reprinted with an English translation by Stefan Bauer-Mengelberg and Jean van Heijenoort in Gödel (1990), 240–251.

————. 1964. What is Cantor's continuum problem? In P. Benacerrraf and H. Putnam, eds. *Philosophy of Mathematics: Selected readings*. Englewood Cliffs, New Jersey, Prentice-Hall, 258–273; reprinted in second edition, Cambridge, Cambridge University Press, 1984, 470–485; also in Gödel (1990), 254–270.

————. 1972. On an extension of finitary mathematics that has not yet been used. Gödel's revision, with extensive notes, of an English translation of Gödel (1958) by Leo Boron, published in Gödel (1990), 271–280.

————. 1990. *Collected Works, Vol. II*. Oxford, Clarendon Press.

Hallett, Michael. 1990. Physicalism, reductionism and Hilbert. In Andrew Irvine, ed., *Physicalism in Mathematics*. Dordrecht, Holland, D. Reidel, 183–257.

Heath, Sir T. L. 1925. *The Thirteen Books of Euclid's Elements*, 2nd ed. (3 vols.) Cambridge, Cambridge University Press; reprinted by Dover, New York, 1956.

Heijenoort, Jean van. 1967a. Logic as calculus and logic as language. *Synthese* 17, 324–30.

————. ed. 1967b. *From Frege to Gödel: A Source Book in Mathematical Logic.* Cambridge, Mass., Harvard University Press.

Hertz, Heinrich. 1894. *Prinzipien der Mechanik.* Leipzig, Johannes Barth; reprint 1910; English translation by D. E. Jones and J. T. Walley, *Principles of Mechanics,* London, Macmillan 1900; reprinted by Dover, New York, 1956.

Hilbert, David. *1891. *Projektive Geometrie.* Vorlesung, Sommersemester 1891. Niedersächsische Staats- und Universitätsbibliothek, Göttingen, under Cod. Ms. Hilbert 535.

————. *1894. *Die Grundlagen der Geometrie.* Vorlesung, Sommersemester 1894. Niedersächsische Staats- und Universitätsbibliothek, Göttingen, under Cod. Ms. Hilbert 541.

————. *1894–95. *Analytische Geometrie der Ebene und des Raumes.* Vorlesung, Wintersemester 1894–1895. Niedersächsische Staats- und Universitätsbibliothek, Göttingen, under Cod. Ms. Hilbert 543.

————. 1895. Über die gerade Linie als kürzeste Verbindung zweier Punkte. *Mathematische Annalen* 46, 91–96.

————. 1897. Die Theorie der algebraischen Zahlkörper [*Zahlbericht*]. *Jahresbericht der deutschen Mathematiker-Vereinigung* 4, 175–546; reprinted in Hilbert (1932), 63–363. Page numbers in the text refer to reprint.

————. *1898–1899. *Grundlagen der euklidischen Geometrie.* Vorlesung, Wintersemester 1898–1899. Niedersächsische Staats- und Universitätsbibliothek, Göttingen, under Cod. Ms. Hilbert 551.

————. *1899a. *Elemente der euklidischen Geometrie.* März 1899. Ausgearbeitet von H. von Schaper. Mathematisches Institut, Georg-August Universität, Göttingen. Also in the Niedersächsische Staats- und Universitätsbibliothek, Göttingen, under Cod. Ms. Hilbert 552.

————. 1899b. Grundlagen der Geometrie. In *Festschrift zur Feier der Enthüllung des Gauss-Weber-Denkmals in Göttingen, 1899.* Leipzig, B. G. Teubner.

————. 1900a. Über den Zahlbegriff. *Jahresbericht der deutschen Mathematiker-Vereinigung* 8, 180–184; English translation in Ewald (1994).

————. 1900b. Mathematische Probleme. *Nachrichten von der königlichen Gesellschaft der Wissenschaften zu Göttingen, mathematisch-physikalische Klasse 1900,* 253–296; English translation in Ewald (1994).

————. 1903. *Grundlagen der Geometrie. Zweite vermehrte Auflage.* Leipzig, B. G. Teubner.

————. 1905a Über die Grundlagen der Logik und Arithmetik. In Krazer (1905), 174–185; English translation in van Heijenoort (1967b), 129–138.

————. *1905b. *Logische Principien des mathematischen Denkens.* Vorlesung, Sommersemester 1905. Ausgearbeitet von Ernst Hellinger. Mathematisches Institut, Georg-August Universität, Göttingen.

————. *1905c. *Logische Principien des mathematischen Denkens.* Vorlesung, Sommersemester 1905. Ausgearbeitet von Max Born. Niedersächsische Staats- und Universitätsbibliothek, Göttingen, under Cod. Ms. Hilbert 558a.

————. 1909. Hermann Minkowski. *Nachrichten von der königlichen Gesellschaft der Wissenschaften zu Göttingen, gesellschaftliche Mitteilungen 1909,* 72–101; reprinted in Hilbert (1935), 339–364.

————. 1918. Axiomatisches Denken. *Mathematische Annalen* 78, 405–415; reprinted in Hilbert (1935), 146–156; English translation in Ewald (1994).

————. *1921–1922. *Grundlagen der Mathematik.* Vorlesung, Wintersemester 1921–1922. Ausgearbeitet von Paul Bernays, Figuren von W. Rosemann. Mathematisches Institut, Georg-August Universität, Göttingen.

————. 1922. "Neubegründung der Mathematik. Erste Mitteilung." *Abhandlungen aus dem mathematischen Seminar der Hamburgischen Universität* 1, 157–177; reprinted in Hilbert (1935), 157–78; English translation in Ewald (1994).

————. *1922–23a. *Logische Grundlagen der Mathematik.* Vorlesung, Wintersemester 1922–23. Ausarbeitung unknown. Niedersächsische Staats- und Universitätsbibliothek, Göttingen, under Cod. Ms. Hilbert 567.

————. *1922–1923b. *Wissen und mathematisches Denken.* Vorlesung, Wintersemester, 1922–1923. Ausgearbeitet von Wilhelm Ackermann. Mathematisches Institut, Georg-August Universität, Göttingen. Published in a limited edition by the Mathematischem Institut, Georg-August Universität, Göttingen, 1988.

————. 1923. Die logischen Grundlagen der Mathematik. *Mathematische Annalen* 88, 151–165; reprinted in Hilbert (1935), 178–191; English translation in Ewald (1994).

————. 1926. Über das Unendliche, *Mathematische Annalen* 95, 161–190; English translation in van Heijenoort (1967b), 367–392.

————. 1928. Die Grundlagen der Mathematik. *Abhandlungen aus dem mathematischen Seminar der Hamburgischen Universität* 6, 65–85; English translation in van Heijenoort (1967b), 464–479.

————. 1932. *Gesammelte Abhandlungen. Erster Band.* Berlin, Julius Springer.

————. 1935. *Gesammelte Abhandlungen. Dritter Band.* Berlin, Julius Springer.

Hilbert, David and Paul Bernays. 1934. *Grundlagen der Mathematik, Band I.* Berlin, Julius Springer.

Hodges, Wilfrid. 1985–1986. Truth in a structure. *Proceedings of the Aristotelian society* 86, 135–151.

Klein, Felix, 1873. Über den allgemeinen Funktionsbegriff und dessen Darstellung durch eine willkürliche Kurve. *Sitzungsberichte der physikalisch-medizinischen Sozietät zu Erlangen vom 8. Dezember 1873.* In *Mathematische Annalen* 22 (1883) reprinted in Klein 1922, 214–224.

————. 1890. Zur Nicht-Euklidischen Geometrie. *Mathematische Annalen* 37; reprinted in Klein (1921), 353–383.

————. 1921. *Gesammelte mathematische Abhandlungen, Erster Band.* Berlin, Verlag von Julius Springer.

————. 1922. *Gesammelte mathematische Abhandlungen, Zweiter Band.* Berlin, Verlag von Julius Springer.

Krazer, A. (ed.). 1905. *Verhandlungen des dritten internationalen Mathematiker-Kongresses in Heidelberg vom 8 bis 13 August 1904.* Leipzig, B. G. Teubner.

Leibniz, G. W. 1859. *Mathematische Schriften, Band IV.* Herausgegeben von C. I. Gerhardt. Hildesheim, Georg Olms Verlagsbuchhandlung, 1962. Reprint of the original edition.

Nagel, Ernest. 1939. The formation of modern conceptions of formal logic in the development of geometry. *Osiris* 7, 142–225.

Parsons, Charles. 1980. Mathematical intuition. *Proceedings of the Aristotelian society* 80 (n.s.), 142–168.

Pasch, Moritz. 1882. *Vorlesungen über neuere Geometrie.* Leipzig, B. G. Teubner.

Patzig, Günther (ed.). 1986. *Gottlob Frege:Funktion, Begriff, Bedeutung.* Sechste Auflage. Göttingen, Vandenhoeck und Ruprecht.

Poncelet, J.-V. 1822. *Traité des propriétés projectives des figures. Tome premier.* Paris, Gauthiers-Villars.

————. 1865. *Traité des propriétés projectives des figures, Tome premier. Deuxième édition.* Paris, Gauthiers-Villars.

Rickets, Thomas. 1986. Objectivity and objecthood: Frege's metaphysics of judgment. In

L. Haaparanta and J. Hintikka, eds., *Frege Synthesized* (Synthese Library, Vol. 181). Dordrecht, D. Reidel, 65–95.

Russell, Bertrand. 1901. Recent work in the philosophy of mathematics. *The International Monthly*; reprinted as "Mathematics and the metaphysicians." In Bertrand Russell, *Mysticism and Logic*. London, George Allen and Unwin, 1917.

———. 1903. *The Principles of Mathematics, Vol. 1*. Cambridge, Cambridge University Press; *The Principles of Mathematics*, 2nd ed. London, George Allen and Unwin, 1937.

Sieg, Wilfried. 1988. Hilbert's program sixty years later. *Journal of Symbolic Logic* 53, 338–348.

———. 1990. Relative consistency and accessible domains. *Synthese*, 84, 259–297.

Tait, W. W. 1981. Finitism. *Journal of Philosophy* 78, 524–546.

Toepell, Michael-Markus. 1986. *Über die Entstehung von David Hilberts "Grundlagen der Geometrie." Studien zur Wissenschafts- Sozial- und Bildungsgeschichte, Band 2.* Göttingen, Vandenhoeck and Ruprecht.

Veblen, Oswald. 1904. A system of axioms for geometry. *Transactions of the American Mathematical Society* 5, 343–384.

Index